SANDHILL COVE

EMMA

The Many Facets of Emma Thompson

Chris Nickson

EMMA

∽

The Many Facets of

Emma Thompson

Taylor Publishing Company · Dallas, Texas

Published by Taylor Publishing Company
1550 West Mockingbird Lane
Dallas, Texas 75235

Book design by Mark McGarry
Set in Fournier & Bernhard Fashion

Library of Congress Cataloging-in-Publication Data
   Nickson, Chris.
      Emma : the many facets of Emma Thompson / Chris Nickson.
         p. cm.
      Includes bibliographical references.
      ISBN 0-87833-965-5 (cloth)
      1. Thompson, Emma, 1959- 2. Actors—Great Britain—Biography.
   I. Title.
   PN2598.T54N5   1997
   791.43'028'092—dc21
   [B]   97-22634
                                                CIP

Printed in the United States of America
10 9 8 7 6 5 4 3 2 1

For Linda

introduction

A colorful fake parrot hangs above the front door of Number 30. Otherwise, from the outside this house looks the same as the other houses on the street, semidetached with a small front garden, white net curtains at the window for privacy.

The car in the driveway is as ordinary as the house. Older, white, anonymous, blending in with everything else in the quiet suburb.

A few blocks away Finchley Road roars with traffic as cars, taxis, and buses head to and from north London. Pedestrians flood out of the Tube station. But in the blocks behind the cricket ground, there's a sense that very little has changed. This is West Hampstead, upscale without being pretentious, genteel, middle-class to the core, and so perfectly English.

West Hampstead *is* Emma Thompson. She has lived there all her life; it has seeped into her bones and her subconscious. In many ways the small area has defined her. And now, equally, she's come to define it. She is the woman who lives at Number 30, leading a life that, by and large, has been one of great control and conformity, the stiff upper lip and the firm, honest handshake. The parrot, iconoclastic and gaudy, is the only sign that something here is *slightly* different, that the person inside might not subscribe completely to the suburban ideal.

She could afford something quite extravagant, a mansion or country estate, but it wouldn't suit her. These are her roots. Her mother lives, literally, across the street. And until her marriage, Emma's sister Sophie had an apartment around the corner.

Ordinary as the place might appear; cheap it wasn't. This house, which she shared with her husband, Kenneth Branagh, until their six-year marriage collapsed, cost $600,000 at the beginning of the decade. The bathroom was customized, and Ken and Emma added his and hers studies and had the kitchen modernized.

And almost certainly, Number 30 is the only house in West Hampstead with an Oscar in the downstairs bathroom. For Emma is not just one of West Hampstead's more famous residents—she's an internationally lauded actress who also managed to garner an Academy Award statuette for screenwriting. As someone who began her entertainment career by wanting to be nothing more than a comedian, she's traveled a long, strange distance in her profession.

She's found her niche playing women of character and moral substance who hide their insecurities and fears behind a brief smile and a carefully constructed middle-class facade. The Margaret Schlegels, Miss Kentons, and Elinor Dashwoods she's created onscreen have all been three dimensional, living beings rather than cinematic creations. At her best, Emma offers a depth of performance that's almost transparent.

But at her best, she's playing women quite like herself—intelligent, comfortable, and decidedly aligned with the middle class. Strong women, occasionally opinionated, with their own problems. These are people she understands; in many ways, they *are* her. She may not be a proponent of the Method, transforming herself body and soul into a role, but she still manages to project a strong sensibility.

And always, she comes back to West Hampstead. It's her ground, her center, both geographically and emotionally.

Over the course of twelve films, plus cameos and television appearances, she's managed to grow not only as an actress but also as a woman. The maturity she's reached hasn't always been easy—witness the breakup of her marriage—but it's given her a calmness that was lacking before. She's outgrown the self-effacement that masked her own dissatisfaction with her looks and her weight, making jokes about them before anyone else could, and steered into an acceptance of herself as she is.

The one quality that typifies Emma Thompson as an actress has nothing to do with looks. Intelligence is the quality that has been the key to her work. She has dismissed what she does as "blind instinct," but in fact, it's an insight that sees quite acutely, that penetrates to the heart of the matter. It has been apparent in her acting, where she can use a lexicon of small gestures to convey a great deal, and more recently, in her adaptation of *Sense and Sensibility*.

The comedian she once aspired to be still peeks through, even in the heaviest of dramas. Emma manages to keep a lightness of touch about her work. With the possible exception of Dora Carrington, all her characters have, in one way or another, shown their humorous sides, whether it was Miss Kenton relaxing in a pub, Gareth Pierce fumbling files into her purse, or Princess Katherine attempting to learn a few words of English. And that serves to make her roles more rounded, more three dimensional. No person is dour or serious every minute; everyone smiles or laughs at some point. The ability to recognize that only underlines the intelligence she brings to her work.

In the decade since she turned to serious drama, a virtual novice in that field apart from a couple of school and college performances, she has received virtually every award possible and seen herself loaded with superlatives as being nothing short of an acting deity by some American critics. She has achieved a remarkable success in a relatively short time; most actors spend their whole lives plugging away in search of recognition. It's been a case of talent will out. From out of nowhere, she vaulted over the competition to become the leading British actress of her generation, another Vanessa Redgrave or Glenda Jackson, which means that even as she gets older, the strong roles will be offered first to her. And there will be others that she'll write, having proved herself in that arena, as well, making herself a double threat.

And behind it all, the lights, masks, glitter, reviews, the sensible schoolgirl remains, with a clear, sane head, and a firm moral code she might sometimes briefly forget—but only very briefly. Even her hand-rolled cigarettes and occasional dropped "h"s, once signs of solidarity with the people, have taken on middle class trappings and respectability.

And like intelligence, respectability is also at the core of Emma's work.

All of her characters have had it, in differing degrees. They've all been *good* people, stout of spirit and heart.

Even in days of political flux, the backbone of England remains its middle class, where the old virtues—loyalty, decency, integrity—still reside. And those old virtues are what others, especially the Americans, love about the English. They are what Emma brings across innately every time she steps in front of a camera. It goes deeper than any acting; it's her. And adding her natural acting ability to this sense of time-honored virtues makes for an irresistible combination.

However much her personal politics may veer from those virtues—she leans well to the left—those are the qualities she projects, the qualities that inform every moment of her work, whether in the period dramas that seem to be her forte or in more contemporary pieces. Emma Thompson has magic.

chapter one

Howover much she may have tried to avoid it, acting is in her genes. Her mother, Phyllida Law, is a respected actress with a strong classical background, and her father, Eric Thompson, had done both stage and television work before going on to earn a reputation as a stage director and the creator of the children's TV show *The Magic Roundabout*.

So the squalling little baby who came into the world on April 15, 1959, at St. Mary's Hospital in Paddington, West London, was surrounded by things theatrical from birth. It was a normal part of life for her, just as it would be for her sister Sophie, born three years later.

But Eric and Phyllida were the first generation to live that way. Phyllida's background was working-class. Her mother had been a domestic servant.

"She went into service when she was twelve," Emma recalled of her grandmother, "and . . . the butcher's son asked her to marry him and he wanted to emigrate to Australia. She always used to say, 'I wish I'd gone, I wish I'd gone.'"

Instead, she chose to remain in what seemed like the relative security of England only to end up pregnant by the master of the house (the child would be Emma's uncle).

"While the wife was away," Emma recounted at the Woman of the Year Award luncheon in London in 1987, "her husband would enter

Gran's attic in stealthy, stockinged feet and, to coin a time-dishonored phrase, have his way with her. I believed her when she told me she was not entirely aware of what was happening until, through this exercise, she became pregnant."

There was never any question of him crossing class barriers and marrying her; the man was already married, after all.

"Unexpectedly," Emma continued, "both husband and wife were extremely sympathetic and offered to take the child when it came since she had no means to support it."

But she refused, even when the couple offered her money for the baby, and "left their service with dignity, a swollen belly, and no references."

Suddenly she was unemployed, homeless, and close to giving birth. It was a story that, sadly, wasn't too uncommon for the time, when some members of the upper classes thought their stations in life gave them *droit de seigneur* over everything around them.

Being alone and angry led her to become the first politically active member of the family, a daring move for any woman at the time and one that wasn't always well received.

"She was stoned in the streets of Glasgow for trying to introduce contraception to some of the poorer families," Emma recalled with indignation. "Can you imagine that? Women with fourteen, fifteen, sixteen children, who were dead tired animals by the time they were in their twenties—and people wanted to stop my grandmother from helping them. She was a great lady."

∽

BECOMING an actor offered Eric Thompson an escape from his own working-class background, which promised a lifetime of drudgery in a factory job or years on the unemployment line.

"He met my mum when they were at the Bristol Old Vic," Emma explained, "and they courted for years and finally got married when Dad was playing Puck and Mum was playing Titania in *A Midsummer Night's Dream*. They married on Saturday morning, did a couple of shows, and went to the country for their honeymoon on Sunday." Like the real troopers Eric and Phyllida were, though, "They were back onstage on Monday."

After initially struggling, television brought regular work to Eric—for some reason he often played crooks on British cop dramas like *Z Cars*, where Brian Blessed, who's become a regular in Kenneth Branagh's films and was the best man at his wedding to Emma, also received his start—and soon enabled him to buy a house for his new family in the London suburbs. It was a 1920s semidetached in West Hampstead, a good, comfortable address, quiet and quite solidly middle-class. If it wasn't the rarefied, moneyed surroundings of Hampstead proper, neither was it the dubious neighborhoods of Kilburn or Cricklewood, slightly further to the west. This was success—material success—and it meant that Eric had fully broken the bonds of the working class, a remarkable achievement for someone in such a peripatetic profession as acting. It meant that his daughters would have advantages that had never come to him—better education and a greater self-confidence about their place in the world.

Most of all, it was a *family* house. The Thompsons were a close-knit clan, and Emma was especially close to her father.

"He was a tremendous influence as a parent. He was self-educated but expressed himself with such wit and irony, and he was extremely articulate. He taught us the importance of laughter."

And there was plenty of that. Eric Thompson was a man with an off-center sense of humor, the type of person who "always talked about *Romeo and Juliet* as if it were a comedy. So we learned to look at things askance and not take them too seriously." And on at least one occasion husband and wife settled an argument in front of the kids by throwing lemon meringue pie at each other.

That kind of behavior, though, was typical for the household. Guffawing, full of the noise of argument, discussion, and jokes, its gentility shot through with a heavy streak of British eccentricity.

"We spent a lot of time on the stairs and the landing," Phyllida Law recalled, "because nobody could bear anyone else to have the last word." Nor did debate cease when the voices finally quieted. Instead, members of the family would leave each other notes, often quite bizarre in content. Once Eric opened a script only to have a note from Emma fall out, reading, "That'll be two shillings and sixpence for the suspender [garter] belt." What it meant, nobody knew, but she'd put one over on her father, if only for little while.

"They were just a truly brilliant family," remembered Emma's closest childhood friend, Jacqueline Sharpe, "and incredibly eccentric as well: Mum running around stark naked doing the cleaning, and Gran was always there—she was deaf as a post—and her dad wandering around in loud checked suits. And food, just food everywhere all the time. How they weren't all grotesquely fat, I'll never know."

In England, and certainly in a bastion of respectability like West Hampstead, the behavior of the Thompsons, even in the privacy of their home with the front door closed and net curtains squarely in place, was just not what was done. To Emma it seemed perfectly normal, the way family members should act with each other. But her school friends, raised a little more sedately, felt differently; perplexed, she could never understand why they found descriptions of her home life "disgusting."

Eric and Phyllida never treated their daughters as children but more, Emma said, "as adults who just hadn't lived as long. I've rarely seen a more successful marriage, without anybody trying to sacrifice any part of their personality, which quite often happens and mostly happens to the woman. They weren't rich. Mum worked but she was always there when we got home from school, talked to us about the day."

Eric and Phyllida's working-class upbringings were long behind them. As actors, they had reinvented themselves, changing their accents and whole styles to assume the middle-class mantle. Emma and Sophie were raised to speak proper, grammatical English, to have all the mannerisms that would help them be perfectly ordinary and, in their own way, fit in with their neighborhood.

Although that was fine at home, it made Emma something of an outcast when she started as a pupil at the local primary school. Suddenly she was around kids from different backgrounds, and being shown that she was different brought on Emma's first bout of insecurity, not only with her speech—which she managed to change quite easily—but more importantly with her looks.

"I don't know whether I would have liked myself as a child," she mused. "I always feel I was deeply punchable, overweight with a plait. I went to the state primary down the road and suffered at school; I was unfortunate in having a posh accent, I was simply disliked. Then I changed my voice, learned how to swear, and it was all right."

As with most children, she made all the necessary adjustments in herself to be accepted by her peers. She needed to feel part of the group and not like an outsider. But the low self-esteem about her body would stay with her, leaving her ready in later life to beat others to the punch with self-deprecating remarks about her appearance. She often referred to herself as "meaty" or "a great hulking bluestocking."

When she was young, her mother said, Emma was "a serious little creature. I remember when we were walking back from school in West Hampstead one day we passed a dead cat in the gutter that was suffering from rigor mortis. She would not be stopped; she picked it up and walked several blocks to give it to a policeman."

For vacations the family would travel up to Scotland. Not long after Emma's birth, members of the Law and Thompson families joined together to purchase a cottage in the village of Ardentinny. At the time, raising the princely sum of one thousand pounds seemed impossible, but Phyllida recalled, "The entire family—my mother, my brother, and us—scraped [it] together . . ."

It was a place that offered relatively cheap vacations, far away from the hurly burly of London. A neighbor, Mary Murton, had two boys close in age to Emma and Sophie, and the four would play together.

"They were all lovely, innocent, glorious children who went on their ponies, swam together in the loch, picnicked, just played for hours," Murton recalls.

Eric Thompson, though, was beginning to find he had less time for such rural retreats. After months of trying, he'd finally persuaded the BBC to purchase a French series of five-minute animations. His plan was to erase the original dialogue (which had been political satire) and replace it with something rather absurd and surreal, all non sequiturs and off-the-wall comments, the type of humor that could only come from England, working on two levels to appeal to both children and adults.

And so *The Magic Roundabout* was born, with Eric writing the new scripts and narrating them himself. Aired in the early evening just before the news, the characters of Dylan the rabbit, Zebedee, Ermintrude, and especially, Dougal the dog quickly became part of the cultural landscape as the show established a strong cult following. Children adored it, but there was also a hip quality to the show, particularly to Dougal, that made it required viewing for anyone who wanted to appear the least bit trendy.

To Emma, Dougal was simply her father in another guise—cynical, occasionally grouchy, but always looking at life in that slightly twisted, funny way. There was "always a sense of poking fun at himself, yet there [was] also a tremendous humanity and kindness. It's incredibly broad-shouldered, that view of life." And it colored the way Emma would always look at things. When her own book, *The Sense and Sensibility Screenplay and Diaries*, was published in 1996, the dedication thanked three things "for having developed my sense of humour": Jane Austen, *Monty Python* (whose influence would come a little later), and *The Magic Roundabout*. It was a way of dedicating it not just to her father but also to the ongoing influence he had on her.

Humor was also Eric's and Phyllida's way of coping with the ongoing strain of illness. Never physically robust, Eric suffered from mild heart disease all his life.

"He had his first heart attack when he was thirty-five and I was six or seven. . . He was ill all the way through, but somehow it was the way my parents dealt with that—the humor which they brought to the situation. My uncle was also very ill, because he had a serious car accident when he was about twenty-five. . . . He died when he was fifty-one of a brain hemorrhage. I was brought up by very witty people who were dealing with quite difficult things—disease and death. . . . I was brought up by people who tended to giggle at funerals.

"My mother had this kind of nursing home for many years. It made a big difference in how we grew up. I think we all appreciated each other very much, perhaps because of that."

Not that illness stopped Eric Thompson from working hard. Even as the success of *The Magic Roundabout* saw his star rising in television, within the theater he'd moved from acting to directing. He was working with a young, unknown playwright named Alan Ayckbourn, whose comedies would soon prove to be fantastic draws in the West End—all with Eric Thompson as director. Suddenly, after years of just getting by, the family had success and money. If they still weren't rich, they were definitely comfortable—in a way that perfectly suited their middle-class street.

Despite the way they earned their paychecks, Phyllida Law insisted, "We were very ordinary, not a bit theatrical." But how many ordinary families had Alec Guinness—referred to by the children as Uncle Alec—over for Sunday lunch?

"Sir Alec was one of their only grand friends," was Emma's explanation. "We weren't a theatrical dynasty in the same way as the Redgraves and the Richardsons."

৩৩

THE young Emma showed no inclination towards drama. Despite some acting classes when she was nine, remembered as "jolly things, fun for kids," she remained a fairly introverted girl, quiet, thoughtful.

"Principally I was interested in books. They possessed me."

Not only did she read voraciously, but she also remembered and understood what she read, leading Eric and Phyllida to jokingly think she would "either marry Prince Charles or become Prime Minister." But there was also a brief period when she considered a career in hospital administration, impressed as she was when a civil servant came and talked about his work at school; that passed, and Emma returned to her books.

When she was eleven, Emma's days at primary school were over, and her parents applied for her to enter Camden School for Girls. It was still a state school, but it was a far cry from the primary where Emma had been forced to roughen her speech to be accepted. The accents here were all decidedly middle-class and all backed, in varying degrees, by money and privilege. It was a place of good, liberal education for the daughters of people in the arts.

Part of the admission process was an interview—the school made no claims at being egalitarian—and Emma, accompanied by her mother, sat down in the headmistress's study to be questioned. When asked what she wanted to be, the previously bookish Emma replied without hesitation, "An actress."

It was an answer from out of the blue, and one that certainly took Phyllida Law aback.

"I almost fainted on the spot. It was the first I'd heard of it, but that wasn't why I was shocked. I assumed it wasn't the right thing to say to the headmistress. We didn't really talk about it again."

It appeared, though, that Emma had said precisely the right thing because she was admitted to the school. But the idea of really becoming an actress would remain largely on the back burner for a few more years. Although she did appear in some school plays, her stardom didn't immediately shine through to her classmates. Sophie Radice, a couple of years younger, noted that "her role in *Lady Audley's Secret* paled in comparison with her sister Sophie's Saint Joan."

Instead, the reputation that seemed to follow Emma at Camden School was as a good girl, the swot, the "perfect prefect," as Radice called her: "Tall, good-looking, and academic, she was the kind of girl who somehow managed to be popular with staff and fellow pupils alike. . . . The quintessential bright-spark schoolgirl."

As something of a reaction to the freedom and license offered to her at home, Emma at Camden became quite the goody two-shoes, the girl whose homework was always handed in on time, no blots or smudges on the pages, the one who was exactly prepared for class, asking the right questions, her hand raised whenever the teacher asked anything. As fellow pupil Ellen Cranitch portrayed her, she was "conventional and conscientious. . . . She had an amazing ability to take what came her way and do it immaculately." But the innate acting ability in her genes was at work. The person who had never been happy with her body, and who now masked that by exhibiting what her mind was capable of, hid her anxieties from those around her quite well, to the extent that Cranitch found her to be a girl with "a lack of insecurity and self-doubt which is rare."

She made herself work. She was definitely bright, but determined to shine, she forced herself always to do better and find the ambition to succeed in herself, something which would remain with her. It was, almost certainly, the deliberate counter to her insecurity. The more forceful, even bossy, she seemed, the less anyone would notice just how unsure of herself she really was underneath it all. It even extended into her home life.

"She ran over us like that machine that flattens tar on the road," as her mother said. "I'll always remember one parents' day at school when the headmistress took us aside and said, 'I think it's important that you shouldn't push your daughter quite so hard.' We sort of slid down the wall with surprise. We explained, 'It's not like that at all. She's pushing *us*!'"

All in all, it wasn't the type of personality that brought many close friends. Nor, for that matter, did it attract the boys. They wanted someone more easygoing, less serious and determined, someone with the sense of fun that seemed to be missing from most of Emma's teenage years. She would later try to rewrite history, and not coincidentally make herself seem more worldly, by claiming she had "enjoyed a varied sex life since the age of fifteen," adding, in *The Advocate*, that "when I was fifteen, my mother took me to see one of the first proponents of birth control. . . . I was so lucky—but even luckier that I wasn't judged by my parents for having a very active sex life from a very early age and really enjoying it." However, the girls in her class were quick to point out the truth of the matter.

"Emma was a wholesome girl," one said, "and I don't know anyone who has had sexual intercourse with her. There were some very deviant people at Camden but she wasn't one. She wasn't in the really wild set. She was quite emotionally organized."

And novelist Rose Boyt, who *was* in the really wild set, confirmed that view.

"The whole school seemed to be split into us and them. There were the ones who slept with boys, took drugs, stayed out all night, and generally misbehaved. I was in that delightful group. Then there were the others. Emma was just a nice girl."

Of course, there were inevitably boys in Emma's life. But, as her best friend Jacqueline Sharpe said, it was all "in a tame and rather innocent sort of way."

Underneath the prissy veneer, the growing Emma was actually something of an outsider. She portrayed herself as one thing to try and mask another, but was really happy with neither. There were few people around whom she could relax and be herself. With Jacqueline, she spent her free time sitting around "in quite expensive coffee bars, ordering one coffee because we couldn't afford anything else and talking about boys."

But there was never one particular boyfriend. Emma had experienced her first real kiss while still young: "I was twelve, he was seventeen. It took place on a bench in a smoky hall throbbing to "Co-Co" by Sweet. He tasted of beer and cigarettes, and it was the most delicious aroma I had ever encountered." But romance—never mind sex—was still far away on the horizon. "I followed him around for the rest of the Easter holidays," she recounted, "until it became so embarrassing he took to hiding behind trees." Her rather daunting, no-nonsense persona kept the male hormones at bay.

Far more important than any boy in her life was watching *Monty Python's Flying Circus* every week on television.

"Nine o'clock on BBC-2, I think," Emma said. "Jacqueline would come over to the house, and we would sit there, and my dad would sit behind. I would always wait to see if my dad laughed. It was just intensely wonderful when we laughed together—because laughing with somebody, especially when it's your dad, is one of the great pleasures of life."

Monty Python, one of the great watersheds of British comedy, was a pivotal experience for Emma. John Cleese, Eric Idle, Michael Palin, Graham Chapman, Terry Jones, and American Terry Gilliam created a show that was both outrageous and absurd, on the cutting edge of what could be considered humorous—not unlike *The Goon Show* in the 1950s, which also took comedy to places it had never been before.

In many ways, *Monty Python* was the heir of *The Goon Show*, filtered through the political and social sensibilities of the sixties, a factor that made it instantly appealing to a younger generation and largely incomprehensible to an older one. Eric Thompson, with the unique humor he'd shown on *The Magic Roundabout* (which seemed to share a surreal viewpoint with *Python*) was rare among his generation in finding the show funny.

For Emma, it was far more than entertainment; it was a revelation. "*Monty Python* changed my life," she revealed. "*Python* is not less important than Garbo; the Marx Brothers are not less important than Ingmar Bergman."

The show made her realize that there could be far more to comedy than merely standing on a stage and telling jokes. It could say something, have some relevance to life.

Throughout Britain, the day after a *Python* broadcast, school classrooms and playgrounds would ring with pupils quoting from the previous night's sketches. And Emma did that, but she took it one step further. With her friend Jacqueline she'd sneak into a cupboard under the stairs at Camden School and rehearse entire sketches.

"We'd do a line like 'The Right Honorable Patch of Brown Liquid' and just roar with laughter, pee ourselves," Sharpe said. For Emma, though, it was more than just fun. "Looking back you realize it was a very serious business with Emma," Sharpe continued. "You rehearsed like hell."

And on the weekends, when they weren't hanging out in the coffee bars or eyeing boys, Emma and Jacqueline would be in Emma's bedroom, reading the sketches into an old reel-to-reel tape recorder, trying to complete one without laughing.

The show was her real grounding in humor, the course that she used to gather all the basics and gave her the real inspiration to become a comedian. "When I saw Michael Palin once, he said he should have charged me for an education," she commented, and there was more than a grain of truth in the flippant line. A lot of kids took their cues from *Python*; it became the cornerstone of the wave of "alternative comedy" that swept through the early 1980s and was evident in such British TV series as *The Young Ones*. And for Emma it was the foundation of an entire career.

As someone who saw herself as an outsider, someone who had low physical self-esteem, considering herself too big, too "meaty," humor was a weapon. She could use it both to attract people to her, to make herself more popular, and also to defend herself: Her own comments about her appearance, jokingly phrased, would carry far less sting than someone else's.

Python was where it all began. From there she began to look outward and to perform in public. Not at school, where any judgment would inevitably have been harsh, but for family and friends and at parties.

"The first monologue I ever did was written by George Melly [a critic and musician], called 'Hampstead Liberal,'" she recalled, "and it was all about this lady standing at a cocktail party and why she'd invited this black man and it is brilliant. It was the early seventies, and I was only in my early teens. But I do remember very clearly standing on the stage next to a piano, and I remember the feeling of *power* as people laughed. I suddenly realized what it was, and I suppose I was learning instinctively about timing and that helped me get on."

Not that performing became a regular thing for Emma; that would have to wait a few years yet. But she did begin to write her own comic material, trying it out first on the family. She was happy to accept input from her parents when she read her pieces for them, always, like the good schoolgirl she was, wanting each sketch to be as perfect as possible. So she was delighted when her father suggested little touches, like changing the word *cherry* to *cerise* for more impact. She gathered and stored all the knowledge. Everything would be useful later.

When Emma was fourteen, real fortune struck the Thompsons. Eric was offered the chance to direct the staging of one of Ayckbourn's plays in America and not surprisingly jumped at the chance. There was never any question as to whether the rest of the family would stay at home, although they would visit while on vacation.

After the drabness of England, which was suffering through political crises and periodic power brownouts, the West Coast of America was a shock of sunshine and consumerism.

"Dad was directing *The Norman Conquests*, I think. . . . I remember going to the supermarket for the first time. Dad gave Soph and me the cart and said we could have anything we wanted. We came back with four cartons of ice cream, smoked bacon, and makeup."

Another time, on one of the "holidays in America," as Emma referred to them, "we used to get taken off to department stores and told we could choose anything we wanted. All I can remember picking is two absolutely terrible corduroy dresses."

More than anything, though, it was the opulence of the rented house in the Hollywood Hills that stayed in her mind, the image of "the strangest, most alien place" she'd ever seen. "The house had grand doors—like two huge waffles—that led to a room with six inches of bright yellow pile carpet, a conversation pit, and lights like you get in discos. Lots of hanging fruit, thirty-five cupboards in the kitchen—we counted them once—and this little pool with a view across L.A."

To the suburban London girl it was all a bit overwhelming, just too over the top. For all the bounty that America offered, Emma, like her parents, was happier in England. She understood the country, how it worked, and her place in it. The United States, with its relatively limitless possibilities, was quite definitely an alien culture.

At the end of her fifth year at Camden, when she was sixteen, Emma, like pupils all over the country, sat her "O"—level exams. The "O" or "Ordinary Level General Certificate of Education" exams (now known as GCSEs) were administered in all the subjects she'd studied. With good results she'd move on to the Sixth Form (the equivalent of the 11th and 12th grades), at the end of which she'd sit her "A" or Advanced Level GCEs, and then possibly go on to university, or leave and join the burgeoning teenage workforce.

She took exams in nine subjects and passed them all with A and B grades. All the work she had put in, and the way she'd pushed herself, had paid off. With those results, there was no question that she'd stay on and try for a place at one of the top universities, in one of the Oxford or Cambridge colleges.

For the last two years of school leading up to the "A"-levels, she would concentrate on three subjects, and she chose was what considered the "language" option: English, French, and Latin.

As to exactly what she might end up doing with her life after her education was complete, that remained to be seen. But Phyllida took her to a career consultant, a man who questioned her at great length before producing a report that concluded that "they thought she might do rather well in the Church," not really an option for girls at the time, at least not in the Church of England, and something that could hardly have been further from her mind. Instead they suggested Emma apply to Oxford.

Oxford and Cambridge remain the elite English universities, set a little apart from the general system. Usually, admission to a British university depends on passing an interview and achieving good "A"-level results. 'Oxbridge' (as the two are jointly known) works slightly differently. Each is made up of a number of individual colleges, operating under the general umbrella of the university. The candidate applies to a specific college to "read" (or study) a specific subject. After an interview at the college, the applicant sits for an Oxbridge entrance exam. If the interview and exam are both passed, a place is guaranteed, regardless of "A"-level results.

For Emma, the chance to apply to such an institution was validation for all the hours of academic work she'd put in at Camden. There was still a long way to go before she actually had a place, but it meant that all the pushing, all the forcing herself, had been worthwhile. To even be considered meant that you were head and shoulders above the crowd, that you shone academically.

It was something to be justifiably proud of, and she was. But at the same time she met someone who would have a profound effect on her future. Through her friend, Owen Brenman, she met a young man named Martin Bergman. He was a couple of years older than Emma and about to go up to Cambridge to begin his own university career.

When they first met, he recalled, "Em had lots of jewelry on and jangled loudly. I thought she was immensely sophisticated." She wasn't yet, of course, certainly nowhere near as much as she hoped to appear. But she and Bergman discovered they had common interests. He was a performer, a comedian, and as soon as he learned of Emma's own fascination with performing and comedy, he asked her to join him and his friends in a production.

"A friend and I asked her to appear with us at a charity show in a couple of sketches we'd written, and Em was immensely polished with perfect comic timing—a stunning, intuitive ability."

Bergman also saw her performance as George Talboys in *Lady Audley's Secret*, which hadn't particularly impressed Sophie Radice (Emma herself "thought I looked like Cary Grant"). His impression couldn't have been more different, even if told with the benefit of hindsight. "Had you told the audience that in less than twenty years the girl wearing the moustache would be winning an Oscar, I don't think anyone would have been surprised. Emma always stood out, always looked like a professional among amateurs."

Although they were just friends and never dated, Bergman's enthusiasm for things theatrical, and particularly comic, served as a catalyst for Emma's growing interest in acting.

With her parents' permission, when she was sixteen she traveled to France to the Avignon Festival, ostensibly to see a performance of Racine's *Andromaque*, which had been one of her French "O"-level required texts. More than the play itself, it was the atmosphere surrounding it, the magic of theatrical illusion of being able to reinvent yourself as someone else, that captured her. "I went to see the production five times and met the cast and so on. I wrote a letter to my father at about three o'clock in the morning, saying. 'I think I'm going to have to go into the theater.'"

She'd caught the acting bug. Through Eric's connections she was able to find work during school vacations as part of the stage crew at the Royal Exchange Theater in Manchester. It was hardly glamorous, long hours as an assistant stage manager for very little money, but to someone who was newly stage-struck, that hardly mattered. Just the chance to be around actors (and the star of one of the productions, Robert Lindsay who was playing Hamlet, was an old friend of the Thompson family), to be involved in the performances, was enough. At least for now.

Outside school she adopted theatrical mannerisms, becoming in reality the jangly faux-sophisticate that Martin Bergman had envisaged. It was, for the moment at least, all surface. Underneath the glitz her insecurity made her remain the good girl who was slogging her way through Camden. Real teenage rebellion seemed to bypass her completely.

Of course, with the freedom she was allowed at home, there was little to kick against. "Anything I was interested in made [my parents] happy," she said. "I had no rebellious stage, because my parents gave me so much freedom that I didn't need to rebel."

Nor did they try and sway her toward their own professions, even after she'd become so infatuated with acting. As it was, Sophie was already on the way to becoming a full-fledged actress. Her genes had kicked in early. As Emma recalled, "Sophie always knew she wanted to act," and while still at Camden, at the age of fifteen, she was already appearing on television in the BBC children's drama *A Traveller in Time*.

Eric and Phyllida never pushed either child. "They did me a huge favor and let *me* decide," Emma said. "The one thing they didn't want was for me to be a drug addict."

And really, there seemed to be little danger of that. Emma was too consumed by things, by acting, by schoolwork, and by the possibility of becoming an undergraduate at Oxford.

Before her final year of school, after passing the Oxbridge exam, she filled in the appropriate forms, applying to Brasenose College. There was no question in her mind of throwing away such a glittering opportunity as Brasenose to attend something as mundane as drama school, even if the theater was uppermost in her mind.

Only recently, and with a great show of reluctance, had the prestigious Brasenose agreed to accept female students. Given any excuse, it seemed, women applicants would be turned down.

"The dons were backing up against the walls when they spotted a female," Emma recalled. "They noticed on my papers that my parents were actors and asked if I intended to take up drama. I said, 'Yes! Oh yes! I want to do that very much.'"

That wasn't exactly the reply they were looking for. Brasenose decided that Emma Thompson wasn't quite a suitable candidate for a place to read English at the college. It was a blow, if not altogether unexpected. So far Emma had sailed through her scholastic career, indeed through life, without any major struggles or setbacks. Now, on a cusp, things seemed as if they were about to fall apart.

But under the joint Oxbridge pool, her papers were circulated to other colleges and reached the desk of Dr. Jean Gooder, director of Studies in English at all-woman's Newnham College, Cambridge. After reading through them, she had "no hesitation whatever in picking Emma out."

She was asked to go for an interview. After her experience at Brasenose, she approached it cautiously, but arriving home, she knew that it was the place for her. "She came home from the interview and sat down in the kitchen with stars in her eyes," Phyllida Law said. "She said, '*Wonderful women!*'"

The university place was formally offered and accepted. Emma could easily have cruised through her last few months at Camden. It didn't even matter if she failed all three of her "A"-levels, she would still have been able to go to Cambridge. But with the finish line so close, she wasn't about to give up, not after so many years of hard work. And so, like the rest of her class, Emma swotted and spent late nights in revision during the spring and early summer of 1978. In August the results appeared. She'd passed in all three subjects with flying colors.

chapter two

Unlike most cities, where the university is merely a part of the city, less than a hundred years old and tucked away in some nondescript corner, in Oxford and Cambridge the universities *are* the city, its heart, soul, and brains. The individual colleges are spread around the town, mostly through the center. They are, in many ways, its history and claim to fame. For several centuries they've been seats of learning, the final polish of education for royalty, future politicians, scientists, and artists of all descriptions. They were places where intellect was taken for granted and rewarded.

Cambridge was where Emma found herself in October 1978, one nervous fresher among many, a little overawed by the surroundings and the weight of time and reputations that were everywhere she looked. At Camden she'd made her mark. The girls there knew who she was. Suddenly she was a nobody again, another face in the burgeoning student crowd; that, too, was difficult, to become anonymous.

Her college, Newnham, was set apart on the outskirts of town, five minutes' walk along leafy Sidgwick Avenue and over the River Cam from the heart of the city. It had been established a little more than a century earlier quite specifically as a "ladies'" college and had only become fully integrated into the Cambridge University system in 1949.

When Emma arrived, her college was still all-female, and she found herself surrounded by young women like herself, more than eager to exercise their intellects and debating skills on all manner of topics. And that included politics.

It wasn't that she'd been unaware of what went on in the world before she started university, but more that she'd been so busy with other things that there'd been no time to become involved. Besides, it had all seemed an adult world away. Now though, she was forced to consider issues, to think and talk at length about the way these things affected her, and prodded into taking stances.

While she was finding her political feet, she was also thrown into the academic deep end, expected not merely to regurgitate the theories of other writers but come up with her own and be capable of defending them.

This rush of expectations "stunted me for a while," she admitted. "It's hard to explain it without sounding ungrateful for a wonderful experience. I was the first member of my family to go to university and felt quite lost in it. When you arrive the whole image of the place wipes you clean. I found the female teachers at my college wonderful—enjoyment is always the best teacher. But I found that very enjoyment marred by the great weight of what other people had thought about it."

Initially, like many students, she had a love-hate relationship with the idea of Cambridge. Being accepted there had thrust her into an intellectual elite, which was a pleasant enough feeling. But at the same time there was a sense of insulation and superiority that could be very stifling. "Cambridge is an overwhelming experience unless you have been born to it—and that's unattractive," she'd say years later. "It needs to be more open." But it wasn't, and still isn't.

တ

OVER the course of the first term Emma tentatively found her feet. She remade herself into a typical student: big black Doc Martens boots, thrift-shop clothes, her father's old fishing jacket, plenty of long scarves, and wire-rimmed glasses, with her hair still cut short.

"I looked just like a sort of baggy, female Kevin Costner," was the way she assessed her appearance. Needless to say, Eric and Phyllida weren't thrilled by this new look, and when she went home to visit, "My parents just rolled their eyes to heaven."

As she admitted, it was all a part of her personal development. Her newly awakened political conscience took the standard turn to the left. Suddenly she was a feminist.

"I was doing what a lot of young women do, rebelling against looking remotely feminine. I wore dungarees, a donkey jacket, little wire glasses like John Lennon. I went faintly radically feminist—which I still am! I was doing all the things you are supposed to do, discussing things, getting furious, thinking I was the only person ever to have thought things through. There's a point if you're female and growing up where you have to be quite rude and aggressive for a while in order to develop. Being compliant won't get you anywhere. I was very aggressive."

Under the political trappings and the espousal of left-wing politics, though, she remained the nice girl from West Hampstead. One contemporary noted, "We decided that she must be putting it on because she couldn't decide which one of us would become really successful and useful to her in later life, so she was being amiable to everyone just in case."

That was, perhaps, an overly cynical judgment. Emma might have changed on the surface, but for those changes to reverberate all the way through her life would take longer. What she was doing was simply what everyone that age does—trying to discover who she really was. Initially there were no thoughts about the future, ambition, or who could help whom. She simply wanted to be human. "It's not as stupid as it sounds. I think we all start off pretty awful. It's that wonderful thing of learning tolerance . . . how to be wise . . . how to be kind."

But even when she arrived, Emma wasn't entirely friendless at Cambridge. Martin Bergman was there, and he'd firmly established himself in the student hierarchy as the President of Footlights, a position of some standing.

Initially a club formed to put on student comic revues, Footlights had grown in importance over the years. During the 1960s its reputation had skyrocketed when so much comic talent had emerged from its training grounds. There was Jonathan Miller and Peter Cook, who made up part of the Beyond the Fringe team that took the world by storm at the start of the decade, then John Cleese, Michael Palin, and Tim Brooke-Taylor, who between them, were partly responsible for subverting the entire course of British comedy in shows like *Do Not Adjust Your Set*, *I'm Sorry, I'll Read That Again*, *The Goodies*, and most importantly, *Monty Python's Flying Circus*.

As they blazed their trails across the entertainment skies, people began to look more closely at Footlights and the talent it contained. The pantomimes and revues they staged toured the country and always enjoyed a good run at the Edinburgh Fringe Festival. The students involved became Cambridge celebrities of a sort, which could, with luck, enough talent, and drive, translate into a lucrative career.

In its history, though, Footlights hadn't been particularly kind to women. "The first time they had women was in 1932," Emma recounted, "and the revue the following year was called 'No More Women,' so that obviously didn't go down very well." By 1978 things had changed, although perhaps not as much as they should have done.

"It was very male dominated, although obviously by the time I joined, women had been present. Eleanor Bron, for instance, and Maggie Smith, whose career is the only person's I know which is even vaguely similar to mine, because she also went from comedy to more serious acting."

Although Emma might have been starting her university career by concentrating more on herself and her place in the scheme of things at university, Martin Bergman was eager to have her as part of his Footlights team.

"He always believed in her and he was very keen to incorporate her in the Footlights," said Kim Harris, part of the team himself. "He was her Svengali really, and a terrifying figure. He was already being very smooth, wearing leather jackets, going to London and coming back with contracts. To us, still essentially sixth-formers, he was remarkable." Bergman had become a real mover and shaker, used to getting what he wanted. And he wanted Emma in Footlights. By the end of her first term his persuasion had paid off, and she agreed to take part in the annual Footlights pantomime, which that year was *Aladdin*.

At the auditions, a colleague remembered, "She waltzed in, all flowing scarves and fantastically theatrical" and waltzed back out again with the title role in her pocket. Although that might have seemed extreme for a newcomer, it was common practice to cast freshmen in major pantomime roles; this time it just happened to be Emma whose timing was right.

Stop Press, the student newspaper, gave her enthusiastic notices before she'd ever set foot on a Cambridge stage, declaring, "The tradition of always casting a first-year as a lead could prove disastrous, but Emma Thompson as Aladdin is a most successful find. Her dancing, singing and acting ability should combine to produce an extremely competent performance." And when the production opened, the paper enthused that she was "particularly difficult not to laugh at."

Pantomime remains one of those curiously British institutions. Performed at Christmas, it takes a classic children's story—often Aladdin, Ali Baba, or Dick Whittington—and turns it into an absurd stage show, one aimed primarily at kids, with plenty of audience involvement, but also containing something for the adults. There's often plenty of gender reversal—historically a girl always plays the principal boy—and two actors work together as the front and back of the "pantomime horse." It's entertainment, pure and simple, silly, often ridiculous, but equally steeped in tradition.

Becoming part of the Footlights circle brought Emma into the orbit of a number of bright young actors, people who'd already made their mark in the society, like Stephen Fry, Hugh Laurie, Tony Slattery, and others. As a whole they were proving themselves to be the best Footlights group in well over a decade, since the Python crowd, in fact, and some outside attention was already coming their way. Great things were expected of them.

That was the atmosphere in which Emma made her debut as Aladdin. Naturally, her parents traveled up from London to watch and be amazed. "We were a little bit frightened of them, to tell the truth," Phyllida Law admitted. "But it was wonderful. They got it all wrong, they corpsed [began laughing] and so forth, and I remember Hugh Laurie giggling a lot. But in the middle of it all was this magical girl with a wonderful presence and dancing style and singing voice. It was all I could do to stop her father getting up out of his chair and start giving her director's notes."

Bergman's feeling about her talent had proved to be correct. It is an exaggeration to say that a star was born that night, but it certainly offered an indication that Emma was a talent well above the norm. "That was it, there wasn't any denying," Law said. "You just looked at her and thought, 'My God, where did she hide all that?'"

Certainly, she wasn't hiding it any more. All the time she and Jacqueline Sharpe had spent reciting *Python* sketches into the old tape recorder and the hours she'd spent writing, polishing, and rehearsing her own comedy sketches had produced a performer with strong timing and, it seemed, a natural flair for the stage. After *Aladdin* there was never any doubt that Emma would become a valuable member of Footlights.

"There was no doubt that Emma was going to go the distance," said Stephen Fry. "In fact, we used to write sketches to be in, and we always had a private joke because the surname of whoever she was playing would be Talented. Our nickname for her was Emma Talented."

But the Footlights crew weren't the only ones to spot her innate abilities. Those with their eyes on serious drama were also interested in her. Not that she was particularly interested in "real" acting at that point. "I was very aware that there was a divide between the people who were interested in doing drama and the sort of panto hams. I was much more interested in having a good time and doing sketch comedy. . . . I'd meet these kind of putative directors, and they'd say to me, 'You must be my Violet!' I'd go, 'What the fuck do you mean, *your* Violet?' I found it so humorless."

Nonetheless, she did perform in a few "straight" plays. For someone who "never had that thing of thinking, I *must* act," she became involved in a production of Tom Stoppard's *Travesties*, and an outdoor production of *All's Well That Ends Well* (which also included Stephen Fry), portraying, *Stop Press* declared, "a brilliant Helena." It was a unique staging, in the cloisters of Queen's College, and one which imported some non-Cambridge talent—in this case, up-and-coming actress Sophie Thompson.

For Emma, though, performance really meant comedy. "I had this tremendous resistance to the notion of women as a kind of romantic ideal, as something to be wondered at, as something beautiful. The thing I wanted to be was that kind of woman who could be strong and independent and jolly, but make people laugh."

She did manage to make people laugh, but on another, more personal level men also saw her as a romantic ideal. During her first year at Cambridge she managed to gather quite a number of admirers.

"You didn't try to seduce Emma Thompson, you fell hopelessly in love with her," was the opinion of James Gale, a university contemporary who admitted, "I certainly had a crush on her. Didn't everybody?" She had a killer smile. She was a bit dumpy, the individual bits weren't that stunning, but the whole package was very impressive. Everything together, she was very beautiful."

And Gale saw others who came under her unwitting spell, even witnessing one make a big gesture to show how he felt about her. "I drove a motorbike into her study at Newnham once," he continued, "with a guy called Tony McCaffrey. We drove through the double doors, along the corridors, up the stairs, and right into her study because Tony was madly in love with her. It was an amazing protestation of love and flattery, but I don't think she took it in quite the right way. I remember it didn't impress her that much. The bike was an MZ250, the ugliest bike ever built. We had to leave it in the study to hide it, and I think she was terrified she was going to get caught."

Whatever disguise the clothes and appearance might offer, the good middle-class girl was unsure how to react to such extravagance and, in fact, made uncomfortable by it. And although she was part of a comedy team that happily made fun of sexual mores, her own moral code remained firmly grounded in suburbia. "She didn't sleep around, I know she didn't," James Gale protested. "She had morals."

And she also had a regular boyfriend. The Footlights rehearsals had brought her into close contact with Hugh Laurie, and soon the two began dating.

If Emma was resolutely middle-class, Hugh was the perfect specimen of the upper-class. From a moneyed family, he'd been educated at Eton, England's most exclusive school, before arriving at Cambridge. He wasn't one to take his background too seriously, however. Instead, he used it to provide material for his comedy, slyly and subtly playing what *Monty Python* had deemed "the upper-class twit." It was a theme he would continue to explore and one that would bring him international renown, as a perfect Wooster to Stephen Fry's Jeeves in television adaptations of P.G. Wodehouse's classic stories.

For all his talent and brashness onstage, away from the greasepaint Hugh was remarkably shy. He was also quite athletic; as a member of the Cambridge rowing team, he'd already achieved his "Blue" (representing the university) in his first year, in the annual boat race against Oxford.

He was, Emma said, "very, very lovable." She had strong memories of late nights, "walking home with him through the Backs, his arm around me, and he'd be dead on his feet, fast asleep. And you have to realize he was gigantic in those days. Six-foot-two and a rowing blue who'd eat seventeen steaks a day."

It wasn't a particularly deep relationship—certainly neither of them was talking about love—and it didn't last long. And when it was over they remained the friends and colleagues they'd been before.

⟲

IN spite of all her activities during her freshman year, Emma's academic work didn't suffer. "She was one of the more remarkable people who could manage both," her tutor, Dr. Gooder, told author Ian Shuttleworth. And with much expected of her scholastically, Emma spent most of the year burning the candle at both ends, which caused a brief illness. By late spring, though, she was firing on all cylinders again and thoroughly involved in the year-end Footlights revue, *Nightcap*, both as a performer and as a writer.

"The boys were fairly blokish," she said later, "and it was difficult to break down the reservations they had about me writing for them."

As she had in *Aladdin*, Emma shined onstage. This time, though, there were people beyond family and friends to notice. The annual revue always attracted agents and producers from London, eager to spot new talent. In 1979 one of them was Richard Armitage, head of the Noel Gay organization. Impressed by young Emma Talented, he signed on as her agent, even though she still had two more years of study left at Cambridge. Emma, he thought, had a golden future.

During the summer, *Nightcap* went on tour, and Emma became part of the road company, the only woman surrounded by six men for eight weeks. The tour program joked, "We're very worried about Emma . . . might not be enough men," but she was happily accompanied by her new boyfriend, and fellow cast member, Simon McBurney (whose own program biography said, "Ideal holiday: an hour away from Emma Thompson").

No sooner was the show on the road, however, than Emma was forced by circumstances to withdraw, as three tragedies rapidly struck her family.

Eric Thompson suffered a stroke at the young age of forty-eight that took away his ability to speak. Then, in quick succession, Emma's grandmother and uncle—both of whom lived with the Thompsons—died.

Three such blows in such a short time to a close family were almost too much to take. Emma quit the *Nightcap* tour and returned home to West Hampstead.

Eric was in the hospital, but it was obvious that when he was released, he'd need a great deal of care if he was ever to speak properly again. And Phyllida was simply too close to be able to do everything that was necessary. As the older daughter, and now an adult in her own right, the task fell to Emma; she was able to "push him."

"The only things that Dad could say when he came out of hospital were 'fuck' and 'shit.' When you have aphasia, somehow people can always remember to swear."

She worked with him all day, every day for the rest of her summer break. His time was carefully structured, broken into fifteen-minute segments to keep his brain fully stimulated. To return his language skills, Emma used flash cards, anything she could think off. "I was fierce [with him]," she admitted. And on occasion, a little too fierce.

"Once, I must have pushed him a bit too hard, and he went into the study where the piano was. He was weeping slightly. He said—this struck me to the core—'I can't do it, Emma.' I said, 'You can, you can, you *can*.' That's when I thought, 'Everything is upside-down now.'"

She'd become the parent, her father the child. It was an awkward, disorienting situation to be in at any time, but most particularly for a young woman of nineteen. "You're learning about fallibility and mortality and that you can't rely on people not to feel or get run over or fall apart or go mad. It's an incredible lesson to learn—and the earlier you learn it, the more useful it is."

By September the hours of work were paying off. Eric's speech hadn't yet returned to the playful level he'd used before his stroke, and never would, but at least he could communicate his thoughts and feelings.

∽

F o r Emma, the summer had taken a turn she'd never expected. The loss of two close relatives, and the rehabilitation of a third, had made it a particularly stressful time for her. Working with her father had required a patience that most young people don't possess. She'd been forced to look deep inside herself for the reserves to do it all, to simply cope with everything.

The experience, sad as it was, had matured her. In her free moments, she'd had a chance to think, to try and sort out what was important to her. She still hadn't conquered her basic insecurity, her dissatisfaction with her own body, and it would be a number of years before she would; instead, she determined how to use it as a feminist tool in her comedy.

The girl who returned to Newnham in October to begin her second year of university was more thoughtful, not quite as full of herself, more patient and willing to listen and learn from others.

Phyllida had sent a letter to Dr. Gooder, Emma's tutor, explaining everything that had happened at home. It wasn't an attempt to solicit sympathy, just a recitation of the facts. But in her term report on Emma, Dr. Gooder was able to note some of the changes.

"Emma's work is of a different order from last year," she wrote. "She has all the naturalness, frankness and energy which made her so attractive a member of the group, but she has come to some inner decision to put more into her work and has simply deepened humanly, I suspect as she has had to face a succession of family tragedies."

The "new" Emma might have been looking at life and work in a slightly different way, facing it head-on, but that didn't mean she was about to abandon Footlights or her old life. There was still plenty of room for everything.

She decided not to reside at Newnham for her second year. In her adulthood she wanted to live with her new boyfriend, Simon McBurney, and the two rented a house outside the city center, off Mill Road, which they shared with two of Emma's friends, Annabel Arden and Jane Grenville.

McBurney was involved with Footlights, but his real love lay with "legitimate" theater—the radical, avant-garde wing of it at that. During the next "long vac" [vacation], he and Emma traveled to Paris to take classes with a clown.

Although some credited him for both Emma's artistic and political development, McBurney was essentially only tangential to both. She'd spent a great deal of time working on herself, thinking through the things that were important to her and developing her own guiding principles. As Kim Harris, Stephen Fry's roommate and future treasurer of Footlights who met Emma at the beginning of that year, noted, "She seemed to have a full set of political principles and she was never a grinding bore about it, either. She didn't do a Vanessa Redgrave and melt your ears with it."

If McBurney had anything other than a romantic effect on her, it was to point out the skill involved in theater (he, along with housemate Annabel Arden, would go on to run the Theatre de Complicité in London), and the way it could be harnessed. Emma, utterly untrained, had glided by on sheer natural talent, the innate abilities she'd inherited from her parents.

And so far it had stood her in good stead. She was the new success story who'd been lured into Footlights and six months later had a London agent—even if it would be a couple of years before he could do anything for her.

To capitalize on that properly would require a lot of work. The real question was, what did Emma want to do? Some friends felt that she'd already made up her mind to be an entertainer and, more than that, to become a star; they believed that was why she'd ended up joining Footlights, rather than pursue the riskier option of "serious" acting.

"It was a career decision," James Gale said. "She was clearly talented, there wasn't any question about that, but there was definitely a feeling that the quickest route to success—which I think was important to her in view of who her mum and dad were—was through light entertainment, and that meant the Footlights."

Emma, quite understandably, has never said she considered Footlights to be a short cut to stardom. Quite the opposite; she always took pains to emphasize how bad the cast could be (including herself) and how awful and mundane most of the performances were, particularly the "smokers" [performances scheduled after meals, when everyone was allowed to smoke]. "It was ghastly. People in the audience would shout, 'You're CRAP! Get OFF!' We were just students trying to make people laugh."

There was a great deal of work behind any glamour that might be involved in a Footlights production. Working with the troupe helped Emma flourish as a writer and also brought out what the London agent had seen in *Nightcap*—an intuitive gift for comedy that could take her far.

The men who were around her may have loved her, but beyond that immediate circle no one seemed especially captivated by her. Unlike actress Tilda Swinton (*Orlando*), a contemporary at Cambridge, she didn't have strangers stopping in the street to look at her. "Tilda was a fantastic beauty," said Caroline Hardy, another student of the time, "very strange and aloof and different. Emma was not in any way clever, beautiful, outstanding, witty, amusing. She was just a very normal, sensible, sensitive, politically involved sort of person who happened to be a very brilliant comedienne."

But even the normal and sensible have to break out every once in a while, and that was what Emma did during her second year at university when she and Simon shaved each other's heads.

"They got drunk one Saturday afternoon," remembered housemate Jane Grenville. "For some reason I didn't have any sheets and was lying in my sleeping bag. They were being silly and got hold of the razor and shaved each other's heads. Then they came bounding into my room yelling, 'Your turn.' I pulled the sleeping bag over my head and waited for them to go away."

Emma's explanation was a little more prosaic. Depending on the account, they had either been drinking or were stoned "and my boyfriend said, 'Emma, you'd look just like Nefertiti with no hair.' So we went up and cut all my hair off: I looked like Vanessa Redgrave in the thing she did about the violinist. But not bad."

At the time—1980—a woman with a shaved head was just not seen, not even in the most radical of student quarters, and even covered by a watch cap the new cut brought Emma more than her share of attention. It was, however, directed at the baldness, not at her; in a way it made the person underneath more anonymous. Only a few people noticed the way it brought out her bone structure.

"It made me realize how good-looking Emma actually was," Grenville said. "It looked wonderful. . . . At the time it was really outrageous. She came home with me one day and my mother was really angry that a woman could appear in public with her head shaved like that. Once or twice, for social events, she put a hat on, but she didn't go running out to buy a wig."

Although, according to James Gale, "She shaved her hair because Simon shaved his," it was also really her belated little piece of teenage rebellion. Throughout adolescence, and during her first year at Cambridge, she'd been the good girl whose only kick against convention was performing comedy—and she'd even done that with innate flair, aiming at perfection. The shaved head set her apart. It wasn't political, it wasn't even a considered gesture, in spite of the fact that Emma would later tell a shocked Dr. Gooder that "she wanted to see what difference it would make to how people perceived her." At its heart, the affair was two kids who got drunk one weekend and, on impulse, decided to do something that would annoy a lot of people. As Phyllida Law, who was "taken aback" by it, said, "It shows she wasn't always mature. She had to wear a woolly hat. She used to say, 'If you don't behave, I'll take my hat off.'"

In shaving her head, however, her timing proved to be off for once. The day after the event she was due to appear with Sandi Toskvig in *Woman's Hour*, the first all-female revue staged at Cambridge. It was directed by Jan Ravens, who'd taken over Martin Bergman's position as president of

Footlights. Needless to say, she wasn't thrilled by Emma's altered appearance.

"Jan Ravens was quite appalled," said Jenny Arnold, who choreographed the production. "She hadn't banked on Emma looking like that. But she did the show, and in fact looked terrific in it."

Emma described the show as "very feminine female stuff, but not feminist; it wasn't political," although it did contain "all these stupid jokes about women who say they don't care about their appearance, and they do desperately."

That night she "went on to do the stuff about not worrying about your appearance with a baseball cap on. Said I'd been to the hairdressers and had had a bit of a problem, because I had . . . and I took my baseball cap off, and everybody went 'Ohhh!' It was great."

The lack of hair wasn't noted in the *Stop Press* review, where Paul Clarke admitted that "[*Woman's Hour*] is very funny," before feeling obliged to show that he really hadn't understood the objective by writing, "What is less certain is whether this sort of show really helps women achieve equal status on a broader dramatic level. Most of the humor was related to women and their stereotypes. Is there not a danger that this will isolate them from mainstream humor by leading us to think that women can only put on good shows about women?"

The hair grew back, never to be shaved again, and the incident faded in the minds of those around Emma and Simon, who would remain a couple for the rest of their time at Cambridge. The brief glimmer of rebellion was over; now it was time to get back to work.

And Emma certainly did that. She appeared regularly with Footlights and in a number of other comic productions during the remainder of her university career, garnering frequent praise from *Stop Press*, which lauded her Natasha in Chekhov's *The Proposal* as "full of bristling vigor . . . the beady eyes and confident stride of the English huntswomen: argumentative, intolerant, blind to any serious opposition, except in one magnificent moment; a flustered, clucking pause that is over almost before it has time to move, where she realizes that her temper has just chased off the only suitor she is ever likely to have."

B y the time she reached her third and final year as a student, the pressure was on Emma. Not only was she involved in almost every Footlights production in one or more capacities, but she also had to write a thesis to fulfill her degree requirements.

Her academic work had been very sound, according to Dr. Gooder, and in seminars Emma had shown herself to be "open and fearless."

The girl who took up Jane Austen as bedtime reading seemed to have developed a true love of nineteenth-century literature, particularly by women authors, which was why she chose George Eliot for her dissertation topic, arguing that Eliot failed to fully create any female heroes in her novels.

It seemed strange, Emma would say later, that Eliot "had a problem with allowing her female characters to be heroic—she created them and then emasculated them, if that's the word. And what's so odd is that Eliot herself was so brave and emancipated. But morally she was very stringent and judgmental. By far her best character is Gwendolen, in *Daniel Deronda*. On the other hand, Dorothea, in *Middlemarch*, is so damn good. I remember reading that book when I was about twenty-one and thinking, Oh, Christ! I'll never be like her."

Although her contention was good and had some validity, it seemed, as Dr. Gooder wrote in her report, that Emma pulled her punches a little in the execution. "The weight of existing Eliot criticism seemed to inhibit Emma from putting her own thoughts down on paper. She felt that what she had to say could not be novel and must not be radical. In the event I believe her critique of George Eliot had both these qualities. . . . It is in general in the conduct of her argument that her weakness lies. Her sweetness of character (which makes her a delight to supervise) perhaps prevents her from being sufficiently combative to develop a full intellectual vigor."

With the work finally out of the way, Emma was free to devote herself to her last Footlights revue, which was titled *The Cellar Tapes*. It looked as if it might be the last gathering of old friends as Emma, Hugh Laurie,

Stephen Fry, Tony Slattery, Paul Shearer, and Penny Dwyer rehearsed their material, which would be performed in Cambridge before going on the road.

Fry's roommate, Kim Harris, was the business manager for the tour. He saw Emma as someone with "a desire to create order around her. She's quietly practical, she'll get things done with the minimum of fuss . . . very brisk with herself in terms of work. No lateness, no tantrums. She's very considerate, very thoughtful. . . ."

All of which contrasted with the parody biography that Emma wrote for *The Cellar Tapes* program, where she described herself as "[wearing] baggy trousers and little round glasses. Protests regularly. Votes SWP [Socialist Workers' Party]. Refuses to be stereotyped. OK?" That she could recognize some of the more obtuse points of her character was good; that she could laugh at them was even better—it showed she wasn't taking herself *too* seriously.

The sketches themselves were an erratic mixture of the brilliant, average, and horribly banal, just the kind of humor one might expect from students. The single routine that stood out, though, not necessarily for its quality as much as its prophetic abilities, had Emma as actress Juliana Talent accepting an award.

Simpering and unctuous, Juliana stated modestly that "this award doesn't belong to me," before including virtually every acceptance-speech cliché, culminating with the sentence, "And of course I'd like to thank from the bottom of my heart, my husband, Lindsay, . . . the director."

It was, in hindsight, a remarkably prescient moment, and one she would laugh about in the years to come when she and Kenneth Branagh were on the podium together. But good humor should always contain at least a kernel of truth, and Emma seemed to have the knack of grasping for it, even if it could be in a self-deprecating manner. Was it Emma looking in the mirror when she had Juliana say, "All you need is luck. I was simply lucky enough to have been born with the most colossal talent?"

The revue comedy wasn't always great, but the comedians themselves were superb. It was generally agreed that the troupe who presented the 1981 Footlights Revue was the best in fifteen years, since the days of former Python members. Stephen Fry, with his height and lantern jaw, could manage a wonderfully deadpan delivery, while Hugh Laurie's confusion seemed utterly natural and unforced. The two played off each other with ease. Even more than Emma, at that point they seemed the likeliest stars and were snapped up for representation by Richard Armitage, who was already Emma's agent. Tony Slattery, who would also go on to fame, was a little more scattershot, while Emma was the cool, assured woman in it all.

On its tour, *The Cellar Tapes* picked up the Perrier Award for comedy at the Edinburgh Fringe Festival, the first year it had been awarded, and a selection of material from the show was aired by the BBC.

It was a splendid highlight on which Emma could end her Cambridge career, going out in a blaze of glory.

Scholastically she hadn't finished quite as brightly. Not completely convinced by her thesis, the examiners had awarded her a Second Class, First Division Honors (2:1) in her BA. It was a solid, perfectly respectable degree, a little shy of the coveted "First Class" and an indication that her work was well above the average. And *any* degree from Cambridge was a feather in the cap. The work was challenging, demanding, and time-consuming. That Emma had done so well while spending so much time on her other interests was all to her credit. Her intellect and personality had been stretched and expanded in ways she could never have imagined before she entered the institution. It had even been the site of her first real romance, although as college days ended, she and Simon McBurney parted ways.

Like so many before her, Cambridge had really been the making of Emma. She'd come into it largely unformed, without any firm idea of what she wanted from life, and she left much more certain. There was still a large element of insecurity in her makeup, but she was beginning to come to terms with that, to confront it. By discovering and developing her talent (as well as her brain), she'd been able to put herself in a position where she could be accepted for that rather than the way she might look, a basic principle of brains rather than beauty.

That Emma should have embraced feminism was hardly a surprise. To her generation, coming on the heels of the first wave of feminists, it seemed like a basic tenet. Far more than that, it simply made sense to her as a woman. Intelligent and well-read, she knew all too well the way women had been treated in the past, and were all too often still being treated. As a woman, it was her duty to do what she could to affect change. She wanted to be seen as an equal, and fully deserved to be treated as an equal.

From there, given the passion of youth, it was a short step to further political involvement, at least on a conversational level, from CND (Campaign for Nuclear Disarmament) to Kampuchea, El Salvador, and the plight of the British miners.

Her time at the university might have fueled and focused her ambition, but it also taught her to look outward, to be concerned with the world around her.

In practical terms, a BA in English, even from so august a seat of learning as Cambridge University, didn't really prepare her for any career. Perhaps that was just as well, because the main thing she had in mind was performing. The only pressing questions seemed to be what, where, and when.

nitially, those questions of what, when, and where were answered by the lingering spell of Footlights. After Edinburgh, *The Cellar Tapes* transformed itself into *Beyond the Footlights*, as Emma, Stephen Fry, and Hugh Laurie, along with colleague Robert Bathhurst, embarked on a two-month tour of Australia before coming back for British dates, culminating in a short London run, which saw Emma garnering all manner of critical laurels. *The Sunday Times*, in particular, marked her for fame by announcing, "Emma Thompson will go further."

Once that was finished, however, Emma was cast upon her own devices. Since she'd always seen herself as a comedian, and her work with the revues had generated plenty of laughter, she decided to try her hand at stand-up comedy, perhaps the hardest and most strenuous form of entertainment. When it works, it's marvelous. Otherwise, for both performer and audience, the experience can be excruciating.

Even with the wave of alternative comedy that was beginning to lap at Britain, Emma quickly discovered that she simply didn't have what was needed for that kind of work.

"I did a bit of stand-up," she told David Letterman, "but soon it became inimical [sic] to my health." The lessons she had learned with Footlights—"how to make people laugh, hold them, and milk it all night"—just didn't seem to apply when she was alone on a stage. Within a short time she realized that "I wasn't very good at it and it frightened me to death." It didn't help that the style she adopted, so prevalent at the time, was quite confrontational. She could be outgoing, even voluble, but such blunt assertion wasn't in her heart. It was a case of trying too hard to be overtly political and feminist, while possibly ignoring the basic tenet of comedy—that it had to be funny and involve the audience. Instead she was talking about male hygiene, standing in front of men in the audience and demanding of them, "Do you wash it? How many times a week? Do you use a cotton ball?"

"At the time," she said almost a decade later, justifying her style, "men were just going around poking anything they felt like without washing. Hairpieces were on the increase, you know?"

There simply wasn't enough there to sustain a career, either in comedy or feminist politics, and the other idea she'd harbored for years, of wanting to be another Lily Tomlin, just didn't translate into the British comedy clubs. The experience gave Emma her first sense of failure, a new and disturbing sensation, and one that did little to help the insecurity inside her. Being self-conscious and unhappy with her appearance was one thing, to suddenly have her talent—something that had seemed completely secure—cast into doubt was another.

It made her question what she was doing, but it didn't stop her from trying to get more work. Performing was what she knew, and she was good at it. The answer was to work not as a solo act, which she now knew wasn't the best idea, but as part of a team.

And that was where the Oxbridge old-boy (or old-girl) network proved to be very handy.

So many of the graduates from Oxford and Cambridge found their way into various nooks of the entertainment industry, in publishing, or with BBC television and radio, or theaters; almost anywhere one cared to look, there was a former Oxbridge student running things.

That was the case in the Light Entertainment division of BBC radio. Jan Ravens, who'd been president of Footlights for a year (and director of the *Woman's Hour* production) had gone on to become the only female producer there and worked hard to give women as much opportunity to perform as men.

The first fruit of her agenda was a series called *Three Plus One on Four*, Four being BBC Radio Four, and the Three being Alison Steadman (who would go on to achieve recognition in Mike Leigh's films), comedian Denise Coffey, and Emma Thompson, for whom this was a lifeline after the disaster of stand-up.

Three Plus One on Four didn't quite manage to achieve Ravens's goal "to seep insidiously into people's brains that women could be as funny [as men]." The show, which seemed to aim for the outraged gasp rather than the gradual chuckle, only lasted for one series.

But before Emma had the chance to move her professional life ahead, her personal life took a heavy blow when her father died of a brain hemorrhage in 1982. He'd long suffered from heart problems, and now, at fifty-three, he was gone.

"Even as a child I was always aware he wasn't very well, but he managed to be ill without being an ill person. He was dignified, frightened, but willing to accept what had happened. He was spiritually very powerful. When he'd had three strokes and couldn't talk properly, he fought it enough to direct several plays before he died. He thought his voice had been struck because of his arrogance."

Given the closeness of the family, and the encouragement Eric had given both Emma and Sophie from the beginning, the loss was a heavy one for all of them. "There's nothing more painful than watching two people being parted by death who only want to be together. It's horrible, but oh, it teaches you so much about appreciating life and enjoying it."

The fact that she had nursed him so recently, and been something of a parent to her own father, only made it more difficult. At least Emma, Phyllida, and Sophie were able to offer support to each other. But there was little doubt that Eric's absence echoed around all the corners of Emma's life. Like so many girls, she'd looked up to her father as the central male figure in her life, someone to be proud of and someone she wanted to make proud. He might have had "a hard sort of carapace of privacy and secrecy," but Emma had been able to crack that and reach the warm man inside. He was, perhaps, one of the few men she knew who would accept her unreservedly, without any judgment. Her insecurity could vanish around him.

"He taught me not to be cruel. He used to say, 'She's got all the worst and the best of me.' The desire to say things to folks I believe are stupid is very strong. He taught me always to think before I speak. One of the things he always used to say to me I've never forgotten was, 'Only be original.'"

To have that lifeline removed when she was only twenty-three and still finding her way in the world, still a little wobbly and unsure, only made things more difficult. Emma's admiration for her father was deep; she'd looked up to him completely. The result was that she and her mother became close, with a relationship that began to take on overtones of best friends rather than parent and daughter. "My mother's very powerful," she explained. "She's not maternal so much as a tremendous intellectual support. She and Pa never asked us for anything, never demanded our gratitude, which means they have it eternally."

And she had to acknowledge that life went on. She could feel the loss deeply, but other people weren't even aware of it.

Professionally, work was beckoning, and she threw herself into it as a way of numbing the wound. First there was a chance to join the touring revue of *Not the Nine O'Clock News*, a satirical show that had been popular on television for four years. Emma became part of the cast for a brief run. According to Cambridge friend Caroline Hardy, "Emma had a lousy cold and just went on and was brilliant. I remember someone saying they were amazed how small she was—she was so big on stage you expected to meet this giant when she came off."

Back working with others, the sparkle returned to her performance. But whereas the main chances to show her abilities had been in front of live audiences, the specter of being able to entertain the whole country at one time was now dangled in front of her—a part in a television series.

Again, it was the old-boy network in operation. Stephen Fry and Hugh Laurie had been signed for a comedy sketch show that would team them with comedians Ben Elton (better known as one of the writers of *The Young Ones*) and Robbie Coltrane (whose image changed with his portrayal of psychologist Fitz in the *Cracker* series). Emma was invited to join the group and, not surprisingly, jumped at the chance.

With three out of the five having worked together in Footlights, it would have been easy to see the show, titled *Alfresco*, as an extension of the old university revues, but Emma was quick to deny that.

"We're trying to play down our Footlights past," she announced. "We're not trying to deny it, but it has such a powerful aura that, when you leave, you feel a bit wary about the name. We all grew up on *Monty Python*—the other shows we're too young to remember."

The show was written, performed, and filmed with a British sense of inspired amateurism. As Elton recalled, "On occasion scripts weren't finished when we went out to shoot. We spent all day filming one sketch leaving only fifteen minutes for a fight scene that would normally take a day to film."

In spite of all the obstacles the cast seemed to put in their own way, the show was well received when it aired. While Fry and Laurie (and Fry in particular) had carved their own comedic niches, it was Emma who was the most lauded talent of *Alfresco*, with the *Daily Express* critic going so far as to state, "If Emma Thompson doesn't become the brightest new comedy star of the galaxy . . . there ain't no justice."

Her success on television gave her the courage to try solo performance again, and she took a one-woman show (not unlike Lily Tomlin's ventures in America, playing different characters in "scenes") called "Short Vehicle" to the 1983 Edinburgh Fringe Festival. This wasn't the straight stand-up comedy that had terrified her, but it was daunting enough. There were contributions from other writers—including Alfresco colleagues Fry, Laurie, and Elton—but most of the material was Emma's, and virtually right up to show time she was in a panic, wondering if she'd ever finish the writing. Taking herself off to Paris, in the hope that it might offer inspiration, didn't help, and she ended up calling Kim Harris, her old Footlights compatriot, at 3 A.M.

"She was drunk out of her mind. But she's never been a dissipated, swashbuckling, anti-bourgeois, Soho hard-drinking type like so many actors. She's never been remotely self-destructive, and though she is ambitious in terms of her art, she doesn't want power for the sake of it."

With Paris not having provided the magic she'd hoped, she returned home, still sporting a hangover. She traveled north of the border, hoping for the best, but in the light of what had happened before with her solo performances, ready to have the worst happen.

"It's terrifying," she admitted before showtime. "I've been trudging 'round cafes trying to get ideas. I've never been keen on jokes. I like the different ways people speak: They're almost invariably funny."

Perhaps because of Emma's new visibility on television, or perhaps because it was more professional and funnier, "Short Vehicle" was granted a much better reception than Emma's earlier attempts at solo comedy. But it almost seemed as if, having failed once in the field she had to revisit and conquer it, to prove that the failure was the aberration and that she *could* succeed at anything she wanted to turn her hand to.

Creating characters for a show was one thing, though; straight stand-up was another. Emma had failed before, and even though she thought she'd overcome that, a fresh incident that year made it clear that this just wasn't her forte.

"Absolutely the worst moment I ever had was trying to do five minutes' stand-up comedy on Nelson's Column during a Reagan Out CND [Campaign for Nuclear Disarmament, an organization Emma had joined at Cambridge] march I was coordinating in 1983. That occasion was gross—the most frightening thing I've ever done. I should have been warned. Beforehand I was standing in a lorry marshaling, doing the 'Could little Willie please find his mum?' routine. And then I thought, 'It's a hot day. They've had a long wait. I'll do a monologue.' So I started, and halfway through this woman came up, grabbed me and hissed, 'If you can't say something sensible, *shut up!*' It was said so viciously that I apologized. She was there because she was worried about nuclear weapons and quite reasonably thought it was flippant for somebody to do a monologue of a comic nature. It taught me a lot. . . . I realize how easy it is to offend if they don't know you and don't pick up on the irony. I just *died.* I was wearing a bright turquoise summer thingy and couldn't change into a disguise or put on a moustache. I would have been quite happy for the bomb to drop on me immediately."

It was a swift pull down to earth. Emma might have had the ego to believe that she knew what people wanted (and even rationalized her rejection by stating that the audience either didn't recognize her or wasn't intelligent enough to pick up on the irony of her performance) and that they wanted her, but the truth was that she wasn't a star yet—although success was definitely on its way. It wasn't on a huge scale yet, no paparazzi or limos, but within the field of alternative comedy, the leads of *Alfresco* were achieving reputations. Emma found herself in demand for appearances on other television shows, like *Saturday Live* and the short-lived *Carrott's Lib*. She was gradually becoming a recognizable face and voice on the small screen. And with that, at least in the politically oriented field of alternative comedy, came responsibility. Not only did she have to talk the socialist talk—which by now was certainly a part of her—but she also had to prove she could walk that walk.

And so Emma found herself as the emcee of "The Big One," a CND benefit staged at London's Apollo Victoria Theatre at the beginning of 1984, where her "unashamedly upper-middle-class" speech and manners were derided by *New Musical Express*, its blue collar turned up high. Although the reviewer admitted that "Her monologues, patter and sulfurous rapport with her victims in the audience *were* hilarious," a kick still had to be administered by writing "you couldn't help noticing how high she carried her pert, blasé little nose." While it was nowhere near as bad an experience as the one she'd had the year before at Nelson's Column, the words had to sting a little.

Political involvement and commitment were an integral part of the scene at that time, and Emma took it even further into her own life by dating Red Stripe, the leader of a band named The Flying Pickets. It was her first relationship since Cambridge, but it didn't last long—he left her for a woman named Coral Island. Her career might have been on the rise, but it was at the expense of any kind of romance.

"She used to moan all the time about how she was never asked out by men," said someone who knew her at that time. "Mind you, she didn't exactly dress to attract—she'd have her hair scraped back and wore leggings, brightly colored socks, Doc Martens, big, grungy jumpers and anoraks." In other words, her sartorial skills hadn't yet graduated from Cambridge.

Alfresco lasted for two series (six episodes apiece), and then Emma found herself out of work again. However, such was her growing reputation that it wouldn't be for long. Whereas the vast majority of performers seemed to spend far more time "resting" than working, the Footlights graduates seemed to have charmed lives. Emma had been noted as an up-and-coming young comedian, and Channel Four television quickly latched on to her.

Channel Four, part of Independent Television, had been created to cater to minority interests; as such, it wasn't intended to turn a profit but rather to air shows that might not otherwise be seen. After Emma appeared on one of their shows, *Assaulted Nuts*, which threw her into the company of those who'd helped change the course of comedy in the sixties, Mike Bolland, then the senior commissioning editor for Channel Four, offered her the chance to write and perform a comedy special.

The script she delivered didn't match up to the Emma he'd seen. Everything seemed flat and unfunny. Bolland had it marked for rejection, until she appeared in front of his desk and performed the show for him in its entirety, to show how funny it *could* be.

"It was quite extraordinary," Bolland recollected. "She did the whole thing in my office and it was incredibly funny. It had never happened to me before and no one's done it since. When she'd finished, I said, 'OK, let's do it.'"

But convincing Bolland was only the first hurdle. Emma had firm ideas about the show, a few of which ran counter to all manner of broadcasting policy, including the title she fought for: *Sexually Transmitted*. When she lost the battle on that, she opted for *First Offense*, because she said, "it's the first program I've written for television, and it's also quite offensive." A compromise was finally reached with *Up For Grabs*, which was taped over the course of 1985.

It was, as Emma had wryly stated, "quite offensive," with frequent explicit sexual references that were a bit beyond the pale, even for liberal British television. Possibly she'd written it that way with the hope of generating controversy and some attendant publicity. If so, she would end up being disappointed. Channel Four had spent the money on the program, and they were going to air it. But in the best manner of political strategists, they buried it in the middle of the night three days after Christmas, where it was hardly likely to attract a mass audience; which meant that, for all intents and purposes, it wasn't going to offer much help to her cause.

Even so, a few reviewers did manage to stay up and watch, which led to her being "praised for her brilliant character acting and damned for her frequently filthy script." And the version that made it to the screen, Bolland maintained, was greatly watered down from the performance she'd given in his office.

Still, some powers that be saw potential in Emma and on the strength of *Up For Grabs*, the BBC signed her up to develop a series of half-hour shows.

Those, however, would have to be put on the back burner. During 1985 Emma's career had begun to take on some real momentum. Even as she'd been working on her Channel Four show, she'd received her first real stage break—the Oxbridge old-boy network flexing its muscles again.

Following *Alfresco*, Stephen Fry had been approached to write a new "book," or dialogue, to the 1930s hit musical *Me and My Girl*, in preparation for a planned revival. The songs for *Me and My Girl* had been written by Noel Gay, whose son, Richard Armitage, just happened to be both Stephen Fry's and Emma's agent. Script in hand, director Mike Ockrent set about casting the female lead.

"We'd been struggling with somebody for quite a while," he said, "until Richard Armitage suggested Emma—tentatively, because she was a client of his. Stephen then said, 'Well, you should see her.' They were all incredibly young in those days; there was no sense of whether she could act it or whatever."

Still, she got the part, because Ockrent stated later, he was "looking for a sense of reality behind the comedy . . . It's not the normal type of musical casting. We wanted the truth of the play to come through."

It would be a test of the acting ability she'd shown at Cambridge—whether Emma, who was relentlessly middle-class, could accurately portray a working-class, Cockney girl named Sally Smith. Ockrent firmly believed she could, although she had few real qualifications for the part.

"I think it was perceived by Richard that it would be a very good thing for her to do, which it was—it plunged her right into the mainstream of British theater life."

It was legitimate, as opposed to alternative, theater and exposed Emma to an audience who'd never seen her before—people for whom the term "alternative comedy" was anathema.

Initially Emma wasn't sure she wanted to even be in the production. "When I first read the script I didn't want to do it; I thought it was a reactionary piece about class rehabilitation." In the end, though, the instincts for performance won out over the political knee-jerk reaction, and she accepted the role, partly, she insisted, because "I wanted to learn to tap dance."

For everyone involved, mounting the play was a learning experience. Only the male lead, Robert Lindsay (who was a friend of Eric Thompson and Phyllida Law), had ever been involved in any type of musical and that had been merely a "play with music." It meant that both cast and crew were constantly swamped. Problems arose on a daily basis, and solutions had to be extemporized. The actors not only had to learn the songs but also how to sing them. Some, including Emma, were taking dance lessons all the way through rehearsals.

As Ockrent recalled, "There was nobody more amazed than Bob and Emma on the very first performance of the show in Leicester (where all the bugs were worked out prior to a London run), with lots of agents and people from London in the audience, that they seemed to like it. I have to say I shared their amazement, but they had such incredible vibrancy between them that they made the show."

Although Emma was understandably nervous at first, that soon changed as she became comfortable in the part. Acting in a musical comedy was the most demanding job she'd ever had, simply because it pushed the boundaries of all her skills. Not only did she have to be funny, she had to sing and dance—neither of which had figured extensively in her repertoire.

Nonetheless, when the show opened in London, it drew ecstatic reviews, while the critics were lavish in praise of her talents.

"Miss Thompson," said one, "a big girl in a print frock standing out in maximum gauche contrast to the surrounding company of sour-faced well-corseted swells, contributes a character as real as a pair of old boots and sings with a full-hearted relaxation that gets to the core of Gay's style."

Since "Gay's style" here included songs that had long since insinuated themselves into the English consciousness, like "The Sun Has Got His Hat On" and "The Lambeth Walk," nostalgia alone almost guaranteed it a sympathetic welcome from journalists. But no one could have predicted the way the public would react. *Me and My Girl* would run for seven years in the West End, with Emma staying for an exhausting sixteen months, appearing onstage as Sally Smith more than five hundred times.

Considering that it had all been a risk, it paid off magnificently. Not only did it make a rich man out of Stephen Fry, who received three percent of the box-office takings for the duration of the run, but it also legitimized Emma as an actress.

Granted, this was light entertainment, hardly the rigors of Shakespeare or classical drama, but for someone previously known only as a comedian it was another thick string to her bow, particularly with the plaudits she received for her performance.

She also learned exactly what was involved in theater, in going out onstage eight times a week to reprise the same part and having to try and make it fresh each time.

"I used to think that if I had to do the Lambeth Walk one more time I'd commit hara-kiri onstage. I became less than human for a while. But I'm proud of having done it and lived."

Me and My Girl greatly broadened Emma's career options. Suddenly she was no longer defined as just one thing—an up-and-coming young comedienne—but as an all-around entertainer, able to tell a joke, act, sing, and dance. And that moved her into a different, more mainstream arena. In the long term, agreeing to take part in the production was probably the best decision she ever made. Suddenly people were seeing her in a completely new light.

Her time with *Me and My Girl* complete, not only did she finally have the time to write and develop her series for the BBC, she was also offered the chance to have a role in an upcoming comedy-drama series on the network.

Tutti Frutti was playwright John Byrne's gritty look at the misfortunes of an old Scottish rock band who were more or less staggering along. There was humor, music, and plenty of conflict between the characters, their wives, girlfriends, and business associates.

Robbie Coltrane, Emma's *Alfresco* colleague, had been cast in a double role as two brothers, one now dead, the other trying hard to fill his shoes, and it was he who suggested Emma for the role of Suzi Kettles.

There was plenty of meat in the part. Suzi was written as a strong woman, one with a sharp brain and a tongue to match, Glaswegian to the core.

Without her recent stage experience, it's debatable how well Emma might have performed as Suzi. Although she'd done a little stage work at Cambridge, that was long behind her, and there was a marked difference between the earnest amateurishness of student productions and the money-spending seriousness of television. It's also quite possible that without her sixteen months as Sally Smith, no producer would have been willing to take a chance on her in such a piece. Before that she'd been too closely defined as that funny, political young woman.

But her time in the West End, even if it grew tedious, saw her blossom as an artist and become alive to the possibilities that existed for her. Although comedy was hardly a dead end, she began to realize she was capable of a great deal more. And by playing other characters, the "big girl" (as she saw herself) could hide herself, could vanish for a little while.

She'd never decided to change and become an actress; in fact, she said, "I've never made any distinctions between comedy and proper acting, with a big P and A." The opportunities came more or less by accident. "It's like people would say, 'Go on, have a go at it,' and I always used to, because I'm an enthusiast for any kind of activity whatsoever." Or, as she put it more succinctly, "I never had that feeling of, 'Oh, I *must* act. I just fell into it by accident."

And so far, with the exception of comedy, which she pursued since college, "The key . . . is people have approached me with wonderful opportunities. Whatever I've done has always seemed to be someone else's idea."

Never mind that the "someone else" tended to be a member of the Oxbridge Mafia or other people she'd worked with. The fact remained that, when she was called upon, Emma could deliver the goods. She'd done it in high style during *Me and My Girl*, and she did it again in *Tutti Frutti*.

As *Vogue* noted, "When the story had her stepping in to replace Robbie Coltrane as lead singer and guitarist, she slicked back her hair, pulled on leather jeans, and produced top-notch rock-n-roll."

Equally, when Suzi was beaten and raped by her estranged husband, Emma was up to the task of showing a woman who could fight back, then learn to cope with what had happened.

With her hair an unnatural shade of red, Suzi could easily have been a lightweight character, played more for light relief than anything. But Emma, even though she was untrained, managed to invest her with intelligence and a depth of feeling that was quite remarkable. Even her accent seemed mostly authentic, although the vacations she'd spent in Scotland as a child (as well as the fact that her grandmother had come from Glasgow) surely must have helped.

"I learned a lot from playing Suzi Kettles," she mused, "and from the women of Glasgow, too." They hadn't been kind to her grandmother when she was trying to educate them about contraception, but for Emma, "They taught me that you don't always have to be terribly polite to people. And that you can just say look, buzz off. Leave me alone."

As a means of further demonstrating her rapidly increasing range, Suzi Kettles was a raging success. It seemed as if each time Emma was appearing in something new, she was astonishing audiences with her versatility. It wasn't so much a case of what would she do next, but what couldn't she do?

What she'd done had been purely instinctive. The techniques of acting were more or less a mystery to her. She was that rarest of things—a complete natural. She'd proved it in *Me and My* Girl, and now again. Emma Thompson simply had a gift for acting, for being on the stage or on camera. Inevitably she would have picked up some ideas from her parents by osmosis, but making it work seemed to be more a case of doing what *felt* right.

"I don't understand acting," she admitted, "and I have a nasty feeling that if I did understand it, I wouldn't be able to do it. If it's a mystery, why *poke* at it? . . . I know one thing: If you just try and act, you're bollixed! It's to do with letting go rather than holding on. It's like that thing we all did as children. The actor should have the concentration of a child when it's playing a game."

However she approached it, it obviously worked for her. When *Tutti Frutti* was aired in 1987, the series was well-received, with Emma in particular singled out for praise to the extent that it was one of two performances that would win her a BAFTA (British Academy of Film and Television Arts) award the next year.

And the other performance that would win her that award was something even further removed from comedy: Harriet Pringle in the television adaptation of Olivia Manning's novels, under the title *Fortunes of War*.

As Harriet, Emma would be the lead in the series, a massive dramatic weight to carry. And there was really little to indicate that she'd have the ability to make it work. Although *Tutti Frutti* had shown that she could act, and could even act very well, she hadn't been the center of the story, the character around whom everything revolved. And as it turned out, *Fortunes of War* director James Cellan Jones didn't even know of her involvement in that project, which was being filmed as *Fortunes* was cast. His only knowledge of Emma came from her comedy and having seen her onstage in *Me and My Girl*—hardly great tests to pass for the lead in such an extended piece of work.

Jones was operating purely on gut feeling. He believed that Emma was perfect for the role, although his resolution wavered when she arrived for her audition "with dyed orange hair [for her Suzi Kettles role] which was monumentally disgusting."

His rationale, that she would either be brilliant or appalling, seemed remarkably reckless given that the show carried a large budget, and would involve extensive filming on locations in the Balkans and Middle East—many months of work for cast and crew alike. To take a chance on someone who was essentially unknown and untested took either a great deal of prescience or a great deal of stupidity, and going into the project no one was quite sure which was the case.

Even Emma herself couldn't be sure how it would work. However much she might believe in her talent, this was something on a massive enough scale to give her pause, especially as a rising young star of British theater, Kenneth Branagh, had been given the part of Guy Pringle, Harriet's husband. How could she, with no training and very little experience, hope to perform at the same level as the Golden Boy?

chapter four

Ken and Em couldn't have been more different. By her own admission, she approached things on "blind instinct," while he was the adept technician who'd won the Bancroft Medal as best student in his year at the Royal Academy of Dramatic Arts, followed rapidly by *Plays & Players* Best Newcomer Award and the Society of West End Theatre Award for Most Promising Newcomer of 1982. Even though he was only twenty-six, he'd already gained a great deal of experience both in theater and television. Everything seemed to give way before him, and he'd acquired a formidable reputation for his skills; there was even talk of him being the new savior of British drama.

"I didn't know his work," Emma said, "but I did know he was sort of a young lion in the British theater."

Not only was he the professional opposite of Emma, but his family background also stood in complete contrast to hers. For all her surface appearances of hipness and being different, Emma's upbringing had been decidedly bourgeois. Kenneth Charles Branagh had emerged from the working classes to become a rising young figure—and from the working classes of Belfast, Northern Ireland, at that.

Born on December 10, 1960, his father was a carpenter, and his mother worked in a mill. The family lived in a public housing estate, in a row house on Mountcollyer Street.

There wasn't much money, just enough to survive. To try and do better by his family, William Branagh did what so many Irish workers before him had done: He went to England in search of a better job. And he found one, flying home every few weeks to see his wife and children. It wasn't exactly a satisfactory state of affairs, leaving the kids more or less without a father, but the money was more than he could ever have earned at home. With his mother still at the mill, young Kenneth would return home from school and be entertained by the television.

"When I was in Belfast from about ages seven to nine," he revealed later, "my dad was in England, and Mum was out working a lot, and I was left on my own to watch television. It seemed I would watch for hours. *Lost At Sea*, *Hopalong Cassidy*, thrillers, B horrors—I would watch everything. That's when I started a love affair with Hollywood." It was an affair that bubbled under the surface for a long time.

All around him in Belfast, though, things were changing. By 1969, the ongoing tension between the Catholics and Protestants was beginning to flare into real violence. With the advent of barricades and soldiers on the streets, the Protestant Branaghs decided it was time to move far away from the troubles. Canada was the first choice, but William's skills with wood weren't in high demand across the Atlantic, so there was no chance of an assisted passage, which the family would need for the journey.

Then his employers in England offered him a house at cheap rent. It was a godsend. He brought Frances and the children over to their new home in Reading, not far from London.

Ken quickly learned to adapt to his new environment. Ridiculed at school for his Irish accent, he changed it—in the course of a week—so that with other boys he sounded as if he'd been born in the south of England, while at home the Belfast brogue still rang.

Whiteknights Primary School also brought his acting debut, playing, ironically, Dougal in a Christmas production of *The Magic Roundabout*, the show Eric Thompson had brought to English television. The play was performed locally several times, giving Ken his first taste of fame. "I was quite an old pro even in those days," he laughed. "We took it round the nurseries—our first tour!"

What Ken really wanted was to fit in with his new surroundings, to be accepted as one of the lads. He tried to make friends by becoming the class clown. But even with a changed accent and a love of soccer common to most boys, he found himself subject to bullying.

"It wasn't because I was Irish so much as because I stood out as an extrovert. In Ireland I'd had a huge extended family, had known everybody for several streets, and I'd developed into this larky person, an embryonic actor, I suppose. So when I got to Reading, as soon as I was comfortable, this is how I was. I tried to make people laugh. It was enough to mark you out, wasn't it?"

With their house scheduled for demolition, the Branaghs were forced to move in 1972, and so Ken found himself once again surrounded by strange kids in another new school, Meadway Comprehensive. After finally being accepted at Whiteknights, he had to start the process all over again.

This time he didn't go at it quite so hard. He didn't try to win over everybody. Instead, he became more of a loner, a kid who'd go straight home from school and spend most of his free time reading and watching television and films, to the point where he became a trivia expert on supporting players.

More than anything else, it was the media that captured his teenage imagination, and his early ambition. "I used to write to a lot of people," he recalled, ". . . to actors asking about their jobs and to the BBC suggesting a chat show for children. I was fourteen and they wrote back suggesting a meeting, but I lost my bottle and didn't go."

By then he'd also become a local journalist, having talked his way into becoming the writer of the "Junior Bookshelf" column of the *Reading Evening Post*.

Away from books, TV, and movies, his great love remained soccer, both following the game and playing it as part of the school's team. And indirectly, that was what really led him to acting. When Meadway's drama teacher, Roger Lewis, asked the team for volunteers to take part in a school production of *Oh! What a Lovely War*, Ken and a number of others agreed to take part. As the others dropped out, Ken found himself more and more involved—and loving every second of it. The icing on the cake came when Lewis asked if he'd ever thought of becoming an actor.

He hadn't—until now. But once the suggestion was put to him, he realized that this *was* exactly what he wanted to do, and plunged himself into finding out more about it.

What he quickly discovered was that he needed experience. One production didn't make him an actor any drama school would consider. And his parents weren't in favor of their son going on the stage; they "were frightened that acting was a profession full of people who were gay or out of work or both." So with his father wanting him to take the traditional route and leave school at sixteen, Ken had to argue to stay on and pursue his "A"-levels, which would also give him time to act.

He joined the Progress Theatre in Reading, an amateur dramatic company, debuting in *The Drunkard, or Down with Demon Drink*—hardly the most auspicious beginning.

But he labored on, and in a short time had become a regular part of Progress. There he found people he could talk to, and girls he could date, including Tracy Newson with whom he was involved for a couple of years to the extent of trying to be a prima donna on her behalf during a production of Strindberg's *Miss Julie*. As Chris Bertrand, another Progress actor recalled, "Ken was obviously the prime contender for the part of Jean, but there were a number of people who could have played Miss Julie. He was going out with a girl called Tracy Newson at the time and would only be in the play if she were to be cast as Miss Julie, so he started very early with that! On this occasion it meant he wasn't cast."

Theater became Ken's be all and end all. He traveled around the country to see exceptional performances and read everything he could get his hands on. Quite naturally his schoolwork suffered, but Ken didn't really care. He'd become completely focused on getting into one of the top drama schools.

Both the Royal Academy of Dramatic Art (RADA) and the Central School of Speech and Drama invited him to audition, with a view to starting in September 1979, and friends from Progress helped him prepare his audition speeches, one from Shakespeare, one contemporary.

The first round of auditions took place in January 1979, and both schools invited Ken back. At RADA, though, principal Hugh Cruttwell had some reservations about this prospective student. Still, he saw enough potential that he took the unprecedented step of asking Ken to return with a fresh audition speech, which he would work on with him.

Already nervous, Ken forgot his lines while working with Cruttwell, who was infinitely pleased at that. In fact, he declared it a "breakthrough" that Ken's shell had cracked. But it didn't mean the automatic offer of a place.

Instead he went back to Central School for a second round of high-pressure auditions, encompassing movement, speech, and song. At the end of the day, they offered him a place. That evening, at home, he wrote to thank them, but declined the offer; he simply felt he wouldn't be happy there.

He was certain that RADA would turn him down and began to hunt around for other drama schools he could apply to. So when the acceptance letter arrived a couple of days later, he was ecstatic.

The only fly in the ointment was that he still needed money to pay for his course, which eventually came in the form of a grant from Berkshire County Council. Ken was through the door and on his way.

Once his student career began, Ken wasn't the shining light he might have imagined himself to be but merely one of a number of talented would-be actors, all sweating and studying to learn the ropes. If anything set him apart, it was his ambition. By the 1980s, acting was a fairly respectable profession, but it required, in many ways, a middle-class sensibility and adaptability, which Ken, the working-class boy from Belfast, hadn't been born with.

In his moves to Reading and to new schools, he'd been forced to adapt, to become something of a chameleon to be accepted. Even in acting there'd been a sense of his starting behind everyone else, having more to learn and understand. But ambition hid the insecurity of someone who knew he hadn't been born to this but was determined to work harder and be better, to show them all and make a success of it.

Although RADA covered the whole spectrum of drama, there was an emphasis on performance, and Ken soon found himself in a production of

The Merchant of Venice, touring the comprehensive schools of North London and playing to bored audiences of kids who would rather have been almost anywhere else—a reaction that may have colored his later attempts to make the Bard part of popular mass culture.

When he was cast as Chebutykin in Chekhov's *The Three Sisters,* he wrote to Sir Laurence Olivier for advice as to how to approach the role. If he was going to approach someone, why not the very best? The big surprise was that Olivier replied, even if he offered no words of help for the show.

RADA even gave Ken a few opportunities to perform before greats. When it was announced that the Queen and the Duke of Edinburgh would be visiting the Academy to celebrate its seventy-fifth birthday, Ken, in a very forthright move, requested that he be allowed to recite a soliloquy from *Hamlet.* Perhaps surprisingly, Hugh Cruttwell agreed, and after extensive rehearsals, Ken had the chance to show his talent to the Academy's president, Sir John Gielgud. Ken was a bundle of nerves, and, he thought, his rendition went far over the top. Gielgud, though, was urbane and charming with him, offering kind advice. The final performance before the Royal couple was much better.

That success was enough to spur Ken into arguing that he should be given a chance to play Hamlet in a full production of the play, and, having proved himself before a high audience, he was granted the role at the beginning of his third and final year.

The timing couldn't have been better. He needed to look ahead, to think of life after college, to get an agent, to try and have some work lined up so that he didn't start professional life as an actor in the unemployment line. To that end, he wrote to Patricia Marchmont, an agent who'd lectured at RADA, inviting her to see his Hamlet with a view to taking him on.

As a matter of fact, unemployment didn't figure into Ken's plans at all; quite the opposite. He'd spent the summer vacation circulating his photograph and resume and had even auditioned for the lead in a television play, *Too Late to Talk to Billy.* With its working-class Belfast setting, Ken seemed like a natural for the role, and he was offered it but with one proviso: He had to give up the idea of playing Hamlet to concentrate on this part.

It was a difficult, almost impossible choice, and one Ken didn't want to have to make. And in the end, he didn't. A great test of his persuasive powers brought him the best of both worlds—not only did he not have to give up his first Hamlet but also the rehearsals for Billy would begin in London to accommodate Ken's schedule, and the BBC would negotiate with Equity to obtain a temporary card for him (a necessity for a professional production). It was a remarkable coup for him to pull off, early evidence of the silver tongue that would help him in the years to come. He knew he was the right man for both parts, and was able to state his case convincingly enough for both sets of bosses to believe him.

In the strain of preparing for two major roles, one had to suffer, and in the end it was his Prince of Denmark that bore the brunt. His performance was far from the brilliance he'd hoped for. Still, it was enough for the prestigious Patricia Marchmont to accept him as a client.

Too Late to Talk to Billy, though, was something of a triumph. In the *Guardian*, his performance was described as "storing anger like a bomb under his coat, but with an acute sense of duty and responsibility towards his sisters, and a capacity for tenderness that he will not allow to become commitment."

Still, although it put him far ahead of his RADA contemporaries, one television appearance, even in a leading role, didn't make Ken a star. There was a great deal more to be done before that could happen. But the omens were good. On graduating from RADA, he was offered the chance to audition for a new play, *Another Country*, as Tommy Judd, the only working-class young man in a group of public schoolboys. He won the part.

And at the same time, he auditioned for the Royal Shakespeare Company, not for any particular role but to become a member. They, too, offered him a contract. He had his choices, and he opted for *Another Country*.

It seemed he'd picked well. On the heels of his Bancroft Medal from RADA, his performance as Tommy Judd brought him both *Plays & Players* Best Newcomer Award and the Society of West End Theatre Award for Most Promising Newcomer of 1982. Within dramatic circles he'd rapidly gained a reputation for his work. Now all he had to do was live up to it.

After six months of playing in *Another Country*, Ken decided not to renew his contract, a fortuitous move since he was soon offered the lead in a Channel Four television miniseries, *The Boy in the Bush*, to be filmed in Australia. Not surprisingly, he accepted. Then, even as the project was being developed, he appeared for the BBC in an adaptation of Virginia Woolf's *To the Lighthouse*.

But it seemed as if much bigger things were on the horizon. He was asked to read as Mozart in Milos Forman's screen adaptation of *Amadeus*, which had run so long on the stage. There was no quick decision to be made this time, though. Branagh auditioned twice, then Forman traveled to America to test actors there. In the meantime, with *The Boy in the Bush* still not ready to shoot, Ken found more television work in *A Matter of Choice for Billy*, the sequel to his first television play.

Few actors could have been so busy straight out of drama school, but the experience, rigorous as it was, truly helped him advance as an professional. He learned how to play onscreen, how to do less to convey more—something that had seemed to come quite naturally to Emma. Whereas theatrical work depended on playing to an auditorium, projecting voice and personality with broad strokes, film and television work were almost a pointillist counterpart, a layering of small gestures and inflections to build the character. It took a little while for Ken, always the fiery performer, to tone things down and adjust.

It took six long months before Forman decided on his Mozart. Ken's agent had already been told that the part was "ninety percent his." So when the announcement was made that it had gone to a young American, Tom Hulce, Patricia Marchmont had to restrain her client from sending a telegram that read "Thanks for the wait STOP Good luck with the film STOP Why don't you stick it up your ass and don't STOP."

By now *The Boy in the Bush* was ready to film, and Ken left for a three-month shoot in the Australian outback. Then it was back to London and rehearsals for a project of his own, *The Madness*, a solo performance of Tennyson's poem "Maud," all 1400 lines of it, to be staged in September 1983 at the Upstream Theatre Club. When rehearsals concluded, he was jetting off to Belfast to act in the third of the "Billy" plays, *A Coming to Terms for Billy*.

He seemed to be running from job to job. After *The Madness*, which didn't make money, but amazingly didn't lose any, he was St. Francis in *Francis* onstage.

From there it was definitely a case of onward and upward. The Royal Shakespeare Company showed renewed interest in Ken. Straight out of RADA he'd been little more than another member of the graduating pack, another jobbing actor, but now he was rapidly becoming an important young figure in British theater. After an interview and brief audition, they made him an offer for a season, several parts culminating in the title role in *Henry V*.

Naturally, Ken accepted. The RSC was the pinnacle for serious stage actors; it was recognition and acceptance, not just of the status he'd managed to carve for himself but also of his abilities.

In preparation for his starring role, Ken needed to research his monarch, to gain some insight into the way royalty felt and acted. He decided to go right to the top; after all, Olivier had replied to him. So he approached the Prince of Wales and was granted an interview, which began a relationship that would continue into the future.

All in all, however, his time at Stratford with the RSC wasn't a happy one. "I went expecting a family enterprise where you could always knock on someone's door," he said. "Well, you could knock on a door, but there wasn't usually anyone on the other side of it."

His frustration with the bureaucracy led him to organize fringe productions with the other actors, small pieces that caught his fancy, and when his RSC contract expired, he took that idea one step further, putting together his own company to stage *Romeo and Juliet*.

All that took planning, which had never been his strong point and he now had no time for. He was a rising star and in great demand. For television, he filmed back to back *Coming Through*; Ibsen's *Ghosts*; and *Lorna*, the last of the "Billy" plays.

He'd become, he admitted, "a cocky little shit," but he'd earned all his accolades. He worked hard and pushed himself as far as he could. When he was offered the role of Guy Pringle in *Fortunes of War*, he grabbed it. But with five months left before filming began, there was still plenty he could do—he had two film roles lined up (in *High Season* and *A Month in the Country*), which would pay for his *Romeo and Juliet*; the actual production of *Romeo and Juliet*; and he was also co-producing *John Sessions at the Eleventh Hour*, a one-man show starring an old friend from RADA.

Romeo and Juliet lost money, but profit hadn't been the point. It had been an exercise, doing it to show it could be done. And having done it once and acquired a taste, Ken began to realize he could do it again and again, with a permanent company. He discussed the idea of forming a repertory company with David Parfitt, his co-producer on the Sessions show, who was all in favor of it. It seemed viable—with a lot of work. Sessions offered his services on the business side, setting everything up. So as Ken left for Slovenia to begin *Fortunes of War*, things were beginning to move behind him in England.

෨෬

KEN and Emma had never met. What they knew of each other rested largely on public perceptions—that she was a comic who'd moved towards drama, and that he was one of the theater's new glowing stars.

Beyond that, Emma had heard that Ken had a propensity for falling in love with his leading ladies, a trait not uncommon in actors. While it might have seemed that he'd been far too busy to have enjoyed any kind of personal life, there'd been a number of romantic entanglements of varying degrees of seriousness. While still at RADA, he'd met fellow student Katy Behean, and they'd stayed together until 1983. Then there was Joely Richardson, Vanessa Redgrave's daughter, and Amanda Root, another actress.

Ken also came into this production with a reputation as a real "luvvie," a very theatrical type who addressed everyone as "darling" or "love." It was pure affectation, another way of reinventing the working-class Irish kid, another layer of camouflage on the personality. And it made him very much one of the acting crowd, a little loud, somewhat extroverted and full of himself.

As Guy Pringle, Ken was playing second banana to Emma's Harriet. *Fortunes of War* was much more her story than his, which meant that Emma had a great deal more work to do.

"I didn't have a very clear notion of Harriet from the start," she admitted. "People usually either hate Harriet or hate Guy. I didn't much like Harriet myself. She rather got up my nose. It was something I hadn't done before, playing someone not of my own time. The situation for women was so different then. Harriet really couldn't be positive; she didn't have the language to protest. She wanted to be a wife, to have status, purpose. It becomes clear to her that that purpose doesn't exist, that Guy doesn't need her." At the same time, she had to admit that "Harriet is a wonderful character. She is one of these English women who is like a clear stream. Very deep."

She'd obviously taken the time to consider the part at great length and formulate her own ideas about the character. She proceeded from twin bases of instinct and intelligence. That was all she could do. She didn't have the technical skills to work it all through. Flying blind and hoping that it all turned out fine would be the way for her.

"It was like playing someone who finds that they are being slowly immured. But one of the things I enjoyed most about playing Harriet was her wit, her very powerful sense of irony that allows her to survive. I still think it's difficult for people to accept a woman who looks good and has a strong brain, which she uses. I've actually had very intelligent people say to me, 'It's wonderful that you can act and think.' But in any branch of the arts there must be intelligence—that, surely, must be your starting point."

If Emma wasn't too fond of Harriet, neither was Ken taken with Guy. "I wasn't too enamored of him at first," he admitted. "I found it hard to imagine that anyone so intelligent and sensitive about many things could be so insensitive to his wife."

But while the Pringles' domestic problems were the heart of the drama, much larger forces were sweeping around them as World War II raged, separating them and forcing them to lead their own lives, to become independent and self-reliant.

For his own part, Ken was suspicious of Emma's casting, and everything it represented. "I had a . . . suspicion of a certain kind . . . Cambridge Mafia . . . with all the privileges and legs-up, career-wise, that it can provide." But very quickly he sensed her abilities, and soon he was full of praise for Emma's work. "Emma's understanding of the role of Harriet Pringle was complete, and it was enormously enjoyable to work with her."

Initially there was little thought of involvement between the two. The work schedule was grueling, and when he wasn't on the set, Ken seemed to be constantly on the phone to London, trying to put together the company that would become Renaissance, and working on the initial idea of getting well-known actors to direct Shakespeare. Anthony Hopkins had sprung to mind, and "after endless drunken evenings, Emma persuaded me that I should stop talking and simply write to him with my idea that he should direct me in a role that I suspected would never necessarily be mine: Macbeth."

The three months of shooting in Ljubljana, Slovenia, forced Ken and Emma to spend a lot of time together. And it wasn't long before Emma, who started out familiar only with Ken's reputation, began saying that she had been "totally in awe of him before we met"—an abrupt change of tune. At least they "became good friends, thank God."

The first inkling she had that friendship could be something more came on a night shoot. The two of them were resting between takes, huddled under blankets against the night cold. "Ken started to sing, in a little falsetto, to kind of amuse me—and I burst into tears. Because he sounded exactly like my father singing on *The Magic Roundabout*. And it was most strange, because it was, as it were, unsolicited."

It was a tender moment that changed the whole tenor of their relationship, from a professional friendship to "keen interest." Still, as Emma acknowledged, "Our personal relationship grew as slowly as professional relationships do."

While things were starting to simmer between the two of them in Slovenia, Ken was still supposedly involved with Joely Richardson back in England. When they did break up on Ken's return, it was, by all accounts, quite explosive. There was a great deal of fallout—the cast of a play

Richardson was in were asked to take down all Branagh pictures from the theater so she wouldn't have to see his face.

◌◌

THE actors and crew of *Fortunes of War* returned to London to film at Ealing studios, which gave Ken even more chance to spend his free time working on Renaissance matters. Not only was a four-play Shakespeare season in the works for 1988, with Dame Judi Dench, Derek Jacobi, Geraldine McEwan, and Anthony Hopkins now tentatively set as directors and Ken himself directing *Twelfth Night,* but there were also two shows set for 1987, a John Sessions one-man performance and the premiere of a play Ken had written, *Public Enemy.*

Inevitably, all the work involved in this meant that any romance with Emma was kept at a low level. Between hectic arrangements and shooting, there simply wasn't the time. And Emma was announcing to the press, when asked, that she didn't have a boyfriend, saying, "I haven't time for all that. I am up to my neck in work."

And it was early days between the two of them yet. The courtship that Emma would refer to as "like the mating dance of two lobsters. We clashed claws," was barely underway.

Ken seemed like the workaholic, but Emma was quite honest in saying she had plenty to keep herself occupied, starting to write the material for her upcoming comedy series. She was just beginning to realize what a tremendous task she'd taken on. "You end up lying in the bottom of the bath feeling like a deflated balloon, feeling incredibly heavy. That heaviness was what I started with. I had to kind of fill my own bath up."

In January 1987, all those involved in *Fortunes of War* trooped off again, this time to Egypt for more location shooting. Although Ken and Emma were becoming much closer, they gave no indication of it to their colleagues.

For the first third of the year they were together, day in and day out, as filming continued. From Egypt it was back to London, then Greece, with a final stint at England's Ealing studios. By that time Emma was helping

Ken and his business partner, David Parfitt, in the mundane task of stuffing envelopes to send to possible Renaissance backers. When she found herself sending a letter address to Emma Thompson, she left the room only to return with a "generous" check to help the cause.

By the time their work on *Fortunes* was complete, they were both talking, albeit tentatively, about love. For Emma, "Love is a killer; being in love is very difficult, terrifying and it's certainly hard work. I think the propinquity of actors and actresses, that nearness, is responsible for a lot of grave errors. When you work with somebody you often think you've fallen in love. One's watched countless pairings."

If that sounded like a denial of involvement, it was no more so than Ken's pronouncement that, "I am as camp as a row of tents—and I intend to stay that way. . . . As far as I am concerned, the nation can think I'm gay."

Emma also decided that it was time to rewrite her personal history, to spice things up a little, claiming to have had many lovers and to have been "sexually active since I was fifteen"—even though there had only ever been three real boyfriends. It was a way of shedding the goody-goody image that had trailed her all her life and, perhaps, of not letting people see that insecurity about her looks. After all, if she'd been that sexually active, a lot of men must have found her attractive. All of which led to statements like, "Marriage is an extremely dangerous step—don't take it until you have shagged [slept with] everything with a pulse," and "I'm going to have to call a press conference to announce my celibacy."

But she was by no means ignoring the intellectual and political sides of her nature. Commissioned by the *Daily Mirror* in 1987, she wrote an article on the battle of the sexes, in which she stated, "We are being deceived, betrayed, conned and made fools of by the romance-peddlers and, believe me, I hate them almost as much as I hate the high school heroin-pusher who is at least illegal. I feel like turning round and demanding back my lost years, the years when I felt excluded from society because I didn't have a boyfriend, a wasp-waist or blonde hair."

She admitted that "I like men, for instance, but I don't understand them. I have hardly ever met a man who was willing to explain himself to me, his fears, his desires and so on." Ultimately, she explained, "Love is converted into Romance and Romance is a con."

Somehow, the woman who wanted a "friend" and communication didn't quite jibe with the person who seemed to see sex as an open field to be run through at will. And although that was probably true of many women who'd come of age at that time, wanting one thing and being told to enjoy the tail end of the era of free, irresponsible love, perhaps more than a little of her attitude came from the low body self-image she'd carried around for many years.

At the same time, when her defenses were down and she wasn't trying to fashion a "hard carapace" of her own, Emma could give indications of her feelings for Ken. "I've been rather eclectic in who I've been drawn to over the years but I suppose I like broad natures. I don't mean a physical type, but spiritually. I'm attracted to people who strike out in all directions, who see further than self and their own small concerns, natures with whom you can talk about anything, where there are no limits." The hints might have been veiled, but they were there. If anyone was trying to strike out in all directions, it was Ken.

He, meanwhile, was hip-deep in Renaissance (whose Latin motto, *Ingenuas didicisse fideliter artes emollit mores nec sinit esse feros*, translated as "To have conscientiously studied the liberal arts refines behavior and does not allow it to be savage" came from Ovid and was bestowed on the company by Emma, still the girl with scholastic aspirations) and its first shows.

Emma was trying to finish the writing for her series. As time passed, the work was proving more and more difficult, to the extent she'd given it a working title of *A Big Mistake*, explaining in September 1987 that she was hating all of it. "None of it's funny," she wrote. "None of it. I want to die."

Fortunes of War aired in Britain during the fall of 1987 to high acclaim. An expensive production, it was intended to be as "important" as *The Jewel in the Crown* or *Brideshead Revisited*, the type of period piece that the British had always managed so well. *The Daily Express* said it "looks set to become a masterpiece . . . everything about the production shouts blockbuster." But by the time it crossed the Atlantic, the blockbuster tag was working against it. To *People* it was a series where "nothing happens," although *New York* magazine conceded that "brilliant images wed to witty words and actors lazing about like lions add up to a thoughtful delight."

The one agreement was on the real emergence of Emma's talent. *People* (giving Emma her first American notice) allowed that "Only one person—Emma Thompson—brightens things up; she does a fine job playing the ideal woman—graceful, strong, patient, pretty, smart and silent in her suffering. Without her, this would be nothing but a long, long journey to nowhere."

And at home the *Daily Express* noted that "From the beginning it was Emma's wide, all seeing eyes which became our vision. She has a rare talent, not bestowed on many actors, which is the courage to be still. By doing so little, she tells us so much." Elsewhere in the same paper, Rosalie Horner wrote, "As Harriet, Emma Thompson gave an uncompromising performance which highlighted her directness, yet brought out her vulnerability, but never at the expense of her sharp sense of humor. From the opening moments, when Harriet gazed out of the train into the dark, unknown landscape as she and Guy traveled to Bucharest, she drew us into her own personal adventure."

The *London Evening Standard*, in what was more like a love letter than a review, said, "Miss Thompson is not by conventional standards beautiful. But her face has a pert charm; the eyes are large and expressive and there is . . . a firmness to her generous mouth which suggests repressed passion. . . . Week by week, Miss Thompson's portrayal of good, decent Harriet with her sensible clothes and down-to-earth manner, has built up into a powerful and oddly contemporary idealization of brunette women. Men are drawn to her by her enigmatic manner and her swift, graceful movements. Her common-sense practicality as she nests in capital after war-torn capital, surely the least alluring of theatrical circumstances is . . . a convincing demonstration of . . . delicacy and fragrance under pressure." *The Observer* summed it up best, writing that she showed true "star quality," giving a performance that was "English, understated, receptive . . . intense in repose."

But the character-middle class, intelligent if not always sure of either the world or herself—wasn't that great a stretch from the real Emma.

There was enough in there for her to latch onto for her first full dramatic part, one she'd liked "because there's no neat happy-ever-after ending. Life's not like that." The role of Harriet Pringle contributed to her BAFTA award, along with *Tutti Frutti*, which had also been shown in 1987—a recognition that came as a surprise to her.

"It won't happen again," she said during her acceptance speech, "and I doubt I'll be as busy as this in the future so I might as well enjoy it."

Suddenly there was an entirely new perception of Emma. She'd made a very quick, smooth transition from comedian to serious actress. Certainly Ken—who was, admittedly, a little biased—thought so. "I think she has a talent which will resist pigeonholes, rightly in my view," he said. "She's not going to give up the comedy, but she will undoubtedly go on to Shakespeare. What she has is an ability, which isn't arrogance. . . . A comedian has a vulnerability and a natural self-questioning which are actually very useful in straight acting."

As 1987 turned to 1988, it was becoming more and more apparent that Ken and Emma were a real couple. When she was asked about the relationship, she coyly replied, "Do you mind if I don't answer that? Just the question makes me palpitate," as close to confirmation as she'd come. And the fact that it was serious was reflected when she said thoughtfully, "I'd hate to think of myself as too violently independent. I'm a city person, live alone. But I'm beginning to think it wouldn't be difficult to share."

She lived alone, indeed, but it was hardly a lonely existence. The apartment she'd bought was, literally, just around the corner from her mother's house. She knew the neighborhood, the people. She felt comfortable and safe there; it was, in some ways, almost a return to the womb.

In January Ken and Emma took off for Los Angeles to spend three days promoting *Fortunes of War*, which had been bought by PBS to show on *Masterpiece Theatre*. It was, Ken wrote, "a visit which allowed Emma Thompson and I to fulfill a lifelong ambition and visit Disneyland. Both of us were nearly sick on 'The Matterhorn,' but we thrilled to the new 'Star Tours' ride. . . . We emerged like wide-eyed six-year-olds, yelping through our candy floss, and heading for . . . as many rides as we could fit in."

The rumor circulated in Britain that they first slept together at

Disneyland. Ken, though, would later deny that it was true, saying, "Not exactly. We did consummate [our relationship] around the time our trip to Disney happened. But I refuse to say it was the magic of Mickey and Minnie that did it."

Wherever the deed happened exactly, it remains an interesting point that they'd known each other almost eighteen months, and had a relationship for at least a year of that time, before they did finally sleep together. Which would seem to make a liar out of Emma's advice to "shag anything with a pulse" and give a greater indication of her real character—selective and infinitely cautious.

On their return, it was time for Emma to put herself to the test and begin recording *Thompson*, as *A Big Mistake* was going to be known. At her insistence the series of six shows were shot without either a studio audience, which meant no sense of feedback between viewer and performer, or any kind of laugh track. It was naked, take-it-or-leave-it humor, from the pen and mind of Emma Thompson.

"I've been in absolute control. I wrote the whole thing myself and I suffered tremendous terror. I thought, 'I've committed myself and everybody else to piles of rubbish.' But if it's a desperate disaster I have done it. It is an achievement and a bit of me just feels very proud having got through it."

If the remark sounded somewhat apologetic, as if she sensed that the programs weren't very good, then she unconsciously knew the truth. The six months spent filming in television studios in Manchester (where she rented a house for the duration, sharing it with Imelda Staunton, her main partner on the show) should have brought forth more. As a viewing experience, *Thompson* was an unmitigated disaster. The ideas were there, and there were some patches of good, funny writing; but they were too few and far between for anything billing itself as comedy.

Ken, of course, had been roped in to help, appearing in several sketches, and he deemed it "a real pleasure to work together on her television show. . . . I thought it brilliantly original and innovative television. There was an excellent cast, and it was great fun to do."

In fairness, Emma did try to push the envelope of TV sketch comedy in some of the segments, aiming quite squarely at women and addressing her own insecurity in dealing with female appearance. "I tease my own sex," she admitted, "because to me that is more enjoyable than teasing the opposite sex . . . I'm sure that somewhere or other I am exorcising demons. . . . I do not know any woman who has not been on a diet or worried about what she ate."

While that was fine in theory, the execution left a lot to be desired. And if pithiness and insight was meant to be the aim, then the sight of Emma tap-dancing in cherry Jell-O was completely irrelevant, simply a way of demonstrating that yes, she also had that skill. The shows proved to be a hodgepodge of all kinds of comedy—sketches, monologues, musical, visual—an attempt to be all things to all people, which ended up being nothing to anybody. Ken wasn't the only known commodity to help Emma out; Phyllida Law made an appearance as a strange woman who'd spent years living in a tree, and various other famous and semifamous colleagues lent their talents. "One of the nicest things about the show is that I could work with lots of old friends. Robbie Coltrane wrote begging me to be in it, then sent me money as well, so I relented. Prunella Scales is in it, and Charles Kay appears as a Mother Superior."

Overall it ended up being more baffling and ridiculous than funny. Whatever humor was there became lost among ideas that meandered, petered out, or abruptly ended.

Reviewers savaged it, and the audiences switched off in droves. In one national newspaper, a critic went so far as to call it, "One of the most embarrassing things I have seen on television . . . sluggish . . . self-indulgent," while another suggested she take her "smug, self-regarding sketches" and "stick them up her baggy boiler suit"—hardly the kind of words any performer wanted to hear. Before it aired, Emma had predicted, "When it's all over I expect I'll just crawl into a corner and cry a lot," but she hadn't been anticipating doing that from the words written about her.

When a few episodes finally aired in America on some PBS stations in 1990, *Variety* called it "as irregular as it is irreverent. Some bits . . . are mildly amusing. Still, Thompson has an individualistic style and novel, playful spirit that can be very engaging," a remarkably lukewarm endorsement, coming as it did after Emma's big-screen debut in the lauded *Henry V*. Among the press, the show seemed to have only one champion, Suzanne Moore in the *New Statesman*, who stated quite plainly that "Emma Thompson's talent is one that it's impossible to argue with. Having already proved herself as a serious actress . . . Emma is all set to round off her renaissance woman image with this new series . . . And yes she can write—some of the material is very good indeed. At times her cleverness is almost too much to take, smacking as it does of a privileged background of singing and dancing lessons [neither of which she ever endured as a child]. But before you get irritated let me also tell you that she is politically right on . . . underlying many of her skits are serious issues from vivisection to sexual harassment. The woman has it all. . . . What Thompson excels at—perhaps because she understands them—is portraying these horsy, sloany, yuppie women and their ridiculous self-delusions. . . . Some of these observations are as funny as they are disturbing."

But even Emma admitted that her comedy sketches were "more circular than linear, they don't always have a beginning, middle and end with an obvious punchline." Being politically correct and overly feminist was fine. Still, the people had to find something in there to laugh about.

Coming as it did after she'd received her BAFTA Award, there were very high expectations for the series, and *Thompson* simply didn't live up to them.

"She was flavor of the month," said the show's producer, Humphrey Barclay, himself a veteran of sixties comedy. "The combination of all that publicity and the fact that it was on BBC-1 rather drowned our baby."

When some critics accused Emma of exploiting her new success to make the series, the remarks cut deep. "I'd had all this success, unlooked-for, as an actress, and suddenly, when I go back to my roots, which were comedy, I was being accused of somehow cashing in on being a successful actress and trying to be a comedian. I'd never wanted to be a successful actress—all I'd wanted to be was a comedian."

The problem was, really, that she'd been given her chance, let loose, and she'd failed. The failure she could accept—at least publicly—with a philosophical air. "My father told me, 'If you can't fail, you can't do anything.' In terms of public reaction my television series was a huge failure, but to me it wasn't rubbish, it was the most valuable thing I ever undertook. You learn much more from the experience of failing to please than you do from accepting an award."

What she couldn't accept, though, was the fact that some reviewers had looked on it with disdain because she was a woman. "They think I should just be attractive, do serious drama;" she complained. "They're threatened by a moderately good-looking woman who tries to be funny as well. . . . It confuses the signals. We are taught to take women only on a very few levels."

It was a significant remark, one that showed some changes in her thinking. Emma had always subscribed to the feminist creed, but nine months of living with Harriet Pringle day in and day out seemed to have deepened the feeling until it really had become a part of her. Equality was no longer a slogan; it was a need, a right. No one doubted that she'd been a feminist since her days at Cambridge. For any woman, she asserted, "It would be stupid not to be," but it finally seemed to have penetrated her bones, so she no longer needed to shout it from the rooftops. The anger remained, but she'd become more adept and dealing with it and using it. And perhaps because of her romance with Ken, she was finally willing to think slightly better of her own appearance, gone from something she'd ignore or joke about to "moderately good-looking."

Still, it was a rough time for her, and although she undoubtedly did learn a lot from it, she did herself no favors by making some incredibly asinine statements about the series, describing it (in perfect "luvvie" terms) as "an allotment. I've got this little patch of ground. And I've planted all these seeds, and I've come up with a few carrots and a couple of mangy old onions and some potatoes and lots of different vegetables. They've got roots and they've come out of the ground and they were planted by me. Above the allotment is a massive, an incredibly beautiful oak tree, and that's Shakespeare. When you get tired you take a deck chair and you go and sit under the oak tree."

As remarks went, it was funnier than most of the material in Thompson. The only problem was that she was completely serious. She might have been learning and growing, but she was doing it in public, and the British press, always eager to expose idiocy, took her to task.

As colleague Greg Snow recalled, "You must never forget that there was a point when Emma's career seemed as bad as it could possibly be. She was the subject of absolute national hilarity. There were cartoons in newspapers almost daily, taking the piss out of her, saying how useless she was. It's amazing that she came back from that."

Still, she took her licks fairly well. "I was roundly punished for it," she remembered,". . . but it also taught me a great deal. I'm a rather doglike person who will go bounding up to everybody and go, 'Let's play!' and then not understand when they give me a kick in the stomach because they're not interested."

But learn she finally did.

"The question, 'What are you now—an actress or a comedienne?' wouldn't mean anything to me. I just want to do different things," was the way she refused to define herself before the series aired. Afterwards, though, she never performed any more sketch comedy, at least on television. But she did take a comic role in a video called *Managing Problem People*, a training tape for young executives produced by John Cleese's Video Arts Company. Written by old friend Stephen Fry, it brought together two generations of English comedy as Cleese himself shared the stage with Fry, Dawn French (*French and Saunders*), Nigel Hawthorne (*Yes, Prime Minister*), Rik Mayall (*The Young Ones*), and Emma, playing Moaning Minnie, a woman who made "a drama out of every crisis."

Other opportunities were arising, which, in all fairness, would eventually take her far from the work she'd done in the past. But had she really wanted, she could have found the time to have pursued comedy as well. The lashing she took from the press and public simply became a deterrent. Indeed, she said, she hoped that "the experience will have helped me for the next task, hopefully a drama."

There had been any number of rumors about what that next task might be. Talk had circulated about her starring in a musical or making a television film with Judi Dench, but neither of those things happened.

Instead she accepted a film role, a chance to star in a comedy called

Camden Town Boy. It was a small movie, but it did give Emma the chance to spread her wings even further. She'd been a comic, for better or worse. She'd played straight drama, and now she could really combine the two. More than that, it was a chance to grow in a different direction—into film. Television was fine, but even major series like *Fortunes of War* had their limits. Wonderful as it was, it remained somewhat parochial. Movies, though, were very much an international medium. Being noticed in a movie would open up any number of further possibilities for her.

She and Ken were openly established as a couple by now, albeit an extremely busy one. Her schedule was full, and his was overflowing. Nineteen eighty-eight had been the year when Renaissance moved into top gear, staging Shakespeare all over the country. Of the actors he'd approached to direct plays, in the end only Anthony Hopkins had refused, so Ken had played in *Much Ado About Nothing* under Judi Dench, in *As You Like It* under Geraldine McEwan, and was directed by Derek Jacobi in the second *Hamlet* of his career (even taking it on the road to its spiritual home of Elsinore, in Denmark).

As soon as that season was done, he had to prepare for the shooting of his first film, yet more Shakespeare—*Henry V*. Not only had Ken adapted the play, but he was also set to star as the king and direct the picture, an audacious move for someone who was only twenty-seven and who had never made a movie before.

He looked to Emma a lot during this time, as much as they had any chance to be together. The pressure of work was building around him, and he needed her as his stability and anchor, roles that her upbringing had well prepared her for.

"Emma and I are terrific mates," Ken said, "but she is also a great maverick. [We] can talk to each other, but she is very wise as well, and we both go our own way. . . . She also has her own circle of friends, who are a comfort. And you need that, but a lot of the time you are on your own and you do miss a cuddle. A hug is great."

Filming took place in the fall, from October 31 to December 18, at Shepperton Studios. Almost until the last minute, the fate of the movie was up in the air, as financing came, then dropped out. As it was, the pieces finally fell into place—thanks to selling the distribution rights in advance to the BBC and Curzon Films, and to the involvement of financier Stephen Evans, who was able to put together an investment consortium to raise the final two million pounds just a month before shooting began—but it was a tense time for Ken, in more ways than one.

All the pressure was on him. Not only did he have to deliver a great performance, but it was also on his shoulders as director to deliver a great film and do it within the allotted budget of eight million dollars—a paltry amount for such a large production.

Having to do everything, and look after all the details, took its toll on him. "I was pretty close to a nervous breakdown," he remembered. "It was ongoing, deep, deep thoughtlessness to the people around me, which was very wounding to them. Emma particularly, suffered at the hands of it." More than anyone else, he came to depend on her to be there for him. "It was Emma who brought wisdom and understanding and peace and love and became the center of my life."

For her part, she would see that "Ken was so exhausted and stressed out I had to cradle him in my arms after the day's filming." They gave each other tenderness and support. But there was more to Emma's role in *Henry V* than merely offering hugs, backrubs, and love to its star. Ken had cast her as Princess Katherine of France, her scenes to be filmed as soon as she'd finished work on *The Tall Guy* (as *Camden Town Boy* had come to be known).

"I told him to cast someone French," she said. "He said, 'No, I want it to be played this way, and you'll do it the way I want it.'"

Her big Shakespearean moment arrived on December 8, as she filmed the first of her two scenes. Geraldine McEwan played her maid. They were, Ken wrote in his book *Beginnings*, "both brilliant comediennes who transformed the French lesson scene into a beautiful, tenderly comic affair which manages in brief to show the woman's role in this depressingly male piece."

Although she'd naturally read Shakespeare as part of her education, it was Ken who really made her love the words. "He was full of the joy and enthusiasm for Shakespeare that I had for my work," she explained.

Ken's work on *Henry V* didn't finish when the filming ended. Rather, it was just beginning. He had all the pieces, and now he had to finish shaping them into a complete picture, which, of course, meant more months of stress. But that didn't stop him making plans for 1989, including some stage work with Emma in a revival of John Osborne's celebrated kitchen-sink drama, *Look Back in Anger*.

Emma, too, already had much of her year booked. In addition to the play, she'd already committed to two television dramas. And there was the small matter of a wedding to be planned. During the shooting of *Henry V*, Ken had proposed to her, and she'd accepted.

It was something that had been on both their minds for some time. As Emma said, "It is lovely to work and to accomplish things. But [that] does not comfort you if you are alone in the wee small hours of the night. Work is not the be-all and end-all for me. It does not replace all the other things."

Before any of these other things, though, she found time to take part in a student film. *Tin Fish* was the graduation exercise of Paul Murton, whom she'd known since childhood, the Murtons having property next to the Thompson's vacation cottage in Scotland.

He'd based it on the life story of his brother, Gerry, whom Emma had known well, and who had died of leukemia when he was fourteen. When Paul approached her to play the mother, he fully expected to hear that she was too busy—after all, Emma had become a known show business figure, in demand. But she blocked out five days for the filming and worked for nothing, even donating her expenses to the cast party.

chapter five

The path of romance, it appeared, had been quite too smooth for Ken and Emma. They were a real couple, looking ahead to the future, and it should have all been clear sailing from then on. But while visiting Ken's flat one day—she had her own key—Emma discovered some letters to him from a woman. Reading them, it became obvious that they'd had a recent, brief affair.

She saw red. This was a woman who had just recently changed her tune on promiscuity to the extent that she'd said, "I would never be able to handle sexual infidelity," and now she was faced with irrefutable evidence of it.

Rumor had it that before leaving Ken's apartment that day she took a pair of scissors and cut up all his clothes. She definitely told him that she never wanted to see him again and left for New York. He followed—another rumor said that she actually wanted him to follow her—and after a great deal of talking, explaining, and thinking, they were reunited. On his knees in Central Park, Ken proposed.

She never had any intention of making it easy for him. While she'd wanted a reputation and a past, Ken really had one, and she made him pay for it. Actor Brian Blessed felt that "Ken's efforts in those early days were comparable to Richard Harris in *A Man Called Horse*. He had to go through all those ceremonies to earn that lovely Indian girl. I think Ken had to earn Emma, and there's a lot to be said for that."

They agreed to hold the wedding during the summer, although it would be several months before any announcement would be made to the press.

Before that, they both had plenty of work to do. Emma had *The Tall Guy* coming out (it would be released later in the United States); *The Winslow Boy*, Terence Rattigan's play; and *Knuckles*, another television play, to record.

At the time she was still trying to live down *Thompson* in Britain. She'd started the move away from being a comedian, but in the mind of the public she had to prove herself again to be taken seriously. And as Ken's partner, she found herself very much in his shadow. He was the Golden Boy, the working-class kid who'd raised himself by his bootstraps to quickly become the leading Shakespearean actor of his generation, the man who'd made the Bard popular again, the man who, if *Henry V* was successful, would be the new savior of British film. Already he'd been compared—and knowing full well the value of publicity, hadn't refuted the comparison—to Sir Laurence Olivier, *the* British actor of the twentieth century. Next to that, for all her success, for all the praise she'd received (as well as the loud rejoinders), Emma was seen as the second banana, trying to ride to real artistic fame on her boyfriend's coattails—meaning that she had to do exceptional work to be accepted for her own talents.

The two TV plays worked well, confirming that she did have ability as a dramatic actress and that she could work away from Ken and still turn in an excellent performance.

And then *The Tall Guy* proved that her comedic ability hadn't deserted her, even if *Thompson* had left that in great doubt. *The Tall Guy* definitely played to her strengths. As the no-nonsense nurse, Kate Lemon, Emma was impeccably cast. Her talent was all the more evident, if often understated, by being focused on a credible, well-constructed script. She radiated efficiency in everything, even in breaking up with her two-timing lover, Dexter, played by Jeff Goldblum. Kate was a strong, intelligent, perceptive woman, the anchor of reality in a world that was decidedly off kilter. Her facial expressions while watching Dexter in the premiere of the musical *Elephant!* (the first musical based on the life of the Elephant Man) showed just how much she'd learned to play to the camera. With her eyes glittering, she moved through a series of twitching mouths and inclined heads that conveyed the growing absurdity of it all.

"Kate is just the most wonderful role," she said, "because she is exactly that woman who says the thing you wish you had said at the time. She knows what she wants but she's not callous. She's just very practical. [Dexter] is the one who cries because he is the one who has hurt himself. It's so accurate. You know she's upset but she's holding it in. . . . So off she goes and you never see her crying, which is great because normally what you see is man is vile to woman, woman goes away and dies the death. It's lovely to see the other side of it. Man hurts woman and in doing so hurts self badly."

Director Mel Smith was more than happy with her performance. "She's got this fantastic clarity in her acting," he said. "She's very uncluttered in what she does, because she's very intelligent in how she approaches the material. You really do feel an emotional appeal from her."

To many people, the movie's highlight was its sex scene. Philosophically, there was no reason why Emma shouldn't perform naked, but on a personal level, she was still insecure about her body. The compromise was achieved by making the sex and nudity a slapstick business, not erotic but funny, as Dexter and Kate, over the course of an afternoon of lovemaking, managed to completely destroy Kate's apartment. It parodied the overblown orgasm scenes so prevalent in movies and installed laughter in its places.

Emma, especially, loved the scene, although she was in no great hurry to do another. "If I never do another sex scene, I'll be happy," she announced. "It was terrifying at first but the atmosphere on the set for those two days became very compassionate and kind. People talked in slightly lower voices and behaved terribly well. The main thing you notice is that everyone in the room stares you right in the eye all the time. Even when they've made you a cup of tea the crew are terrified to look at you below the neck, which is actually a bit unnatural!"

The idea of that scene—indeed, a lot of *The Tall Guy*—owed a debt to the absurdities of *Monty Python*. It was a very English film, even if one of its stars was American. It didn't pretend to be anything but a small, funny movie, which more or less condemned it to immediate obscurity.

It had moments when it was truly hilarious and others that strained to be but failed, such as the musical interlude set to Madness' "It Must Be Love," which wanted desperately to spoof the whole idea of musical comedy but fell far short of the mark. And that hit or miss quality ultimately worked against it, making it something minor and largely ignored, even in Britain.

The few American critics who saw it seemed to be polarized in their views. The ones who liked it, loved it, and those who hated it really found it beyond the pale. Pauline Kael, writing in *The New Yorker*, felt that "if the SCTV troupe at its peak . . . had made a wild . . . movie satire of life in the theater, it might have had something like the inventive dottiness of *The Tall Guy*." And *People* began its review with the line, "Studiously bonkers, this British comedy makes silliness seem not only hilarious but downright respectable." *Commonweal*, on the other hand, acerbically noted that if any reader "sat down right now and dashed off a comic travesty of *The Elephant Man*, I'm sure you would get at least three more laughs out of whatever audience you cared to show it to than [director] Smith got from the audience I was sitting in."

Given her sizable role, there were naturally words written about Emma's performance. One uncomplimentary person summed her up as "hatchet-faced." *People* noted that she looked "like a sexed-up young Julie Andrews, [who] breathes heavily and laughs hard . . ." The *New Yorker* was at least willing to term her "the precise Emma Thompson," adding, "There's nothing extra about her; she's stripped down to pure flakiness. . . . It's not that she's sane, exactly; she's an original—her face registers tickled disbelief."

The *New Republic's* Stanley Kauffmann discovered the movie somewhat later, further into Emma's career, deeming her "just as delightful as the film and vice versa," with the writer adding, "In one way I'm glad to have missed *The Tall Guy* until after I saw Thompson's Margaret Schlegel [in *Howards End*]. This adds to the wonder: because she plays the nurse . . . as if this mod environment were the only one she could imagine, as if its colors and boundaries were exactly hers. . . . Now I don't believe there's anything Thompson could not do—superbly."

More than anything the movie served notice that, despite *Thompson*, Emma could—in the right circumstances and with the right direction—still be a strong comic force. It also proved that she played at her peak when she was close to home, portraying someone like herself—intelligent, relatively middle-class, and briskly efficient, always in some sort of motion.

At the premiere, though, she and Ken must have winced their way through the end of the movie, because Kate left Dexter for his infidelity with another actress and he finally went to the hospital where she worked and begged forgiveness in front of an ever-growing stream of casualties. Emma's own flight to New York and Ken's pleas that won her back had happened just a month before.

For better or worse, *The Tall Guy* died a quick death in the theaters. Jeff Goldblum wasn't a big enough star to attract the crowds, Emma remained a question mark to American audiences, and the film itself wasn't consistently funny enough to start word-of-mouth support and be a sleeper.

By the time of its release, though, Emma had moved on. The television plays had been filmed, and there were new challenges to be sought, the first of which was her stage debut with her husband-to-be.

☙

EMMA'S stage experience as a serious actress was, at best, sketchy, no more than a couple of pieces at school and a few roles at Cambridge—certainly not enough, normally, to be considered for a leading role in a play. The theater was a completely different kettle of fish than film or television, less subtle, requiring a much greater projection of the voice and emotions. But when Renaissance decided to stage *Look Back in Anger*, Ken wanted Emma to star with him in the production, which was to be directed by Judi Dench.

It was a natural decision. They were a couple about to be married. They'd worked together before. She'd shown she could act, even if audiences had yet to see her Princess Katherine. And perhaps, it was his piece of indulgence.

Certainly there was irony in it. They'd yet to tie the knot that would supposedly bind them for life, yet they were going to portray one of the most ill-suited couples of modern drama; it hardly seemed like a great omen.

Actually, it seemed like it would barely happen at all. A tour had been set up, but playwright John Osborne initially only gave permission for one London performance, on June 11, 1989, which would hardly contribute to making the production a financial success. But, with the out-of-town shows scheduled, Renaissance went ahead anyway.

As Alison Porter to Ken's Jimmy, Emma had a thankless task. Her character was little more than second banana, a cipher and catalyst for the male lead, which was largely the way people viewed the relationship between her and Ken. But she was willing to credit the play with more depth and felt that it had gone beyond its "Angry Young Man" history.

"I think the play has sloughed off its first skin," she ventured. "Men are much less willing to identify with the character of Jimmy than they once were. It has become about how hate occurs and how people invite it. About fear of women. About the way people persuade themselves that other people aren't actually human and that you can do what you like to them."

In 1958 it had been a revolutionary piece of drama. In hindsight, though, its whole attitude was quite chauvinistic, and that inevitably raised Emma's feminist hackles. If she'd found herself confronted with a Jimmy Porter in real life, she said, "I'd lay him out cold. When I read the play I did think, I can't do this. It's so depressing and misogynistic. But I think it is saved by the quality of the writing."

There was some question as to whether this version of the play did any justice to the quality of Osborne's writing, though. Reportedly, one woman noisily left the theater, yelling, "Dreadful! Dreadful! Absolutely the worst performance I have ever seen!"

There seemed to be some debate over the authenticity of the incident. Some dismissed it as a publicity stunt, and the publicity certainly helped the show—to the point where Osborne relented on his earlier decision and allowed a four-week London run. However, it seems likely that the incident was genuine. Consummate publicist that Ken had been forced to become, he still had his artistic integrity and wouldn't have interrupted a performance in such a way.

Reviews were mixed. Some felt that Ken just didn't have the fire inside him to play Jimmy properly. If he managed to summon up the hatred, it was unfocused and weak. Other critics said the whole production was marvelous. As Alison, Emma had more of a reactive role, one that didn't tax her growing dramatic abilities, although she did play with some bristle, as the London Times noted, "not as a defenseless drudge, but as a wife who knows how to defend herself with tactical silences." But her work was largely lost in the discussion over Ken's performance. At the time, after all, he was the star.

Prior to the London run, the play did manage to tour several cities, including Ken's hometown of Belfast, where audience reaction was quite marked. "Our audiences in Belfast, they really hated [Jimmy]," Emma said. "He was the angry young man, now he's seen as the vicious young man who doesn't know when to stop."

By the time the production was established at the London Coliseum, it had gain a sort of notoriety, most for that vocal walkout, that was not quite warranted by its quality. It was filmed, shown by Thames Television, and even released on video cassette.

But if Ken and Emma occasionally seemed distracted onstage, they could have been excused; they had other things on their minds. Since the reconciliation in New York, they'd been carefully planning their wedding, and it was going to be a big theatrical party. Which meant, of course, that although the press wasn't invited, they had to be told, and in great detail prior to the event. That way Ken and Emma could try to have the best of both worlds—private and public.

There was one attempt to fool the media. The press release, circulated in mid-August, announced that the wedding would take place "by the end of September." In fact, it was scheduled to happen in less than a week, on August 20, 1989.

No written invitations had been issued, hoping to stop leaks, but rumors still flew around London. Members of Ken's family were hounded for details, and the couple themselves were followed. "I found it offensive that

Emma and I were chased all over the place before, during and after our wedding," Ken said later. "We were both in the West End at the time, and we were followed—no, pursued—everywhere. Worse than that, [the press] tried to get to my family and friends as well, by all sorts of devious means. They lied, they impersonated people. It's just not on, I'm afraid."

The location and date of the ceremony had been kept as secret as possible and full security had been arranged, but that didn't deter the few tabloid journalists who managed to ferret out the truth. Kenneth Branagh's marriage was big news.

Finally, immediately prior to the event, another press release was issued, giving every detail of the event, from the wedding breakfast of roast lamb and smoked salmon to the "costumes" of the bridge and groom.

"Branagh will be dressed in a hand-tailored, double-breasted, navy blue linen suit," it was announced. "But Emma's close friends, who have been sworn to secrecy over her wedding dress, will say only that she is not planning to wear white."

The wedding party had hoped for privacy by holding the ceremony in the gardens of Cliveden House, well outside London in Berkshire. Unfortunately, they hadn't checked with the National Trust, the organization that owned the property and that refused to close the estate to the public on the whim of an actor, no matter how big a name he might be. It seemed as if it had never occurred to Ken that such a thing could happen.

In fact, the entire wedding had elements of farce about it. Two days after the ceremony, the Reverend Johnson, who had officiated, pointed out that the service had only been a blessing and, contrary to their expectations, Ken and Emma were not legally married at all, which led to a rush to legally conclude the business, quietly carried out at the Register Office in Camden a few days later.

The wedding, which cost the couple a cool thirty thousand pounds (around $50,000), was one of the theatrical parties of the year. Brian Blessed, the actor who'd been so supportive of Ken during the filming of *Henry V* was best man. Readings—including Shakespeare, naturally—were given by Judi Dench and Richard Briers. Apart from family, the guest list of two hundred included a virtual who's who of the entertainment world—Stephen Fry, Hugh Laurie, John Sessions, Ben Elton, and any number of other celebrities, who were treated to a concert and a fireworks display. The Branaghs wanted a celebration that would be memorable, even to the glitterati. Their names were established, and even though Renaissance seemed to keep teetering on the financial brink, both Ken and Em were reasonably well-off; although they were far from millionaires, they were hardly starving artists.

Emma, who could have worn anything, chose to appear in a none-too-flattering pastel dress and white veil, looking like a cross between a decorated cake and a harlequin. For the happy couple, who firmly believed they were newlyweds, there would be no honeymoon. As with Emma's own parents, it was a case of one night off, and then, the next day, a return to stifled lives in *Look Back in Anger*, which was still in the middle of its London run.

The assembled crowd made it very much a "luvvie" gathering, but then again, Ken was well established as a luvvie, and now, by association, Emma became a luvvie, too, which seemed to suit her perfectly. She was becoming much more the theatrical actress, moving in a few different circles. She had, after all, earlier that summer performed Shakespeare in front of royalty, joining Ken and other members of Renaissance to entertain at a party thrown by Prince Charles.

Mr. and Mrs. Branagh immediately became the golden couple of British drama. They both acted and acted well. Marriage to Ken somehow seemed to erase the debacle of *Thompson* from memory, and Emma was roundly lauded by the press again.

Inevitably, writers scrambled for comparisons—Olivier and Leigh, Burton and Taylor—but there was none that was quite apt. About the best thing that could be said was that there was a rosy glow about the couple that boded well for future productions.

Ken had always shown a strong sense of timing and publicity, so the arrival of the first part of his autobiography—at age twenty-eight!—to coincide with the opening of *Henry V* that fall surprised nobody. Written, as he admitted on the first page, for money, about the only astonishing thing was how little it revealed about himself. Emma warranted no more than a few lines of warm words, and those were all related to work. But then the majority of the book dealt with his work. Work had been his life, at least so far. What marriage would do to him remained to be seen.

The book helped the film, and the film had been a prime focus of his life for well over a year. Even before its release the critics were hailing him, not only for his acting but also for his vision as a filmmaker.

For someone who'd never directed a film before, and who'd almost given himself a nervous breakdown trying to complete it, Ken had done a remarkable job with *Henry V*. It was—as it had to be—very different from Olivier's 1944 classic. But Ken wasn't afraid to pay homage, with a forties feel to the music, stirring, swelling, and melodramatic. Nor was he afraid of going over the top at times and becoming sentimental, even maudlin—as in a couple of the flashback scenes with Falstaff (played by Emma's old *Tutti Frutti* and *Alfresco* colleague, Robbie Coltrane).

Over all, he'd done an excellent job. But he'd put himself in a position where anything less would have meant utter disgrace. By Hollywood standards his budget was minute, but from that he'd managed to fashion an epic of sorts, if a little short on the crowds of extras that the battle of Agincourt really demanded.

Above all, he'd succeeded in making Shakespeare accessible, exciting, and populist, quite an achievement for the late twentieth century. He was the underdog in the movie business: He'd made a film that left the English feeling good about themselves, and that made him into an even greater hero in the British press.

It was a movie that glorified the spirit of war, or the spirit of a nation at war, while still making battle itself an horrendous thing—quite a fine line to tread, perfect for a generation that had lived through the brief Falklands war with its dichotomy of images, and vastly different from Olivier's interpretation. But, as Ken had noted, "The play is about a young monarch achieving maturity but at some cost to himself. We are addicted today to the media images of people who make decisions that affect hundreds of thousands of lives. . . . Now is the right time to explore the paradoxical aspect of Henry's character."

In the end, though, it was an uplifting piece, at least if you were English. Henry won the battle and the war against overwhelming odds, and as part of the peace treaty, even got the girl. A perfect end to the tale.

And the girl was, naturally, played by Emma. As Princess Katherine she only had two scenes, which were more or less the light relief in a relentless film. For the English lesson, given by her maid, Emma adopted a flawless French accent—the result of good schooling and a few trips to the country—laughing and giggling as if mass slaughter wasn't about to happen. Which, for her, it wasn't. There was airiness and delight around, a very girlish charm about her that fell to the ground when she opened the door to her chamber and saw the grim faces of her father and his counselors. But her dancing and joking had been a reminder that life was going on and there could be some happiness.

In her other scene, being clumsily wooed by Henry at the end of the film, she played in an understated manner, letting her large eyes do all the work and controlling everything with her silence and supposed incomprehension. By his own admission, Henry was no practiced lover, no speaker of sweet words, but Katherine made him sweat in asking for her hand in marriage and even then teased by refusing him a kiss until after the ceremony. Although just a supposedly powerless woman, as Emma played the scene—on Ken's instructions—she displayed more strength than her father, who would give in to all of Henry's demands.

"It's a strange episode to place at the end of such a play," Ken wrote, "and needs playing of the utmost delicacy if it is to tell us any more about [Henry], and this strangely sensitive princess. The scene is both funny and tremendously sad. The princess has no choice, but she is spirited and intelligent, and subtly challenges Henry, who is unusually vulnerable in the scene."

On its release, the film elevated Ken in British estimations and made him a newcomer worth noting in Hollywood. To the English he'd not only had the audacity to take on the role that Olivier had made his own, but he'd also managed it as well, if not better, than the master. To American reviewers, not familiar with the young legend, this new actor-director was simply a revelation. Jack Kroll called it "a *Henry V* for our time. . . . [It] echoes not just the war against Hitler but the ignoble adventure of the Falkland Isles," mentioning that Branagh's "boyish toughness adds savor to his outstanding performance and helps to explain his astonishing success at an early age." To the *New Yorker* it was an excellent film, but Ken's lack of film expertise showed through the cracks, noting that "his attempts at spectacular effects strain his inventiveness" and that "he's trying to make it into an anti-war film, an epic noir. But he can't quite dampen the play's rush of excitement."

In *The Nation*, Stuart Klawans was full of praise, to the point where: "I like it so much I don't even want to write about it. I would prefer to leave my desk right now and watch it again." Not only did he find it superb art but also excellent entertainment, noting that, "You can eat popcorn with the same abandon as at a John Ford matinee."

Stanley Kauffmann, in the *New Republic*, harbored a few doubts but was willing to concede that Ken "is a genuinely gifted director," with "a good eyes for a cinematic flow that seems to bear language along." As an actor, though, Kauffmann felt he suffered in comparison to Olivier with "his long trumpet-call speeches" coming out "more like electoral campaign speeches pleading for support than like kingly inspiration and command."

Given her small role in the proceedings, and a name that was still basically unknown in the United States, it wasn't surprising that most critics ignored Emma's Katherine, overwhelmed as she was by the rest of the movie. But some did sit up and take notice of her. Kauffmann felt she had "an exceptionally interesting face and a subtle manner; but she is a highly assured young woman, not a cloistered, shy princess. In the English-lesson scene, I expected her to correct her teacher's pronunciation, and in the wooing scene, I thought she would tell Henry to pull up his socks and get on with it."

The Nation felt she made "a delightfully droll Katherine, making you laugh out loud at her scenes, instead of smiling at them out of respect for the author." Even if there wasn't much of it, she came away well-praised, if not quite covered in her husband's glory.

In a slightly different context, the "spirited and intelligent" comment of Ken's in his book could also have applied to Emma's other film role, Kate

Lemon, as well as Harriet Pringle and Suzi Kettles. Very early in her dramatic career Emma seemed to be busy carving a niche for herself, one that played close to her own personality.

For she was, without a doubt, intelligent, and she could definitely be spirited when the occasion arose. She was still discovering what she could and couldn't do, and so far she had merely dipped her toe into the pool of acting. It was notable, however, that her two movie roles had still been "light" ones. The women she played might have had brains and a keen sense of perception, as well as their serious sides, but they were shown in a more comic setting. It was as if she was still serving an apprenticeship of drama, that her past as a comedian was forcing her to make small, transitional steps to something new.

But there seemed to be little doubt that there was, slowly, a new Emma emerging, one who was very much an actress. And certainly, much of the influence for that had to be attributed to Ken. Although he genuinely believed in her abilities as a comedienne and would never have tried to stifle her—Emma was strong enough not to let that happen, anyway—he'd seen firsthand what she could do with a true serious role, how she could project it on the screen, and he gently encouraged her in that direction.

Considering that she'd never imagined herself in serious drama, had never really taken acting lessons other than a few childish pieces of music and movement, it was evident that she had a marvelous natural talent. Ken had worked long and hard to hone his abilities, to make himself into a fine interpreter of Shakespeare. With Emma, as she noted, it was all "blind instinct"; but her instinct always seemed to be exactly on target.

Some of that blind instinct could well have been inherited, given that her sister Sophie had also developed into a wonderful actress, one who specialized in the classics and who'd worked both with the Royal Shakespeare Company and Renaissance (she'd played Ophelia to Ken's Hamlet). But some also undoubtedly came from her intelligence, the ability to read and understand a part, and the natural intellectual inclination to explore and deconstruct a character, to see her motivations and background.

Not surprisingly, she and Ken were eager to do more work together. They were newlyweds, both involved, in one way or another, with acting.

What could have been more natural? "It was a good marriage of ideas," she said, "because we agreed the important thing was to celebrate and tell these stories with as much joy and abandon as we could."

Before they could make that happen, though, Emma was committed to work without her husband, in yet another comedy. *Impromptu* was the story of authoress George Sand's romantic pursuit of Chopin, retold as bad French farce. The subject didn't seem ripe for humorous interpretation, and for good reason—it wasn't. Although the script had a number of good lines, it was their acerbic nature that made an audience laugh, rather than anything inherently funny.

The cast was a bizarre international mix. Judy Davis played Sand, striding around for most of the movie in a man's suit and giving George a decidedly Australian lilt to her speech. Mandy Patinkin and Bernadette Peters represented the Americans, while the rest of the cast was made up of familiar British faces, including Hugh Grant as the consumptive Chopin. It was the kind of combination that might well not have worked, and Emma proved to be the oil that kept the cogs of the film moving.

"If it ever came down to a choice between her and another actress, I'd tell a producer to hire her, because you're going to have a better time," producer Stuart Oken said later. "She was happy to be there and worked to keep other people laughing even during difficult times. She could assess a situation where tensions existed, and she'd take on the mother role to make it okay. She do something like give you the back rub you need to make it all right."

While set in nineteenth-century France, there was very little, if any, French feel to the story. Instead it seemed quite English, not merely because of the accents but from the utter absurdity of the characters. Emma only added to that by playing the brainless Countess D'Antan, who attempted to bring culture into her country life by inviting a number of artists (Chopin, Liszt, Delacroix, and Sand) to her estate for two weeks, where they could sponge off her generosity, and found herself severely lampooned for her troubles. Her interpretation of the Countess was as a younger Joyce Grenfell, the English comedienne who almost created the archetype of the female upper-class twit.

"The woman's a complete idiot," Emma said of her character, "but actually very touching. I loved the script, so baroque and unusual, and the language, the full-bloodedness of it. I'd always wanted to work in France, and I wore a lot of very funny dresses. I think sometime actors get terribly serious because they want to deny the fact that a lot of it involves getting dressed up in exciting clothes that make you feel different. You get to wear them all day and wander around and actually be that person—it's bliss."

But it wasn't the clothes that made the woman, it was Emma's acting. The sheer breathless dizziness she gave the Countess, the blank, horse-faced smile—so typical of the English upper classes—all contributed to offer a performance that came perilously close to stealing the film from its stars. Certainly she was the color to their monochrome, a burst of energy and hopefulness. Even faced with the ridiculousness of the script, she was one of the few in the cast to actually project humor.

Amazingly, *People* liked it, granting it "a whimsical charm," while pointing out that neither script nor direction paid "undue attention to the problems of anachronism or literal history." The *National Review*, however, was far less kind, calling it "the most pretentious, silliest, and inadvertently funniest film in years . . . an absurd farandole" with "stilted dialogue and amateurish direction . . . trampling everyone and everything into the mud." At least the *New Republic* was able to single Emma out as "a surprise pleasure as a flutterly culture-vulture duchess. . . . She delights twice, with her acting and with her revelation of range."

Emma, though, did have one problem with the film. Nothing to do with her acting but instead with her physical appearance onscreen. "During *Look Back in Anger* my metabolism just gave up for a while and everything made its way quietly on to my hips." However, her less willowy shape pleased *Impromptu*'s costume designer. "He got the corsets out and said, 'This is the sort of body you can do something with.' I was like a tube of toothpaste."

At one point during shooting, it was even suggested that she might need to diet. Instead, when the person who'd made that remark appeared in the canteen, Emma had gathered all the cast's desserts in front of her and was nibbling at them, her feminist response to the affront. However, once the filming was complete—and the only person she really had to prove anything to was herself—the self-doubt about her appearance reasserted itself, and she checked into Grayshott Hall health farm in order to lose some of that weight quickly.

Luckily for everyone concerned, the embarrassment of *Impromptu* vanished quickly from the theaters on its release in spring 1991.

Meanwhile, Ken had come up with the next project for Renaissance: stagings of *King Lear* and *A Midsummer Night's Dream*. Unlike previous Renaissance theater productions—and by now Emma, if not a major part of the Renaissance group, was definitely a member of its family—these two would be performed worldwide, in countries like Japan and America. It was a smart move, well-timed to take advantage of the couple's new international fame from *Henry V.* And by concentrating on territories outside Britain, they'd be away from the eyes of writers who both loved them and loved to hate them.

Emma had already been offered more television work but turned it down in favor of performing with her husband and stretching herself in Shakespearean roles, as Helena in *Dream* and the Fool in *King Lear.*

The Oscar nominations, and the ceremony itself, occurred while Ken and Emma were on tour with the Shakespeare plays. For the nominations they were actually in Los Angeles, performing nightly at the Mark Taper auditorium and living in an apartment that hardly seemed to befit their status.

"We were living in the Oakwood Apartments in Burbank," Emma said. "Rain was coming in through the ceiling and we had the four posts of the bed set in water-filled ashtrays to keep the ants out of the sheets." Although the physical deprivation might have been slightly exaggerated, it was almost certainly true that Ken, firmly believing he had a chance at a nomination "was up all night on the couch waiting for news. . . . There was a receiver-shaped dent on the side of his head." After he heard the news, she continued, "It took all morning to get him off the ceiling. After that, the scripts came in by the truckload."

He'd been nominated for both Best Actor and Best Director for *Henry V*, and the film had garnered other, more technical nominations. Big things had been expected of it, and it delivered; any awards were merely icing on the cake—and the icing was already piled high. The British Film Institute had, perhaps predictably, awarded it Best Film of the Year. At the European Film Awards it was voted Young European Film of the Year, with Ken as European Actor of the Year. But the Oscars were in a completely different class. They were the awards that everyone knew and recognized. One of those statuettes could be Ken's passport to true international fame and fortune.

Many felt he had a good chance of winning. Shakespeare, after all, was revered; he had class in an industry that showed little. And that meant that Ken had class. And the shadow of the young Orson Welles, writing, directing, and starring in *Citizen Kane* still hung over the Academy. Its members liked young men of ambition who could deliver the goods.

Certainly no one would ever have thought that Emma would beat her husband to an Oscar. At the time the very notion seemed absurd; he was the truly talented and ambitious one. She was merely the good actress on his arm wearing his wedding ring. She'd yet to spread her wings properly. Then again, she'd yet to be given the chance to show what she could really do. Quite probably she herself didn't even know what she was capable of.

The nomination alone suddenly made Kenneth Branagh a hot property in Hollywood. He was feted, lauded, and would have been wined and dined if he wasn't working and on tour. By contrast, Emma, who had three movies on her resume now, was largely ignored and passed over. She remained Mrs. Branagh, an appendage, rather than being credited as a strong actress in her own right.

And a strong actress was what she was rapidly proving to be, one who could turn her hand to any role and draw something fresh from it. Whether that was because with a lack of dramatic training she saw things in less formally theatrical terms, or because she was able to dissect her parts in a literary manner, the end result was impressive. Most intriguing was her interpretation of the Fool in *Lear*, which drew mixed reviews. Traditionally a male role, she made the character quite asexual, a grotesque caricature of a person who, because of her/his deformities, could look at people from the outside and how funny their lives were and speak both sharply and wisely about them. It was a daring interpretation, but on the whole it managed to click with audiences. Branagh wanted Shakespeare to be entertainment again, rather than a long, scholarly evening at the theater, and the interest in the Fool helped make his *King Lear* precisely that.

Newsweek said that "Emma Thompson . . . does a brilliant double as the Fool in Lear and the dippy Helena in *Dream*. She plays the fool as a plague-crippled hunchback. Her exquisite face emerging from a ravaged frame, Thompson scuttles and hops about like some mutant beetle or toad, her deformity giving added force and pathos to her verbal trade."

In America, the *Chicago Tribune* looked more deeply at the role. "Thompson took Shakespeare's most insightful court jester and turned him-her into an it, a 'swamp thing' as she puts it, a deformed, tongue-tied ghoul that slashed Shakespeare's wit with razors and found extraordinary layers of pain and suffering in the character."

Variety agreed that "Emma Thompson does a fine job as the Fool, Shakespeare's cleverly disguised voice of wisdom, moving around the stage like a human toad, distorted and twisted of body, but clear of vision."

King Lear was generally better received than Branagh's frothy interpretation of *A Midsummer Night's Dream*, which *Los Angeles* declared had "the feel of Shakespeare that has been polished and high-teched to appeal to people who don't care for Shakespeare . . . rather than just going with the Shakespearean fast flow. I found my mind wandering."

Updated to the 1920s, with Branagh taking the part of Peter Quince, it was, *Variety* said, a treatment with "no single strong vision . . . some scenes work, some don't; some performances are polished, others need help." And *Time* felt it was "radical chiefly in its frivolousness," noting that "Freud has nothing to do with this version. Its inspiration is more on the order of *Me and My Girl*."

Finally Renaissance brought the plays home to Britain, as one of the main attractions at the 1990 Edinburgh Festival staged in August. Tickets for the shows sold out well in advance, and the interest wasn't so much in Shakespeare as in Ken and Emma, to the point where they had to remain in virtual hiding every day from crowds eager to see and meet them. "It got completely stupid," said Ken's business partner David Parfitt. "Everything happened at once. They're just trying to stay out of the limelight now."

The opening in Edinburgh marked the one hundredth time the company had performed the two plays in nine months, and the *Sunday Express* had nothing but praise for Branagh's direction, calling it "powerful and breathless," as well as all the performances, singling out Emma, whose "crippled and cadaverous-looking Fool is mordently witty and brilliantly observed," just as she was "both funny and dignified" as Helena in *Dream*, which the paper noted as "also highly recommended."

However, in the *Daily Express*, Maureen Paton was much more sanguine, calling the plays "two mediocre productions . . . with all the basic values of a school show." Even she, though, was convinced by Emma "as a brilliantly conceived tragicomic Fool . . . she holds all the emotional power," and praising her Helena as "all lanky wounded pride."

Ken pronounced himself very impressed with all that Emma had brought to the parts. "One of my favorite performances of Emma's was as the Fool," he said. "She was absolutely magnificent—one of the best pieces of acting I've ever seen. She obviously does have a very sharp sense of comedy—but also of pathos."

In this case it was apparent that much of Emma's interpretation had come from the course she and Simon McBurney had taken in Paris some years earlier with Phillipe Gaulier, during the Cambridge summer vacation. Gaulier had theorized that there were three disciplines, "which were Tragedians, Clowns, and Buffoons," and her Fool seemed to be heavily drawn from the notion of the Buffoon: "sort of the people from the swamps or the leper colonies who were brought in to amuse *la jeunesse doree* and who had nothing to lose and, therefore, whose gift was parody. They always trod a very fine line because they were brought in to be grotesque, but if they went over the line, they would lose their lives. . . . It's very ancient, but it's still a part of our nature." And while Emma saw herself as one of nature's clowns, her Fool was far more bizarre, an intelligent, perceptive grotesquerie.

On Oscar night the plays were being performed in Japan. Emma stayed with the production, in the spirit of "the show must go on," while Ken, accompanied by old friend John Sessions, went to the ceremony. He didn't walk away with any of the statuettes, but for a first film he'd still managed to do astonishingly well.

༄

SUDDENLY he had a large Hollywood profile. He was bankable. And that inevitably meant scripts coming to him from everybody and his brother. Initially, the majority of the scripts that deluged Ken were "Period things. Kings! Endless kings! Or anything with a robe. 'We've got this great 15th-century story about a monk, and there's a king in it and . . .' Oh, Christ! Anything [with] an alleged weight to it." He had considered adapting Thomas Hardy's *The Return of the Native* for the screen, "but I don't think most of the studios knew quite how to take me. Then I picked up *Dead Again* off the script pile and literally could not put it down."

chapter six

Dead Again had begun life in 1986 when writer Scott Frank came up with the idea. When Ken stumbled onto it, it was being pushed by producer Lindsay Doran, who was working for Sidney Pollack's company, Mirage, which, Doran said, "made movies based on our hearts' desires, not on whatever material happened to be submitted from the agencies."

She believed in the script and had been trying to get it made. Some directors had turned it down, and Doran had rejected a few who'd wanted to make it. The right person hadn't come along, at least not until she saw Branagh in *Henry V*. Doran realized Ken was the director she needed—"someone who could be visually dazzling and deliver strong emotions."

After Ken had read the script, and been captivated by it, he and Doran met. But he came in with some ideas of his own. Doran had expected him to be just the director; he also wanted to star. She'd envisaged some strong American movie names in the lead roles; he wanted to play *both* male leads. And he wanted Emma for both female leads.

"Ken's thing is he just didn't want to do it on his own," Emma told *Premiere* later. "He really needed the support system, because it was a very frightening job. . . . I don't see the point of putting yourself through something as hard as that if you can't share the adventure with your witness.

Also, he wanted me as an actress, not only a wife. I mean, he actually thinks my work is good."

And there was no reason why he shouldn't have thought so, since she'd shown her range and her quality. Working in Hollywood, away from the Renaissance team and the friends who'd helped him so far, at least he'd have one sympathetic pair of ears.

Although she wanted Ken for the movie, Doran was initially skeptical about his ideas. Scott Frank "had originally written it for four people, with the idea that there were many more twists to the plot. But Ken said to me, 'Let me be your Lon Chaney,' I thought of *Dr. Strangelove*, and I realized this could work."

Convincing Doran was relatively easy; convincing the executives at Paramount to take such a chance on a relatively unknown filmmaker, and a British filmmaker at that, however talented he might seem, was altogether another matter. Still, at least Ken and Emma were there together. "We'd have some ghastly experience with some executives in a boardroom," Emma recalled, "and at least we could recover by locking ourselves in a bathroom and hissing at each other for ten minutes about how awful they were."

It was time to turn on the Branagh charm that had worked so well in the past. "Ten minutes with Ken, and he can talk you into anything," admitted David Kirkpatrick, the head of Paramount. "We all knew very well that when you buy Ken Branagh, you buy the whole package."

But they did force Ken to include some Americans in that package, as a way of hedging their bets—Donald Sutherland, Andy Garcia, and Robin Williams (who played without a credit) were added to the cast. (However, when Donald Sutherland dropped out of the cast, Branagh insisted that Derek Jacobi replace him as the film's villain, allowing himself to be surrounded even more by a British support system.) Ken and Emma remained largely unknown in America, and weren't likely to draw in audiences at the box office. To make sure Ken couldn't do too much damage, the budget was set at $15 million, making it, by Hollywood standards, a small film.

For Ken, though, who'd been so used to being involved in helping raise the finances for his own work, it seemed like a fortune. "I can't help taking it personally that people have said, 'Here is $15 million of somebody else's money, could you please make this film work?' But responsibility—for me—is a very useful creative pressure. I like to return the faith, as it were."

As soon as the commitments for the Renaissance Shakespeare tour had been fulfilled, Ken and Emma packed their bags, left London, and moved to Los Angeles to prepare for *Dead Again*. It wasn't something that had been anticipated in England, and suddenly after being praised as the golden couple, they found themselves vilified in the press for leaving the country and chasing the money.

It was seen as a betrayal, after Ken had been so loudly heralded as the savior of British cinema, one who'd seemed to put his artistic ideals in front of cash in the bank. And the press, having helped make his reputation, was now unleashing its fury on him—and on Emma for going with him. For a while, at least, the newspapers would have no kind words for them.

But Ken and Emma were several thousand miles away from the furor, working hard. Emma had spent time in America before when her father was directing, but for Ken it was a new experience, although, Emma noted, he seemed to adjust to it very easily. "He's got an instinctive understanding of the place. He just arrived there and started to work it out, because that's the kind of brain he has."

For this "reincarnation romance," as it was billed, they both had to do plenty of preparation. Since an English private eye in America wouldn't have been too believable, Ken had to master a California accent, for which he worked with three separate dialect coaches.

Meanwhile, Emma began to delve into the subject of rebirth. She even announced that, "I once went to a psychic and he said that in a past life I had been married to my mother, and that my father and sister were our children. I'm sure Kenneth could have been my servant, my Egyptian toyboy or my pet turtle." Luckily she was joking; however, after a few of the gaffes she'd made in the past, it wasn't always easy to be certain.

While Ken was taken with the idea of the movie, Emma had ambivalent thoughts about her role, which required her to look good more than act.

"I found it stressful to be in a part that was supposed to be beautiful, for a start. I loved the story, it was well told and a good thriller, you know, but it's not nearly as interesting as the stuff that I normally do. I just find it's important to play people you're not sure about."

Of course, Emma had her ongoing doubts about her looks and appearance, and any role that required beauty and glamour would have scared her a little, since she felt they were qualities she didn't possess. In fact, she initially suggested to Ken that he find another actress to star in the movie—although she ended up looking marvelous herself.

"I thought Ken really wanted, *needed* a star, but he said he wanted someone he could do emotional shorthand with. And I think we look right together. I'm sure Michelle Pfeiffer would have been wonderful, but would she have looked right with Ken?"

Pfeiffer could have added a distant sexiness to the film, but in Lindsay Doran's estimation, Emma brought her own brand of sex appeal. "There are a lot of people who think being smart is sexy. A lot of people think being funny is sexy. Also she's a sexual person, she creates a sexy atmosphere and she's very earthy, which is a big surprise to people who think she's got her nose in a book all the time."

Between preparation, a three-month shoot, and post-production work, Ken and Emma were committed to spending almost a year in Los Angeles. Luckily, they both enjoyed being there—at least as visitors.

"Every day I drove to work," Emma said, "with the radio on and the breeze blowing through my hair; I thought to myself, 'Good heavens, this is quite thrilling. It's like Ken and Em's Big Adventure,'" adding elsewhere that "It was just wonderful, but I think it would have been a grave mistake for us to give up our status as foreigners." For Ken's part, "It was very exciting. But it's just not home. I'm a northern European, so I'd always rather be [in Europe]."

It was the first time the two of them had worked together so closely, and for such a long period, which could easily have caused tensions, especially since Ken was Emma's boss on the movie.

"Strangely enough, even with all the lighting breaks and delays on the set, we didn't find that we were in each other's hair all day," Ken said. "What we've always had, which is nice, is a shared sense of humor. One of the things Em was able to do was make me laugh."

As he'd anticipated, she became his prime support and sounding board for ideas. "We've never used the set as a place to work out personal differences. . . . If he was not my husband, I might be more difficult. I don't want to hurt his feelings so I hold back."

It was the third time they'd played a married couple, although, as she noted, "I think it's interesting that the couples we've played have, generally speaking, had fairly disastrous relationships. . . . Let's just say that in professional terms, Romeo and Juliet we ain't!"

California even seemed to bring out a little of the "new man" in Ken, and for the first time in their marriage, he cooked for Emma. It was a two-course meal: cream of mushroom soup and chicken casserole. Ken might have known how to act and direct, but in the kitchen he definitely needed instruction. The soup consisted of mushrooms sliced into hot cream, and "I don't know what he did with the chicken," Emma said. "I didn't ask for the recipe." After that sole culinary foray, Emma returned to preparing their meals.

Even on the movie set she was initially thought of as Mrs. Branagh. As in England, Ken was deemed to be the star, the name, and she was extra baggage, riding on his ticket. As soon as filming began, though, that was proved not to be the case. She brought a cool, chuckling intelligence to her two roles.

"She's very insightful," writer Scott Frank soon discovered. "She kind of gets at you with humor, while at the same time she's being really honest. One minute she can make you laugh at yourself, but the next minute she's got you *examining* yourself. She's that way about herself."

She and Lindsay Doran had quickly become friends, discovering a mutual passion for Jane Austen. "My top-favorite author," Emma said. "I started reading her when I was about ten or eleven and she just gets better and better."

"I'll read those books and I'll get to a point where I'll have put the book down because I'm laughing so much. People don't associate that with Jane Austen."

As if it were a ghost she couldn't quite exorcise, two weeks after the filming of *Dead Again* had begun, KCET, the Los Angeles public television station, began airing *Thompson.*

However much Emma shuddered at the idea of the series following her around, Lindsay Doran and her husband "found ourselves glued to it every week . . . we found it hilarious."

"There were a couple of skits in *Thompson*," she recalled, "especially the 'Victorian Mouse' skit, as Emma calls it. It was in the first episode. She plays a Victorian woman who comes to see her mother on the day after her marriage. Her little sister is there also. They're having tea and very polite conversation. Emma's character tells them that the oddest thing happened last night, that after dinner her husband said to her, 'Have you ever seen one of *these?*' She then says to her mother and sister, 'He opened his trousers and out came a sort of bald, pink mouse.' It was hilarious. It wasn't that it was raunchy. It was the language was very precise and very funny."

What Emma didn't know was that for some years Doran had also harbored a desire to make a movie of Jane Austen's *Sense and Sensibility*. The main—or perhaps first—stumbling block had been that she couldn't find a writer to adapt the novel. But "Emma's ability to write in period language seemed effortless. In short, it was exactly the kind of writing I'd been searching for. I knew that Emma had never written a screenplay before, but there was enough sense of story-telling even in those two- and three-minute sketches to indicate that writing a full-length script wouldn't be too difficult a leap."

And, indeed, Doran did talk to Emma about writing a screenplay. It was an offer that came quite out of the blue, and a task that would take a great deal of work before it would see fruition. Initially she was surprised at Doran's choice of book, but reading it again, she came to understand its dramatic possibilities and took up the challenge eagerly, feeling that "even if I fail it will be worth it to have a go."

More immediately, there was *Dead Again* to finish. Ken had done something quite rare in Hollywood—he'd filmed Scott Frank's script word for word, although he altered it some by deciding that he and Emma should play both sets of lead characters, an idea that hadn't occurred to Frank. "[He's] very respectful of the word," Frank said. "Because he comes from theater, he's very clear and precise about not deviating from the text. When there's something that doesn't work for him, he's very good about letting me come up with the solution. He would never impose one."

∾

As a boy in Belfast, Ken had been enthralled by Hollywood movies, by Jimmy Cagney and Alfred Hitchcock, and this was his chance to make that kind of film. The fact that it was so different from *Henry V* was only part of the appeal to him. It also enabled him to offer his own small homage to a childhood in front of the television.

At sneak previews, though, *Dead Again* didn't fare at all well. Members of the audience treated it as low comedy; some even walked out. It was a gutting moment for its director. Even re-cutting didn't help. The film was going to be shelved until Ken suggested that the flashback scenes with Roman and Margaret Strauss be run in black and white instead of color.

Surprisingly, this small change made a huge difference. It invoked a forties glamour and gave the movie a sense of style it otherwise lacked, a brooding and menace that was heightened by the shadows and monochrome.

In fact, those were the scenes where *Dead Again* came to life. With a goatee, swept-back hair, and a German accent, Ken was perfectly convincing as composer Roman Strauss; he even managed to emanate a faint sex appeal. Emma, playing Margaret Strauss, had to convey the character's personality in a quieter way, with less dialogue. But although she seemed more aristocratic than glamorous—and for someone who was a cellist in an orchestra, Margaret never seemed to practice, or even have an instrument around—she did invest Margaret with an amused, concerned intelligence.

The contemporary story was a completely different matter. Ken had worked on his California accent for several weeks before filming, attempting to make it "as weirdly West Coast as possible," but it simply wasn't realistic, although "I spent some time wandering about Los Angeles trying it out, buying things in malls." In her low-key way, by not trying too hard, Emma sounded more believable as the American Grace.

Most vitally, he simply didn't look the part of a hard-boiled detective.

105

His face was too boyish and unformed, as if he had barely experienced life let alone spent time on its darker side, seeking answers.

As Grace, the amnesiac whose identity he'd been hired to discover, Emma didn't have too much to do. Initially mute, she had to keep her eyes wide in wonder, look lost, be regressed, and gradually find herself. Still, she managed to maintain a coolness of attitude, a certain dignity, that kept Grace interesting. However, unlike Ken, her performance was all she had to concentrate on.

Even in its new form, *Dead Again* received very mixed reviews on its release in summer 1991. Most American critics seemed to enjoy it. One reviewer even found Ken's American accent convincing, stating it "may be the best performance of an American ever played by a Brit, filled with subtle ticks [sic] and a kind of hidden edginess. And the accent is dead on. It's almost as though Branagh is using *Dead Again* to audition for the U.S. studios."

Glamour called it "a movie with genuine style *and* satisfying creepiness," pointing out that, in a season that offered plenty of special effects—this was the year of *Terminator 2*—very few films had real characterization. *Newsweek* deemed it "cotton candy," with a "cleverly convoluted and frankly preposterous story," which was true, but at the same time admitted it was "highly entertaining claptrap, an exercise in artifice that's more sophisticated than most summer fare." To David Denby, though, writing in *New York*, Ken didn't have "sufficient command of film style, or the right actors, to bring off his boldly old-fashioned experiment with complete success."

Meanwhile, in *America*, Richard Blake rhapsodized that "[Branagh's] work offers convincing evidence that the film industry has a few brainwaves left. . . . It's a summer movie that can satisfy the sophistication of a fall audience." *People* summed it up by saying, "Suffice it to say that anyone who in a previous incarnation—or even this one—loved *Laura* should love this film." In *The Nation*, Stuart Klawans also compared it to *Laura*, saying that Ken had made "a 1940s-style melodrama that plays as if it had been released the day after" *Laura* had and also offering that "it gives you the satisfaction people used to get from an old-fashioned form of drama, which in recent years has been ironized almost to death. . . . Such are the wonders Branagh promises to work, if Paramount Pictures will only keep him in America."

The views of Ken's performance were more mixed. Some loved it, others hated it. Emma, though, received a greater share of praise, although almost every review felt it necessary to point out that, in real life, she was Mrs. Branagh. Not only was it a good selling point for the movie, it was also an indication of just how little known she still was in America.

"Thompson has everything," *The New Republic* said, "talent, style, intelligence, and (like Streep) an instinct for avoiding platitude in run-of-the-mill reactions and responses. . . . Thompson is the romantic actress Merle Oberon wanted to be. . . . [She] does her impressive best to escape the conventions of her role." *People* was also impressed with her qualities, noting she "projects palpable intelligence and wit." *America* felt that she "switches comfortably from the American Grace to the British Margaret, and she becomes lovely, sympathetic characters in both instances."

However, although the praise was definitely there, not everyone was raving about her performance. *New York*, decidedly tepid, felt that she didn't "have the intoxicating Hollywood glamour for her forties great lady. Thompson is a serious, talented, funny woman, but she's probably too honest an actress for florid kitsch." And the reviewer went on to point out that "neither in the past nor in the present-day sequences do Branagh and Thompson strike sparks as lovers," a view echoed elsewhere when a reviewer offered that "in and out of clinches, Branagh and Thompson seem about as lyrically intimate with each other as the leads in your average high school play. This, from actors who are actually married to each other and whose courtship scene in *Henry V* had both youthful charm and animality."

And it was true; on camera there appeared to be little chemistry between them. While, given the storytelling rules invoked by the script, it was obvious from the beginning that they'd end up together, there was never any sense of a growing bond between them. Even the one contemporary romantic scene, where Mike took Grace to a bar to hear some music, only to find it had been closed down, had the awkwardness of a teenage first date rather than any impending sense of sensuality. Had they become so comfortable with each other so quickly that it was impossible to reproduce the sparks? After less than two years of marriage, that seemed unlikely. If the fault lay anywhere, it could have been in Ken's direction. This was, after all, only his second film and his first in Hollywood. He was still learning the techniques, and was bound to make mistakes. He'd played romantic scenes as an actor, but as a director they remained new; his reach was still exceeding his grasp.

Still, as an homage to Hollywood's golden era, *Dead Again* had its moments. While the influence of Hitchcock and Welles lay heavily upon it, that also helped the fun. In the final analysis, though, *Dead Again* just didn't fulfill its potential, perhaps because as Ken said, "I still think of myself primarily as an actor." He could even take a reasonably objective view of his directorial abilities in *American Film*, calling it, ". . . very up and down. There are occasional moments of blistering clarity where I know where to put the camera and what size the shot should be. Then there are moments when I realize how fucking difficult it is."

However much he protested that he had no wish to be seduced by the American movie business, saying, "I'd hate to become too familiar with America. Whenever I'm in America, I feel I'm in a movie—I like that distance," the British press wasn't about to quickly forgive Ken and Emma for abandoning Pinewood Studios for the back lots of Tinsel Town. He'd been the great hope, and she was starting to show promise, and then they'd jumped ship.

That inevitably meant that *Dead Again* received a hostile welcome in Britain from most of the critics. That, really, was par for the course from the British media, a beast that loved to build up stars and then show its power by tearing them down again. "Our media continues to be a wee bit strange," Ken mused, "but I think it's just part of what happens. There is some degree of what I call 'setting up and knocking down,' meaning that it's particularly British to resent people who appear to be successful in a sort of overblown way."

Emma, always more domestic, preferred to see the relationship they had with the press as familial. "They're like very, very grumpy parents," she suggested. "They can be thuggish, but then they can turn around and be sort of incredibly sympathetic."

For the moment they were being decidedly grumpy, to the point where Emma commented, "I'm just glad we weren't sent home in unmarked crates," and Ken tried to defuse everything by saying he was "relieved, completely and utterly relieved. I'm brilliant at taking bad news and find it very hard to deal with the rest of it. That's a troubled, puritanical, Protestant upbringing for you."

Ultimately, *Dead Again* served two purposes. Whether completely successful or not, it consolidated Ken's reputation as someone who could direct a film and bring it in on time and without going over budget, which would be important for any future plans. And it offered Emma her first extensive serious movie role. The concept behind the picture might have been somewhat kitsch, but her acting wasn't. She showed an instinctive grasp of the form, never overplaying to the camera, and projecting a likable, eminently sensible personality; this was someone who was never going to be swept away by tides of emotion. More than most, she embodied the British stiff upper lip characteristic. While many actors change themselves to fit the parts they are playing (Robert De Niro being a prime example), Emma looks at the role and latches onto the pieces that come closest to her own personality, then emphasizes those to color the character.

And although that is an untrained way of proceeding, it works. Combined with the warmth she casts, it makes her easy to watch and hear. What could seem like artifice with some actors on screen appears perfectly natural in her. Emma quickly developed her own take on the art of acting, a series of small ebbs and flows that could work in certain contexts. She wasn't cut out, for example, to reprise Elizabeth Taylor's Cleopatra, with all its grandiosity, but *Dead Again* continued to establish a niche for her as someone who could bring a great deal to the more strait-laced roles and make them more than the sum of their words. And this made for an impressive start.

But comedy wasn't going to immediately vanish from her life. While on the West Coast, Emma was offered a chance to appear in her favorite sitcom, *Cheers*, which had a history of drawing in slightly unusual guests—John Cleese had also been on the show. She played Nanny Gee, a thoroughly awful children's' entertainer who visits the bar and who turns out to be the former wife of regular Frazier Crane. Nanny Gee was over the top, impossibly ridiculous, and Emma loved every minute of playing her. Being able to act on a show like *Cheers* was real celebrity to her. And although, she said, "I only got the part because Glenn Close had to drop out," the fact that she was even asked meant that in some quarters her talent had been noticed.

But once *Dead Again* was finally ready, Ken and Emma's Big Hollywood adventure was over. It was time to return to London and the life they were used to, far from large rented houses and convertibles. What they needed, first of all, was a vacation, and finally they took one, the first time they had been able to spend together where work wasn't constantly intruding. For three months they disappeared, on a walking tour of Scotland and Ireland. It was also time to think about putting down some real roots. Emma's small flat had been fine for her but was too cramped for the pair of them. Even though one or the other usually seemed to be gone, they needed a larger place where Emma could have an office of her own to start work on the *Sense and Sensibility* project, for which she'd signed to write the screenplay. And just prior to going to America to make *Dead Again*, they'd bought the perfect place. Now they had a chance to settle in.

There had never been much point in looking beyond West Hampstead. That was Emma's neighborhood; it always had been. It was the only place she seemed to want to live, where she felt truly relaxed and at home (when the opportunity occurred a couple of years later to buy a larger house in Hampstead proper—which Ken and Emma could have easily afforded—they chose to stay where they were). So when a house went on the market directly across the street from Emma's mother, it seemed like serendipity, and they had no hesitation in snapping it up, even at some $600,000, hardly a bargain for a neighborhood that was nice, but not exclusive.

Her mother had actually taken a hand in the dealings, informing the executors of the estate handling the house that Ken and Emma were interested in the property.

A suburban semidetached house hardly seemed the place for such an artistic pair, but for Emma it was ideal. The life of the suburban middle class was in her blood. In slightly different ways, it infused all her film roles. Innocuous and bland as they might have been, those were her roots, and she was determined to stay as close to them as possible. Although behind the ordinary facade, the house was quite luxurious, with two studies and a shower with a raised tiled bed on which to sit and let exhaustion wash away. For Ken this was part of his climb up—from Belfast, from Reading, from south London—his rise to prosperity and creature comforts.

Emma was also pleased to be so near to her mother. There had always been a great deal of affection between the family members, and Eric Thompson's death had brought the remaining members even closer together. Sophie Thompson, now fully established as an actress in her own right, bought Emma's old flat just a few blocks away.

As the year progressed, though, there was a more pressing need for them to be close. Emma's Uncle James—Phyllida Law's brother—died, followed shortly by Ronald Eyre, Emma's godfather. It seemed as if the men she knew were all dying young. "It was like some medieval curse," she said. "We can't get over the fact that all these divine men managed to drop off the twig with such alarming alacrity. . . . Thank God for Ken."

Ken, and her mother, were Emma's support system. Since she'd become an adult, and then joined the theatrical profession, Emma and Phyllida had enjoyed a good relationship. Now they could, and did, pop in and out of each other's houses, friends and neighbors as much as family.

Ken, luckily, also liked Phyllida. He'd already cast Sophie when Renaissance had performed *Hamlet*. And as he geared up for the next film, he offered Phyllida a part.

Emma had become fully integrated with Ken's theatrical friends. In turn, he'd been accepted by her set, the comic Mafia and the old Cambridge Footlights crowd.

Emma's original mentor, Martin Bergman, the boy she'd met some fifteen years before who'd ended up as president of Footlights when she was just starting out and had persuaded her to become involved in it, had moved to America and married the comedian Rita Rudner. These days he operated very much behind the scenes, involved mostly with is wife's career.

But his memories of the good times at the university hadn't faded. In fact, he'd written a screenplay with his wife that unashamedly and nostalgically celebrated them. The fact that it had a part ideally suited to Rita—at that point about to hit the zenith of her career—was conveniently coincidental. The script interested Ken. Although still a workaholic, marriage had made him realize that there was more to life than movies and theater. "I've certainly reached a point in my life where I'm very interested in maintaining friends and valuing friendship in the face of a difficult world," he said, and that was exactly the message of *Peter's Friends*. And perhaps most importantly, it enabled him to work with Emma again, back in England.

"It is set in modern Britain and is very much a contemporary piece," Ken announced. "It features mainly British actors and will be shot around London," before adding, possibly for the benefit of the assembled journalists, "I'm very excited about projects in England, and I was less excited about being asked to live in America and do some other things." In typical fashion, he did hedge his bets a little, by allowing that, "I would go back at the appropriate time for the appropriate project."

For all its intimations of *The Big Chill*, the very successful movie that more or less defined the baby boomer generation, Paramount wasn't too eager to become involved with financing, although they had a deal with Renaissance, which in effect, meant directly with Ken.

"*Peter's Friends* cost $3 million; I'd just made *Dead Again*, which cost $15 million and made about $40 million in America, so they said, 'We'll do anything you want.' I told them about *Peter's Friends*, they said, 'Fine, we'll read it over the weekend and ring you on Monday.' They never do, of course, because they can't stand to give you bad news. . . . They finally said, 'We don't know how to make a film like this.'"

But Ken did, or at least he believed he did. Not only did he want to direct, but again he wanted to take one of the roles as well, making himself, at least for the duration of the movie, into a Cambridge graduate and part of Footlights—on an even keel with Emma and her friends.

It had been written for the Footlights group that had taken *The Cellar Tapes* on tour and then gone on to their own fame and fortunes, and they seemed happy to be involved with it. It made for a family reunion of sorts, for which everyone was being paid, if not over-generously by movie standards.

Peter's Friends dealt with the adult issues of AIDS, alcoholism, SIDS, and infidelity, among others, but it merely glossed over the surface of each one before moving on to the next topic, as if there was a list to be checked off. That meant that the roles tended to be stereotypes, rather than real flesh-and-blood. And while any group of people was bound to amass problems as they grew older, in the ten years since leaving Cambridge this fictional group had gathered far more than their share. Even worse, every single stage of the script was telegraphed far ahead of time. Though the acting helped in part to offset the clichés, the screenplay's predictability was its greatest downfall.

Using music that had been popular in the late seventies and early eighties, by such artists as Bruce Springsteen, Queen, and Tears for Fears, only heightened the comparisons with *The Big Chill*, as if this was a faint English echo, one generation later.

For all its faults, and there were many, the movie did have a warmth about it that could only have come from so many old friends working together. And that, really, was what made the movie possible. Shot on such a small budget, in such a tight time frame—five weeks—it would have been impossible without a core of people used to each other, knowing each other, and above all, liking each other; no egos to be stroked or fed. "Did we laugh!" Emma said. "It was great fun, as it should have been."

In terms of professionalism, they'd all come a long way since Footlights. Fry and Laurie had established themselves as international television stars with their interpretation of P.G. Wodehouse's Wooster and Jeeves. Tony Slattery was known as a comedian. And Emma now had a reputation in the movies.

Given that the part of Maggie was written for her, there were definite echoes of Emma in the character she played. She was wrapped in the type of heavy sweaters and cardigans Emma had always favored as a way of disguising her body. And the idea of leaving Post-It notes for the cat while she was gone merely parodied Emma's own tendency to leave them all over the place.

The only difference was in their love lives. Maggie was the single woman who really didn't want to be single, with a life that wasn't so much self-contained as isolated. When she did look for love, it tended to be in the wrong places, such as the gay Peter, appearing at his bedroom door and throwing off her robe, or with Paul, the housekeeper's teenage son.

The cast made as much of the material as they could, giving it a warmth and emphasizing the wit over the occasionally maudlin sentimentality. And in that regard, under Ken's direction, they did manage to create a pleasant small film, with moderately credible characters and an obvious plot. Imelda Staunton, who played Hugh Laurie's wife, said hopefully, "We want the audience to care about the characters. We don't want them to see us as a group of rather uppity people on a posh weekend and say, 'So what?'"

However, given that it all took place in the large ancestral country house that Peter had inherited, and that everyone was involved in some way in the media, it would have been difficult for audiences to think otherwise. But in some ways the smug elitism of Cambridge and the media glorifying itself did work in its favor, creating a group that could be looked at from the outside, with either fascination or horror.

In Britain, it was the Branagh-Thompson-Fry-Laurie connection that was the draw. In America, the movie's charm was twofold. Not only was it so English, at least superficially, in its banter and the polish of its acting, it also offered a chance to see Rita Rudner on the screen playing the gauche Yank. However good she might have been as a comedian, however, she proved to be no comic actress, making the scenes she was in drag as if huge weights had been attached, whereas everyone else managed to tread quite lightly over the material.

To Americans, less familiar with most of the cast and their backgrounds than British audiences, it was seen as a witty, urbane film, something almost worthy of *Masterpiece Theatre* in the quality of its repartee and act-ing. In England, though, the reviewers weren't particularly charmed by it. The comparisons to *The Big Chill* were inevitable, and *Peter's Friends* suffered from them. One writer succinctly put it that "The British cast, which includes Stephen Fry, Emma Thompson and Branagh himself, isn't in the same league [as that of *The Big Chill*] and neither is the theme." However, *People*, giving it a strong review, called it a "tart, tender, ravish-ingly funny rendering of the first—and perhaps final—reunion of a nearly incestuous group of college grads . . ." singling Ken out for "bringing roguish charm and touching desperation to the role," and Emma, who "provides the joy we've come to expect from her as a virginal bookworm not altogether resigned to spinsterhood." For the most part, though, it just slipped in and out of release, ignored by American critics, a small movie that seemed to aspire to bigger things but lacked the mettle for the climb.

So while it wanted to be something deeper, in the end *Peter's Friends* turned out to be nothing more than a frothy confection with pretensions of greatness. There were no stars as such (although Rudner seemed to want to be one); it was truly an ensemble piece, where the interaction of char-acters was far more important than any single performance. Although hardly a high point in the career of anyone concerned, at least it wasn't a disaster, either. It simply existed.

However, making a movie that was to all intents and purposes autobio-graphical seemed to go to the heads of all concerned and elevate the luvvie factor. When the film premiered at the London Film Festival, the audience was ordered to remain seated until the Branagh party—in other words, all the stars—had left the building, something normally done only for royalty, as the *Daily Express* was quick to point out. It was a ridiculously conceited and grandiose gesture that did them no favors and which served to let peo-ple know that Ken (and by implication, Emma) might be getting above themselves.

Peter's Friends had both delighted and angered the British press. To some it was pure self-indulgence, utterly lacking in redeeming qualities or any thoughts of social responsibility, to others it was Ken and Emma mak-ing amends after running off to Hollywood and the almighty dollar.

It was, by and large, a peculiarly English film, with its middle- and upper-class characters and its reserved approach to revealing aspects of those characters.

Like *The Big Chill*, *Peter's Friends* centered around characters who were basically successful. But at least the characters in *The Big Chill* had a background of social protest and conscience (although not as much as the characters in John Sayles's *Return of the Secaucus Seven*). *Peter's Friends*, in which the characters had come of age in the material eighties, never questioned their right to own things. This failure in the characters, unfortunately, seems to have been a natural result of the privileged, if not sheltered, backgrounds of the Cambridge-educated cast.

Indeed, of the cast it was only Emma who was truly politically active. The awakening of her Cambridge days had stayed with her. During the Gulf War in early 1991 she'd demonstrated and spoken, trying to use her weight as a celebrity to change things in a country that—like the United States—was solidly behind its troops.

"I don't believe you can hit strategic targets without killing people," she told the crowd in Trafalgar Square. And at a press conference by the Committee to Stop the War in the Gulf, she'd joined a number of speakers, including some Labour politicians, to complain not just about the bombing of Iraq but also the way the media had covered it: ". . . the tone of [their] language is either hysterical or sterile. We are not being told about people who are dying. Talking about death is tasteless."

It was an attitude that gained her no friends in the media; it got her vilified in the popular papers, with headlines like "This soap-box actress doth protest too much, methinks," criticizing not only the fact that she'd spoken out, but also her "particularly hammy delivery," "stagey gesture," and suggesting that "Emma Thompson should stick to a script."

She wasn't about to let herself be so easily muzzled, of course. Although actors and the press enjoy a symbiotic relationship—she needed them to publicize her new projects, they needed her to have someone to write about—that wasn't going to be a consideration when it came to something she believed in.

And this wasn't the first time her political involvement, which was usually on a personal level, had reached the public eye. In 1989, shortly after her marriage to Ken, she joined actresses Julie Christie and Caron Keating in Downing Street to present a petition with twenty thousand signatures condemning Pol Pot's return to power in Cambodia to Margaret Thatcher, amid revelations that Britain's SAS was training Pot's troops. "If we help Pol Pot back to power, it will be like re-electing Hitler," Emma said.

However, as one reporter tartly noted, "it wasn't even one signature for each pound spent only three months before on her lavish wedding to Branagh."

Her socialist views put Emma in a difficult position. They were deeply held and firmly rooted, there was no question of that. But at the same time, through Ken (who notably stayed quietly in the background through all of this) she'd become a friend of royalty, spending time socially with Prince Charles. He was the Royal Patron of Renaissance, and they'd become friends—he even sought their advice before giving a speech on Shakespeare and invited them to a party on the Hebridean island off the Scottish coast, where he'd learned a music hall song, "Aunty Mary Had a Canary," to entertain them (although due to car problems, Ken and Emma missed the ferry).

But it put her in the position of having to reconcile the two opposing sides within herself. It was perfectly possible to be a socialist and still live well, possibly even lavishly on occasion; socialism had come a long way from its working-class origins. But to be a socialist and a friend of the heir to the throne, that was a little harder. And really, there was no way to resolve the contradiction between the personal and the political while remaining the person she was.

And one thing she'd always fought against being was Mrs. Branagh, although that was how the media on both sides of the Atlantic seemed to view her. To a point it was even understandable; she'd done roles without Ken, but the ones that had been noticed, and generated publicity, had all been with him. Some journalists who hadn't cared for her work even asserted that she'd only been given parts in his films because she was his wife, not because of any demonstration of talent, and that she might end up being the albatross around his neck.

Realistically, though, it was simply a matter of time before they'd work apart. However much they enjoyed being together, at play and at work, there would be projects that interested them separately. And in spite of the occasional snide comment, Emma had proven herself as a perfectly capable actress, able to hold her own against anyone, and not merely an Adam's rib adjunct of her husband.

She was her own woman and would remain so. Her political activities had proven that. To be seen that way publicly, though, she needed a very visible role away from Ken, and even before *Peter's Friends* began its hectic schedule of filming, tucked between commitments, she'd found what she was looking for.

Over the course of thirty years, James Ivory and Ismail Merchant had accrued reputations as makers of quality films. On remarkably small budgets they shot films that looked like epics. From concentrating on movies about India, they'd broadened their palette, and most recently seemed to have settled on bringing novelist E.M. Forster's work to the screen, in *A Room with a View* and *Maurice*.

Now they were adapting Forster's best-known novel, *Howards End*, and, hearing of the production, Emma desperately wanted to be involved. As someone who'd previously taken whatever part was offered to her, she'd never had to go after film work, but this time she wrote to Ivory requesting the part of Margaret Schlegel, the story's real focal point.

What she couldn't have known was that serendipity was once again with her. Even as she was sitting to write to Ivory, he was writing to her, asking if she'd be interested in the role of Margaret; their letters crossed in the mail. So when his offer came, she jumped at it, and he was very happy to have her as part of his cast. "She is a bit like Margaret anyway," he explained, "enormously rational, highly intelligent, and very assured. She has a great sense of society, and she played that to the hilt."

Howards End interested her because it was that rarest of things in movies, "a complex, human story . . . Modern films don't tend to have that. Their stories and their characters are often very simplistic. The complexity of Forster's story—and I think it's a masterpiece—is even more accessible in the film than it is in the book. There are a lot of problems in the

Emma in the comedy sketch TV series *Alfresco*, which also featured Stephen Fry, Hugh Laurie, Ben Elton, and Robbie Coltrane. (Photofest)

Emma poses for a publicity shot for her TV series *Thompson*. Although it was a critical disaster, Emma's writing for *Thompson* later helped convince producer Lindsay Doran that Emma would be the perfect person to adapt Jane Austen's *Sense and Sensibility*. (Photofest)

As Harriet Pringle in *Fortunes of War* Emma made a smooth transition from comedienne to serious actress. (Photofest)

Emma and future husband Kenneth Branagh met while filming the seven-part miniseries *Fortunes of War*. The two played Harriet and Guy Pringle, newlyweds who find their marriage and their lives threatened by the chaos of World War II. (Photofest)

Emma and Geraldine James in a scene from *The Tall Guy*. (Photofest)

While small, Emma's role as Princess Katherine in Branagh's motion picture adaptation of Shakespeare's *Henry V* was a memorable one. (Photofest)

Emma and Kenneth Branagh on their wedding day, August 20, 1989. (Duncan Raban/All Action/Retna)

Emma and Branagh watch a video playback of a scene during the filming of *Dead Again*. Behind Branagh are producer Lindsay Doran (*center*), who would later produce *Sense and Sensibility*, and screenwriter Scott Frank (*left*). (Archive Photos/Fotos International)

One of Emma's roles in *Dead Again* was that of Margaret Strauss, a renowned concert pianist. (Archive Photos/Fotos International)

In this scene from *Dead Again*, Franklyn Madson (Derek Jacobi, *center*) shows Mike Church (Branagh) and Grace (Emma) an old magazine article about Roman and Margaret Strauss. (Archive Photos/Fotos International)

Emma and Branagh in a scene from the film *Peter's Friends*.
(Clive Coote/Archive Photos)

In the Merchant-Ivory film *Howards End* Emma (as Margaret Schlegel) had a
chance to act with one of her acting idols, Vanessa Redgrave (as Ruth Wilcox).
(Archive Photos)

In what would soon prove to be a bit of irony, Emma and Helena Bonham Carter played sisters Margaret and Helen Schlegel in the film *Howards End*. (Archive Photos)

Anthony Hopkins, Emma's co-star in *Howards End*, gives Emma a kiss as he awards her the Best Actress Oscar for her performance in the film. (Reuters/Blake Sell/Archive Photos)

Emma poses with producer Ismail Merchant (*left*) and director James Ivory (*right*) at the Independent Spirit Awards. (Reuters/Sam Mircovich/Archive Photos)

From left: Denzel Washington, Branagh, Emma, Richard Briers, Brian Blessed, Kate Beckinsale, and Robert Sean Leonard in the film *Much Ado About Nothing*—the last film that Emma and Branagh appeared in together. (Photofest)

After the success of *Howards End*, Emma and Anthony Hopkins co-starred together again in the Merchant-Ivory film *The Remains of the Day*. (Archive Photos)

Prince Charles leads a procession of celebrities, including Emma and Kenneth Branagh, at the premier of *Mary Shelley's Frankenstein*, which Branagh directed and starred in. (Reuters/Fred Prouser/Archive Photos)

Emma with Helena Bonham Carter at the party following the premier of *Mary Shelley's Frankenstein*, in which Bonham Carter appeared. Rumors that Bonham Carter and Kenneth Branagh were having an affair abounded during the filming of *Frankenstein*. (Reuters/Pool/ Archive Photos)

Emma starred in the one-hour television drama *The Blue Boy*, written by her childhood friend Paul Murton. (Photofest)

As the socially inexperi-
enced Dr. Diana Reddin
in *Junior,* shown here
with co-star Arnold
Schwarzenegger, Emma
was really able to tap
into her comedic
impulses. (Photofest)

From left: Director Ivan Reitman, Danny DeVito, Emma, and Arnold
Schwarzenegger smile for the cameras at the Los Angeles premier of *Junior.*
(Reuters/Fred Prouser/Archive Photos)

Emma starred as the painter Dora Carrington in the film *Carrington*. (Photofest)

Jonathan Pryce played Lytton Strachey opposite Emma's Dora Carrington in *Carrington*. (Photofest)

Busy actress and screenwriter Emma Thompson still found time to share a laugh with producer Lindsay Doran on the set of *Sense and Sensibility*. (Archive Photos)

From left: Kate Winslet, Gemma Jones, Emilie Francois, and Emma in a scene from *Sense and Sensibility*. (Clive Coote/Archive Photos)

Hugh Grant (Edward Ferrars) and Emma (Elinor Dashwood) in *Sense and Sensibility*. (Archive Photos)

Emma and co-star Kate Winslet pose with their British Academy of Film and Television Arts awards for their roles in *Sense and Sensibility*. Emma won the award for Best Actress, Winslet won Best Supporting Actress. (Reuters/Kevin Coombs/Archive Photos)

Emma and Kenneth Branagh announce their separation on October 1, 1995.
(Express Newspapers/Archive Newsphotos)

Less than three weeks after Emma announced the separation of her marriage, her sister, Sophie Thompson (*Four Weddings and a Funeral*), married fellow British actor Richard Lumsden, who played Robert Ferrars in *Sense and Sensibility*. (Big Pictures/ Archive Photos)

Emma and her mother, Phyllida Law, at Sophie's wedding. (Big Pictures/Archive Newsphotos)

A thoroughly modern Emma attends the June 1997 premier of the movie *Face/Off*, starring John Travolta and Nicolas Cage. (©Pacha/Corbis)

book because of Forster's own attitudes about 'the lower classes.' He's vile about them. I think he had a lot of problems with women. Margaret is a wonderful creation, but I think the reason for that is that he's put so much of himself in her."

So as Ken plunged headlong into a festival production of *Coriolanus*, followed by a triumphant return to the Royal Shakespeare Company, Emma took a deep breath and began her first major serious movie role alone, not expecting it to transform both her career and her life.

chapter seven

Even before she assumed the persona of Margaret Schlegel, Emma knew she had a busy year ahead. As soon as *Howards End* was completed, she was due to join Ken in Tuscany to act in a film version of *Much Ado About Nothing*. And she also needed to find time to be able to work on her screenplay of *Sense and Sensibility*, which was slowly taking form on her desk and in her mind.

But she was lucky that not having enough time was her biggest problem; for most people in the acting profession, it's the other way around. Even her sister, Sophie, who continued to receive critical raves for her work, frequently found herself working other jobs to cover her bills.

As it was, Emma had even turned a part down, and a starring role in a major Hollywood production at that. On the basis of *Dead Again*, director Paul Verhoeven had approached her about taking the lead in his new movie, *Basic Instinct*, at that stage most notable for the fact that the studio had paid $3 million for Joe Eszterhas's screenplay. In a moment of extreme good sense, she turned it down, and the role went instead to Sharon Stone, catapulting her to both infamy and stardom. But the character contained absolutely nothing of Emma, and she needed those points of contact to make her work come alive. The fit, had it been able to happen at all, would have been appalling.

"I went to see Paul about that part," she admitted in *People*. "But I stay away from those roles, darling, because there's not a chance in hell that I'd ever be cast in such a thing. . . . I don't think there are many women out there thinking, 'Hey, I really want to be made to look stupid and take off all my clothes in a film.'"

In that, though, she was wrong; if it would make them into stars, there were plenty of women (and men) willing to do just that. Certainly, in its exploitation of women (although Eszterhas would have argued that in the movie the women were the powerful figures), *Basic Instinct* ran counter to everything Emma believed in, personally and politically.

Emma wasn't in a strong position to speak out and be heard, but that didn't mean she couldn't have her beliefs and stick to them. What she sought in serious parts was a sort of "female heroic," which didn't come along too often in the movies. She wanted her roles to be "three-dimensional. That they're real people, and they're not appendages, and they're not marginal, and they're not morally irrelevant. That drives me mad more than anything. It's the sort of patriarchy of our culture."

In other words, taking up the offer of *Basic Instinct* had never even been a fleeting option for her, since it fell into every category she despised—which made *Howards End* her greater good fortune. As casting director Celestia Fox pointed out, "It was the perfect role for her to play. Margaret Schlegel is an intellectual, and Emma has a genuine, believable intellect, which is rare in actors. Emma's very real. You think that she's really like the person she's playing, because she's not technical and you can't see her acting. You forget how much of an actress she really is. She's quite tough, but she's tremendous fun and terribly kind to people."

To James Ivory, one of her best features, and one of the reasons he wanted her for Margaret, was that "She projects a quality of mental health. I know that sounds absurd, but in this day and age you meet so many actresses who seem screwed-up. You couldn't have a screwed-up Margaret Schlegel." This made Emma, who permanently carried an air of sensibility, the obvious choice.

"Margaret's kinder and more patient than me, of course," was Emma's own assessment, "but it's one of those parts that make you think, 'I understand this person, I won't have to shift very far to inhabit her.'" And there was a great deal about Margaret she truly understood. Like her character, she'd lost her father. "I wasn't as young as Margaret; I was twenty-four. But it changes her attitude completely." Emma might not have gone through quite the same changes, but she knew them well.

As the moral linchpin of the story, it was Margaret who had to keep her head—and keep the peace between the Schlegels and Wilcoxes—as everything around her was falling apart. Even Anthony Hopkins's character, the bluff, extremely stolid Henry Wilcox, a man who seemed like granite much of the time, could crumble. The only one to really keep her head above water, to make compromise after compromise without ever losing sight of her real self, was Margaret.

"Margaret married Henry Wilcox because she wanted sex," Emma said. "This is a woman who, we assume, never had a full-blown sexual relationship. Who finds that she is a great deal more interesting than most of the men in her circle, then meets a man who is yeoman-like and deals with the practicalities of life tremendously well, and she understands that in order for life to be full, you have to have both—the life of telegrams and anger, as Forster puts it, and the emotional life where you attempt to understand and accept all the vagaries of human nature. She understands that compromise is really about the art of living. It's no good being like Margaret's sister Helen and saying life has to be all about art—God! What a prig!"

For all Margaret's good qualities, though, she was a product of her time and class. She was a woman who'd inherited a good income, affording her a life of leisure with her sister and brother, who was able, with the condescension of the true middle classes, to talk loftily of ideas and ideals, and with Helen, to take on the "project" of Leonard Bast, the working-class man who wanted to make a living and possibly even better his lot. In the end it was their interference that ultimately killed Leonard, shattering the Wilcoxes in the process and letting Margaret show her strength of character in keeping things together.

Even if it could oftentimes be very bloodless, *Howards End* did have a great deal of her in its story and its characters. For Emma, who was beginning to see herself as someone who wasn't quite "a modern" in some ways—a huge turnaround from the Emma of five years earlier, when her morality and ideas had been thoroughly contemporary—Margaret was something of a dream role, not just for its presence but also because "I've always been fascinated by the nineteenth century and [Forster's] characters walk right off the page. Forster put a lot of himself in Margaret because she's a humanist and modern writers don't write like that any more." In fact, she argued, the twentieth century and its events altered the course of literature. "People became cynical after World War I; there was so much killing it changed people. That's why I don't like the language of twentieth century writers, because I think the depth ended with Forster."

Of course, as someone who'd studied the period and read much of the material for her degree, it was perhaps natural that she would bring some literary analysis to bear on her character. But this was definitely a case of the intellect informing the heart, the kind of thought processes that made it clear Emma did not belong in Hollywood, where research tended to mean the Method form of living the role, rather than trying to place it in a social and literary continuum.

For all the seriousness of the story and the tightness of the production, forced to stretch each pound so tightly it could sing, the set of *Howards End* proved to be a fun place to work. The cast was as good as it could possibly be. Along with Emma and Anthony Hopkins was Vanessa Redgrave as Ruth Wilcox and Helena Bonham Carter as Helen Schlegel, the sister with the beauty and the fire whose heart ended up ruling her head.

To play Margaret, it wasn't necessary for Emma to appear as any kind of ravishing beauty, which worked well within her image of herself without feeding into any of her insecurities. "I'm not an ingenue or a pretty face," she admitted. "That's not how I'm seen or have ever been seen. I'm lucky in a sense. I don't have to lose twenty pounds or have various things done to me to maintain some kind of look."

"She's got a good perspective," Hopkins said. "A 'this is only a job' sort of attitude. . . . Unique and a lot of fun. She comes well prepared, she is precise about the objective." And he went so far as to call her "one of the best actresses I have worked with"—high praise from someone who'd already had a long and splendid career.

What she did have that were prerequisites for the role was intelligence that sparkled in her eyes, truly bringing Margaret alive, and her own sense of wit that meshed well with her character's; for all her earnestness, Margaret could exhibit a wicked sense of humor.

The filming took place during the summer of 1991, mostly in Devon, in England's West Country. But trying to capture some of the idyll of a simpler Edwardian English life was hampered by the weather, offering chances for shots only in the brief sunny spells between the rain. But even the downpours didn't dishearten the cast too much, as Emma pointed out. "Everybody is happy because Devon is so lovely even in the rain."

And she became the focal point of entertainment even when the cameras weren't rolling, telling jokes and playing small tricks with cast and crew, displaying a wicked and bawdy sense of humor.

By now Emma had acquired enough film experience to have a sense of confidence in herself and her abilities as a serious actress. She came to Margaret with a definite sense of the role in her mind and how Margaret needed to be played, and she wasn't above arguing points with James Ivory as to how some of her scenes should be handled. With Ken as her director it had been a different matter; much of the discussion could take place at home, or wherever the two of them were together alone. And as her husband, he didn't present quite the separate authority figure that Ivory, who had thirty years in the business, did. Ivory, though, was more than willing to listen, argue back, and even use her input at some points, which made the experience much more pleasurable.

"I really enjoyed it," she said. "And I've never really done that before. I think that's to do with being over thirty and being married. You suddenly think, 'Goddamn, I'll say what I like.'"

In reviews, much was made of the scenes between Vanessa Redgrave and Emma, reading something symbolic into the sprig of heather that Redgrave, who played the traditional, conservative first Mrs. Wilcox, passed to Emma, as if it was a flame or token from the old doyenne of British screen acting to the new.

It made good copy, but it was little more than wishful thinking. Ismail Merchant recalled, "Emma went and kissed Vanessa for giving her the opportunity to work with her, whom she had admired for so long. Vanessa hugged Emma and said it was such a pleasure to work with her. It was a unique and touching moment."

The two of them did have plenty in common; both were politically active, at the left end of the spectrum, and both were the products of theatrical families—but to talk of anything more, any crown being passed, was simply poetic license.

After all, Redgrave was hardly a doddering old woman about to die, and prior to *Howards End*, Emma had still to prove herself as a great serious actress. The closest she'd come had been with Ken in Shakespearean roles, and none of those had required her to carry the plot; her parts had been more the punctuation. So while the expectations for her as Margaret were necessarily high as the center of the film, no one could really have anticipated what the results would prove to be.

Special effects and Arnold Schwarzenegger blockbusters seemed to rule the box office in the early part of the decade, competing for something more violent, more outrageous, with bigger body counts to have the audiences put their money down at the box office—which they seemed only too willing to do.

What Merchant-Ivory made was small films. They looked grand, but they were driven by story, character, and dialogue. They appealed to an audience that wanted articulate thoughts rather than blood and guts. And in *Howards End* they succeeded in that goal more than ever before.

With the dream cast they'd assembled, there was no reason it shouldn't have worked superbly, but in the end the production went far beyond that. The chemistry between the characters ignited flames that stayed luminous for the entire film. Even Samuel West, whose Leonard Bast could have easily come across as a caricature of a working-class man with aspirations, made his character into a living, breathing creation with real feelings, something that Forster had never managed in his novel.

Hopkins's Henry Wilcox was as far from the role that had brought him international fame—Hannibal Lecter—as it was possible to go. His portrait of a smug man in control of his life, used to getting everything he wanted, only to find events gradually overwhelming him, to find himself being held together by a woman stronger than himself, was a study in acting.

But it was in the small gestures—the hand to cover his face when he broke down and revealed his emotions, for example—that he gave real life to Henry. In the scenes where Henry could have been bombastic, Hopkins played him as someone who was so used to being right and being obeyed, making any force of voice completely unnecessary. Even when he proposed to Margaret, having lured her to London from the country under false pretenses, the nervousness barely showed, covered by the indelible politeness of his class and wealth.

It was all underplayed to the extreme, but that was what made it so remarkable and realistic. And in Emma he had the perfect partner for such work, for underplaying was her natural way of acting. The two of them combined to give performances of extreme subtlety, where what was not said was every bit as important as the words uttered. It demanded concentration on the part of an audience, but repaid it tenfold.

While Hopkins played Henry as a very closed man, Emma made Margaret into a very open woman, one whose nature was giving, thinking of everyone else before herself. Before marriage her loyalty had been to her brother and sister. Afterward it went to her husband and to the family name, until Henry forced her to choose between himself and Helen.

Her Margaret was bright, living in a world of intellectual activity, of theories rather than realities. It was a life she enjoyed; Emma's eyes sparkled as the conversations twisted and turned. Marriage dulled her, her eyes seemed to glaze over. Life with Henry offered none of the cut and thrust she'd been used to. In its place, though, came comfort, and having made her decision—her most dramatic gesture in the whole film was to kiss Henry after his proposal—she was determined to stick by it. So she cut Henry off as he tried to confess to having had a mistress. Forgiving was easier than argument.

For all that her performance depended as much on expressions as any words spoken, Emma still made Margaret sprightly, full of life, inwardly acknowledging and accepting the fact that she denied so many things to make life easier, more livable. If Margaret slowly unclenched the closed fist that had been Henry, slowly making him into a full human being, then Emma's Margaret herself was transparent, almost luminous. The ability she had to convey so much with her eyes and her hands was remarkable. It wasn't minimalism, but a full dictionary of nuances.

It would perhaps have been asking too much to have had everything go smoothly, but at least the sole gaffe connected with *Howards End* waited until its premiere. Emma was the perpetrator. It was a gala showing, attended by Princess Margaret, Queen Elizabeth's younger sister. Protocol demanded that no commoner speak to her until spoken to first. But Emma, with her political list to the left, wasn't about to conform to such outmoded ceremony. As the Princess shook her hand, Emma quite deliberately flouted convention to tell her, "You're looking gorgeous tonight, as usual," and the two of them began a short conversation.

Princess Margaret didn't seem to notice the faux pas, or if she did, chose to carry on as if it hadn't happened. The press, however, pounced on it, taking Emma to task for her behavior. In response she came out with a perfect luvvie remark: "Because we know Prince Charles I'm used to being able to do what I like," adding later, "If I did offend then that's tough. But I'm sure not. Princess Margaret has a far greater sense of humor than that." Neither remark endeared her to people, and once again she was briefly vilified in the press, the British tabloids never having cared for anyone who put on graces that weren't theirs by birth.

For a couple of days the incident received more publicity than the movie itself. But once the air cleared, people could begin to voice objective opinions about *Howards End*. Merchant-Ivory films had always been well received by a certain segment of the public and admired for their craft. America, in particular, held them in something close to awe. While the majority of their productions fit well into the *Masterpiece Theatre* category of high middlebrow, this transcended everything they'd done before, largely thanks to the work of Emma and Anthony Hopkins.

Reviews on both sides of the Atlantic were glowing. Only the *Daily Express* seemed to dissent from the general tide of opinion when Compton Miller wrote that, "for me, the two central romances lacked conviction.... I remained under-awed by this overlong exercise in schmaltz."

But the general view was that Merchant-Ivory had produced their finest film with *Howards End. Vogue* called it "literature on screen at its absolute best." *Commonweal* agreed, deeming it "an adaptation that honors its literary source by being lively cinema." *Newsweek* felt that it was the "crowning achievement of [Merchant's and Ivory's] careers, that movie that seems to incorporate all they have learned about filmmaking—and life—and raised it to a new plateau" in "a film of dazzling visual splendor, powered by a dream cast. . . ." *Cosmopolitan* perhaps summed it up best by saying, "My only criticism of *Howards End* is that it comes to an end."

And it was a triumph, not only of the filmmakers' art and the script writing but also for the actors involved. None escaped praise, but as the focal points, most of the printed words dealt with the performances of Hopkins and Emma. He was the known quantity; with his past everyone expected superb work from him. But until *Howards End*, Emma had been something of a mystery. There'd been nothing in her previous screen or television appearances to properly prepare critics for the luminous revelation of her Margaret Schlegel, and with justification, they were overwhelmed.

"As for Emma Thompson," *America* declared, ". . . she is a master of chordal acting: she hits two or three emotional notes simultaneously, thereby drawing a layered response from the viewer. At one moment she can be both an overwrought 'old maid' sick of her own virginity and an ardent woman genuinely roused by love, an overopinionated bluestocking and a true pioneer for the social advancement of women, a silly goose and a noble swan. . . . Emma Thompson manages to embody Forster's vision of what humanity can be like at its fragile, vulnerable best."

In *The New Yorker*, Terrence Rafferty espoused the line of Emma being "a worthy heir" to Vanessa Redgrave but went further: "She never seems to be copying Redgrave's style, but we can feel that she has been inspired by it. She finds her own way: the performance is thrilling and original. Her previous work has been marked chiefly by a wicked adeptness at caricature, but here her acting is unmannered, daringly straightforward. Thompson is required to carry the movie, and she does, with an unusually graceful combination of wit and feeling."

The New Republic said, "We're tempted to believe that Thompson moves and speaks the way that Margaret moved and spoke in Forster's head as he was bringing her to literary being. . . . To be a great novelist's collaborator, as she is here, is to join two arts that are often forced together but are not often truly wed."

But *The Nation* summed it up perfectly: "As Margaret Schlegel . . . Emma Thompson seems to be making up her character with every breath. She's so smooth, you can't get your grips into what she's doing; you just accept her and marvel."

And that was exactly what audiences did. On the basis of its stunning reviews, *Howards End* did excellent business, and not surprisingly, garnered a total of nine Oscar nominations. Among them was one for Emma, as Best Actress.

In fact, there hardly seemed to be any award she wasn't nominated for that year. In England it was another BAFTA, for both her *Howards End* and *Peter's Friends* performances, the *Evening Standard* British Film Award for Best Actress (with Ken picking up their Peter Sellers award for comedy for *Peter's Friends* and the Michael Balcon award for his contribution to film), and another Best Actress award from the London Film Critics' Circle. And that was merely the beginning. The biggest question seemed not to be how many awards she'd win, but where she'd keep them all.

Initially, no one involved with the film had expected it to do well in America. It was so English that it was assumed much would be incomprehensible. Certainly Emma had entertained no high hopes for it, which was why, on the days the initial reviews appeared, she'd called Ismail Merchant, full of anxiety, worried that they might not be good.

"Not good?" Merchant replied. "Have you read the reviews? NOT GOOD? THEY ARE SENSATIONAL!"

And Emma went on to add to her shelf of awards. The National Board of Review, the Los Angeles Film Critics Association, and the New York Film Critics Circle all named her Best Actress. And then came another, bigger, Best Actress award: the Golden Globe Award. She should have been used to it by now, but when Emma found herself on the podium, facing millions on live television in January 1993, all she could manage to say through the breathlessness was "Oh crumbs! We are not used to this sort of thing in England. I've borrowed everything I've got on."

It was an endearing speech, and while it was true that England had no televised awards shows on the scale of the Golden Globes, both alone and with Ken she was a veteran of the awards circuit, even if her own trophies had just recently started coming. And as a luvvie, and a woman who if not rich was definitely comfortable, she should have had a wardrobe that would extend to the occasional grand night out.

There was only one award left, and that was the Oscar. After being lauded so much, and having won almost everything in sight, she knew there had to be a possibility. Winning that would have been the ultimate accolade. As it was, she could no longer really be thought of as Mrs. Branagh, but an Oscar would put the seal on the appellation "Emma Thompson, serious actress," and to have achieved it before Ken, in her first major role, would have been something remarkable.

Everything else had been a build-up to this. Learning of her nomination for the Academy Award for Best Actress in February, knowing it was almost in her grasp, brought out two things in her: nerves and ambition.

The nerves brought on a chest infection and a rash, causing her to check back into Grayshott Hall health farm in Surrey, the place she'd gone in 1990 to lose weight and where she shambled around in "an old dressing gown and my old Oxfam slippers" looking "sort of white and pocky, positively Elizabethan." Her diagnosis for the sudden illness was that "I might be a tad allergic to too much of that kind of attention."

However, given her feelings about her body and looks, it was possible that she was there—at least in part—to be sure she looked her stunning best at the Academy Awards in late March, although she insisted her real reason for being there was to take "the infection out of the house so Ken [then playing Hamlet with the Royal Shakespeare Company and up for an Oscar of his own, for his short film *Swan Song*] didn't get it." It was the perfect excuse, making her sound completely altruistic and as though she didn't really care about the upcoming event.

Something she didn't tell the press was that she'd been lobbying toward the Oscar for several weeks. For over a month everything in her mind was geared to assessing her chances and doing everything she could to bring the award her way. She even made several trips to Los Angeles to further

her cause, while the studio advertised the film heavily. For the woman who'd had everything happen by sheer accident, and who'd seemed perfectly content with that, this undercurrent of ambition was quite alarming, a streak of careerism raising its ugly head.

It was all an important business, and under the jokes an self-deprecation, Emma took it most seriously indeed. For over a month everything in her mind and actions was geared to that award.

When Emma found out that one of the British Sunday papers had interviewed a Hollywood studio executive who'd worked with her and Ken, she faxed the newspaper, demanding (not asking) all the details of his comments.

Emma had always taken great pains to ensure she was seen as a woman of intellect, whose brain was far more important than her body. Suddenly, though, she asked Lord Snowdon to photograph her nude, albeit most artistically, in the style of Velasquez's *Rokeby Venus*. The timing—just before the Oscars and after her stay at the health farm—seemed to smack less of a love of art than a love of publicity, and it did make many of the newspapers.

At the same time, there was no doubt that Emma's nerves were real. She spent the time between the nomination and the Awards themselves on herbal tranquilizers and admitted, "I probably don't quite realize how nervous I will be at the Oscars. I'm probably going to have some sort of frothing fit before it and be flown home to England in a wooden crate."

She wasn't able to attend the Awards with Ken (who was still involved in his run as Hamlet), and so she took the other person closest to her—her mother.

With a perverse sense of irony, the Oscar for Best Actress was due to be presented by Anthony Hopkins. The deal he'd hammered out with Emma was that, if she won, he'd simply say, "Oh fuck," and walk off the stage. In reality, of course, Hopkins wasn't about to screw up his lucrative Hollywood career with something like that, and so he just announced her name.

"As Best Actress came up, Mum turned to me and said, 'You haven't a snowball's chance in hell!' and I said, 'Absolutely!' Then I don't remember much—Tony Hopkins says I floated up there in slow motion."

She might have worked hard to win and look good doing it, but the time still seemed utterly unreal. "All I could think was, oh no, your hems are going to get caught," said Emma. "And I could see my mum sitting forward in her seat with the sort of expression she used to have when I was in school assembly." But the Dorothy Chandler Pavilion was a long way from North Camden School for Girls and a teenager who'd harbored no thoughts of acting. So after Emma reached the stage and accepted the statue, she began a speech that she'd taken a great deal of time preparing.

"I've thought long and hard about each speech," she explained to Robbie Coltrane in *Interview*, "and I've tried to make them short and sweet and yet say something, and also express genuine gratitude. You do feel completely gob-smacked by it all."

This time, after thanking all the usual people, she dedicated her Oscar "to the heroism and courage of women," stating that "I hope it inspires the creation of more true screen heroines. . . ."

After her speech, which had been guaranteed to raise a few eyebrows in an industry that still seemed to view women as sex objects rather than actresses, Emma was escorted backstage where "I walked straight into Morgan Freeman and Gene Hackman and we clinked Oscars. "They told me, 'You look terribly pale. You'd better put on some makeup!' I said, 'What, more? I've got on half a pound already!'"

But the biggest moment of the night came later at the post-award party, where she was able to sit with one of her movie heroes, Clint Eastwood. "We grinned and I said to him, 'I hope you're going to give me a job one day,' and he said, 'But you'd have to obey me!' and I said, 'I'm very obedient.' And I just hoped James Ivory wasn't standing behind me, ready to chip in, 'Are you kidding?'"

Not only did she suddenly find herself accepted among the Hollywood A-list for a little while, but she was at the head of the pack, although, she admitted, "I was kind of queen for five minutes. Jolly nice, I must say!"

As soon as it was over she was on the phone to Ken, waking him in the middle of a post-performance night. "I said, 'Yes, I did get it, and no, you're not dreaming.'"

Afterwards, as she'd hoped, there were questions about her acceptance speech, and the way she felt about women's roles in movies. "If there had been more roles like [Margaret] for all the great actresses in America, I certainly wouldn't have been up there on that stage. . . . She was a complex, ambiguous, and fully rounded human being," Emma explained. What she railed against was the virtual deification of the female body and the idea of being over the hill at thirty. She wanted more roles in the movies for women who didn't conform to some bizarre physical ideal and roles for women who were past that "prime" age. As she pointed out, "I can't compete for the roles Michelle Pfeiffer gets. Or Annette Bening or Sharon Stone. I don't look right. Even if my voice were right, my body's not."

Of course, there were plenty who thought she looked wonderful exactly the way she was. But that wasn't the point. The truth was, by Hollywood standards, Emma was not a bombshell, and those were the people who were offered the prime roles. "And if you think I'm going to spend four months on a fat farm trying to turn my body into something it never was and never will be, forget it. Because my life's too short."

Although she was willing to spend a week in one, making sure she looked as good as she naturally could, it was understandable that she wouldn't want to go further. Her appeal came from her natural beauty and the sexy combination of intelligence and humor. Campaigning for better roles for women was partly a result of her feminism; it just happened that it would aid her career in the long term. Her ability was in her acting, not her body. As one Hollywood agent assessed her, "She's not a classic beauty. She's not X-ray thin, and she hasn't yet had any ribs removed. She has hips, she has a regular woman's body, and that means she can play almost any woman."

What the world needed, Emma thought, were women's roles that would "negate all that rubbish and present a fully rounded individual." Not only like Margaret but also like some of the strong female stars of the past. "Betty Bacall, Katharine Hepburn, Bette Davis, Barbara Stanwyck—these were women around whom movies were *built*. There's been a regression. Women's economic status has improved, but other things have been clawed back. Today we're brainwashed by images of what women should look like.

"You have to be six feet tall and one hundred and twenty pounds. Take Sharon Stone. As far as I could see from *Basic Instinct*, they molded her body out of tough Plasticine. She was making love to Michael Douglas and not an inch of it moved! I thought, 'What did they do, *coat* her with something?' Had that been me [and it could have been, although she chose not to remember that], things would have been flying around and hitting me in the eye."

That she was genuine and honest in her beliefs was beyond doubt. And with the Oscar, she was in a position to say these things and be listened to and quoted. She did not, however, mention the problems she had with her own body-image, preferring to take the old route of self-deprecation by saying, "Luckily, I'm not known as a beauty, even if I do photograph all sort of glammy. If you asked people, 'Do you think she's beautiful? Do you think she's sexy?' I think 99.9 percent would say, 'Not particularly, but she's a good actress, and she's intelligent.'" Her intelligence was more important to her than her looks; but in an ideal world she'd have liked to have been blessed with them both.

∞

WINNING the Academy Award not only firmly established her as Emma Thompson, rather than Mrs. Branagh, but it also led to numerous predictions of her American success, that mountains of scripts and offers would land on her doorstep. A few months later, however, she was saying, "After all the heat generated by winning an Oscar, I haven't been offered any scripts yet by Hollywood. There are lots of ideas, but no offers." Except for a television sitcom, which didn't interest her in the least because, "You have to work on them for five years—it's like a prison sentence."

She attributed the lack of offers to her looks, and the recurring fact that she didn't match up to that impossible Hollywood ideal. Of course, such an explanation didn't completely dig to the root of the matter. Meryl Streep wasn't a beauty in that sense, either, but there was no lack of parts being offered to her. In truth, Emma had been partly the source of her own problem. She'd spoken out loudly for better women's roles at the Oscars, and in doing so had broken an unwritten rule: Don't criticize the industry at its big yearly celebration.

The fact that she'd been quite correct in every point she'd made was irrelevant; she'd opened her mouth and shown herself to be something of a troublemaker. And now she was paying the price. As an outsider, and someone who was a virtual American unknown before *Howards End*, she'd come in and criticized the big studios in their own backyard. Someone like that needed to be taught a lesson, and the lack of offers was precisely that. Hollywood was more than capable of dealing with its own prima donnas; the movie business had years of experience in that. But when it came to politics in any shape or form, they tended to shy far, far away. And Emma had raised a very political issue. The fact that she'd chosen to do it in 1993, the Year of the Woman, only counted further against her. You simply didn't rock the boat.

The surprising thing was that a woman of her intelligence didn't see it. Or at least, she chose not to see it, preferring to blame it all on her looks, that old insecurity of hers.

In truth, though, she need hardly have worried. By the time reporters were asking what had happened to Hollywood, she already had two more films under her belt and was preparing for a third in a bout of workaholicism that very nearly equaled Ken's.

The Oscar created another unexpected circumstance. With all the other awards Emma had garnered for *Howards End*, it meant that in the public eye—most certainly in America but also to an extent in Britain—she'd eclipsed Ken. Not only had she shaken off the "Mrs. Branagh" tag, in some circles there was a danger of him becoming known as "Mr. Thompson." In the nearly four years since their marriage he'd been the more visible one, the person who received most of the press. Now the situation was reversed; Emma was the one they all wanted to interview. To audiences in general, she'd become better known than he was. For all that they both protested there was no jealousy between them, this new situation must have added an odd dynamic to their marriage.

Over the course of their wedded bliss, the question of children had come up several times. As a pair of celebrities, it had been asked in public. More importantly, it had been asked in private, and both Ken and Emma had flip-flopped on the issue. They wanted them; they didn't want them. There seemed to be no consistent answer.

In April 1991 the couple, thinking very seriously about becoming parents, had looked after the children of some friends, an experience that seemed to make Ken want to postpone fatherhood. "We spent last weekend with two great friends of ours who have two kids," he explained. "One is two, one is nine months. We had three full days of being parents. I know this sounds pathetic, but it was a nightmare. After three days I never want to wipe another kid's bum again. You know how it works: you're charmed by other people's kids for half an afternoon, but after that they're fascinating only to their parents."

That time, which Emma dubbed "The Weekend of the Long Nappies," seemed to fire their resolve to continue full-tilt with their careers. Then nearly a year later, they baby-sat again, and Emma said, "We enjoyed him very much."

It reawakened her maternal instincts, and she realized that "I can't wait that much longer because I'm thirty-three. I'd like to have a child." She realized, in a moment of reflection, that "the pinnacles of my life have always been personal. Meeting, falling in love and marrying Ken is what really matters to me."

At that point, though, Emma was poised to film *Much Ado About Nothing*, working with Ken for the fourth time. There was a commitment of time and money, which meant that any thoughts about babies would have to wait. Again. And by the time she'd really be able to resurface, after her other film engagements and the Oscar, it would be almost 1994.

As to the Oscar itself, she needed the perfect place in the house to display it, and after trying the statuette in different rooms, she finally found its ideal home—in the downstairs bathroom. It was nominally a humorous gesture, but it also served another purpose—guests could stand in private, holding it, and practice their acceptance speeches in front on the mirror. Besides, she added, "It looks really good there, I don't have to bother running upstairs every time someone asks to see it."

chapter eight

The role of Beatrice in William Shakespeare's *Much Ado About Nothing* could almost have been written for Emma Thompson. Quick-witted, feistily independent, intelligent, yet with a romantic streak a mile wide, she was one of the strongest female characters he ever created.

The Shakespearean comedies often had a dark side, and this was no exception. The Bard recognized that comedy and tragedy were merely opposite sides of the same coin, and so his lighter plays contained deep shadows—abuses of power, faked deaths, Machiavellian struggles—even if they ended happily, with the bad guys getting their just desserts. But, Branagh felt, "I regard *Much Ado* as truly one of the sunnier plays; it doesn't sit as strongly on the melancholy side as some of the others."

Once again he was directing and starring in the movie, and it was his decision to film in Tuscany, to draw the warmth of the countryside, and the villa where the action takes place, into his adaptation of the play.

It would be the last Renaissance film—the strain of keeping the company going, along with all his other work, was proving too much for Ken, so he'd decided to wind it up—and in terms of scope and cast, by far the biggest. The usual suspects were there—Richard Briers, Brian Blessed, Phyllida Law—but added to them were some big American names—Denzel Washington, Keanu Reeves, and Michael Keaton. Not only would their names on the marquee help draw in the crowds, but it was

an indication that Ken had decided to put his money—and his reputation—where his mouth was after saying that he'd "always admired
American film acting for its emotional recklessness . . . and I think that's
how you should do Shakespeare."

The six weeks of the shoot turned out to be as much vacation as work
for the cast. In a bright stroke not only to save money but help everyone
bond, Ken made the villa where he was filming—Villa Vignamaggio—the
headquarters for the production, so it effectively also became a hotel.
Emma, in complete contrast to the character she was playing, was able to
indulge her love of cooking, producing bowl after bowl of fresh pasta for
everyone involved.

As Beatrice and Benedick, Emma and Ken were involved in constant
verbal sparring, which, she contended, was "pretty close to Ken and me in
real life. We are both very vulnerable and garrulous and banter is very
much a part of our relationship." She found the give and take to be "an
archetypally perfect blueprint for a relationship. Total equals. We made, I
suppose, as feminist a reading of it as possible, without changing the
meaning of it altogether. It's a remarkable part, for me anyway, because
she's so angry, she's so fucking angry! They went off to learn how to ride
and joust and things and she wasn't allowed to go because she was a girl,
and I think the anger and confusion and bewilderment started then, and I
think it's still very much with us."

Seriously reading the play made her realize "how relevant Shakespeare
is for our age, or any age. I wanted to use the opportunity to play for the
first time female anger and rage, which I don't think people find very
acceptable. . . . I was really looking forward to venting rage and having a
good old shout, and that's unusual because it's not very feminine."

She wasn't the only one to see echoes of herself and Ken in the movie.
Branagh adapted the play himself and agreed that "Emma and I are not a
thousand miles away from the characters of Beatrice and Benedick. We
had both experienced long-term relationships before. You sort of dance
around a bit."

If Ken's *Henry V* had been his idea of Shakespeare for contemporary
Britain, trying to make it accessible and relevant, this was his Bard for the

world, and specifically, America. With elements of sitcom and a wholesale homage to Emma's beloved Monty Python in Michael Keaton's Dogberry—his riding an imaginary horse was lifted directly from *Monty Python and the Holy Grail*—as well as some fine pieces of acting, it really did offer something for everyone. He made Denzel Washington's Don Pedro into a man who was both playful and thoughtful, the epitome of a just ruler, while as his bastard brother, Keanu Reeves seethed.

Ken's adaptation highlighted the central battle of the sexes between Beatrice and Benedick. But as writer, star, and director, "it was quite a strain for Ken," Emma said. "He goes quiet when he's got a lot of work on and I know when to stand back and keep out of the way." Over the course of three films together, they'd learned how to cooperate well.

"We have a shorthand. . . . I never disagree with him on the set. If I've got something to say, I'll say it to him well away from everyone else. I know when he's about to blow up about something and I can help take a bit of the pressure off. Directing is really about people management, looking after large groups of people, and I can be of help to spread the load." Working to make everything run smoothly, helping iron out the minor problems, was something that just came naturally to Emma, always the sensible one.

And she thoroughly enjoyed the chance to be working with her husband again. "It was fabulous, being in Italy, making this terrific piece," she recalled. "I know some couples prefer to have space, but we prefer being around each other more of the time than less. *Howards End*, when I was away from Ken, was much more difficult."

And Ken, in turn, was more than happy to have her as part of the company. "She's on a run of great form at the moment," he said. "*Howards End* was a great piece of acting, and she's excellent in *Peter's Friends*, funny and touching. She's come into her own, and she's an important figure in British films now. She's a *significant* actress."

Even allowing for marital bias, his words were nothing less than the truth. There was little doubt that she'd come a long way as a serious actress from her small role as Princess Katherine, or even from her performance as Harriet Pringle, which seemed tentative when compared to her more recent work. She'd learned, instinctively, how to harness the power inside her, whether it was through the small gestures of Margaret Schlegel or the sharp tongue and flashing eyes of Beatrice.

As with her previous roles, becoming Beatrice was a journey of discovery. "I suppose I discovered how to play her as we went along, as happens with most films," she explained. "That's why filmmaking is such a mysterious and interesting process. You can prepare as much as you like, but until you get there you don't know what the hell you're going to do. You prepare beforehand and then you let it go."

This time, so much depended on her screen interaction with Ken. The sexual sparks had to be there, but there also had to be an attraction and repulsion between the pair. Unlike *Dead Again*, where the fire had never caught, this time it crackled from the first onscreen glance, due in part to the dialogue, but also because they were obviously relishing their roles.

"It was great fun to create that relationship," Emma said. "They really like each other and they know each other. It's not really about romance, it's more about recognition of your equal, your match, your pair."

Emma's performance made Beatrice into a perfectly recognizable contemporary woman. The line between someone independent and someone shrewish was fine and she walked it carefully, as did Ken's adaptation of the play, which chose to emphasize those elements familiar to modern audiences, particularly the volleys of words and insults between Benedick and Beatrice, which were not only witty but also locked onto issues as normal today as then.

"That's why Beatrice is such a great part. The first fighter for rights!" And by Elizabethan standards, Beatrice was extremely outspoken, even rebellious, in her craving for equal acceptance. As Ken was quick to note, "Three hundred years after *Much Ado* was written we still have all the same problems."

That was one of the reasons it was such an inspired choice as a film. The issues and relationships made it easy for audiences to slip past any potential problems with the language into the characters and the plot. But there was also much credit to all involved for using Shakespeare's words carefully and bringing a clarity and accessibility to them. So much of the play was driven by speech, rather than action, that it would have been easy to trip up over problems of scansion and meaning. Instead, it all came across as something natural and easy, and—as intended—often devastatingly funny. As was actually the case, all the actors seemed to be thoroughly enjoying themselves, with Ken and Emma positively reveling in the opportunities to top each other in argument.

And the whole thing was bathed in a very Italianate, earthy sensuality, established early on by the bathing scenes with nudity as the most normal thing in the world. Ken had insisted on rehearsal time for the ensemble before filming began, and it paid off, not only in the way they all performed together but also in the healthy glows everyone radiated from the extra time in the warm sun.

Emma in particular looked better than she ever had, someone completely unlike Margaret Schlegel, fiery instead of conciliatory, unleashed rather than repressed, and a person who was quite believably sensual, even deliberately sexy.

With a background that now took in both serious acting and comedy, Emma was well grounded for the part. Her experience with Shakespeare might have been limited, but no more so than others in the cast, especially the American contingent.

The finished product presented England's greatest writer not as someone to be studied line by line, the meanings dissected, and each allusion noted and explored, but someone to be *enjoyed*. It was entertainment, as it had originally been intended to be, a "merry war" that ends in peace and reconciliation, with all except the bad guy living happily ever after.

Quite openly populist, and proud of it, *Much Ado About Nothing* was significantly slated to open in America before England, largely because much of the financing was American. Granted, it followed fairly quickly on the heels of Emma's Oscar, and was thus able to capitalize on her increased visibility. But more than that, it was one of the first times a modern film had tried to take Shakespeare out of the art houses and into the multiplexes. In America, where the plays didn't have the same historical and cultural baggage, there was a greater chance of it being judged on its own merits.

Before it opened, Emma—whose award had now made her far better known than her spouse in the U.S.—was scheduled to fly to New York to give publicity interviews. However, the night before her departure her baggage, including wedding ring and passport, was stolen from her London hotel room, leaving her with only a birth certificate as proof of identity. It was a tribute to the power of celebrity in America that that alone was able to get her in and out of the country. At JFK's immigration control she was waved past with the words, "Fine, an Oscar winner. Go through." The incident, bizarre as it was (why was Emma staying in a hotel room in the city where she lived?), showed that Emma Thompson had firmly established a reputation in her own right and become a star.

There was another reason for letting *Much Ado About Nothing* find its feet first in America. Throughout their careers, both together and alone, Ken and Emma had enjoyed a love-hate relationship with the English media. Sometimes they'd been the toast of the town; at other times, they'd been the subjects of all manner of potshots. Ken, backed by the studio, decided that it would be "too risky to open first" in front of a media "which loves to just take the piss."

Economically it proved to be the right decision. Two years earlier, *Dead Again* had briefly bettered *Terminator 2* at the box office. Now as *Much Ado About Nothing* opened, Ken and Emma found themselves out-grossing Arnold's *Last Action Hero* as language written almost four hundred years earlier proved more popular than special effects, muscles, and car crashes.

It succeeded with audiences partly because Branagh had the sense not to try and film a stage play but make a real movie out of it. For economic reasons, he largely confined himself to one location—the villa—but within those parameters there seemed to be constant movement, a business that kept things rolling right along. His adaptation of the play had been designed for precisely that, and what appeared on the screen confirmed that he was Shakespeare's most accomplished modern interpreter.

For all its success, there were moments of unwarranted excess. The musical interlude as Beatrice and Benedick admitted to themselves that love was the emotion coursing through their veins was an embarrassment—

nothing short of rococo, syrupy, and totally unnecessary. This was a battle of the sexes, after all, not a soap opera.

Once he reined himself in, however, his direction worked marvelously. With such a strong cast, he wisely kept his cameras trained on facial close-ups, forcing his actors to say as much with their expressions as with their words—a virtual necessity when using Shakespearean language for a modern crowd.

The plot essentially consisted of two stories—Hero and Claudio and Beatrice and Benedick—and quite wisely the focus was on the latter. It was stronger by far, much tougher and leaner. Robert Sean Leonard and Kate Beckinsale (who played Claudio and Hero) were young and lovely, but as actors they were thoroughly outclassed by Emma and Ken.

And even Ken was eclipsed by the talents of his wife, which seemed to have begun taking quantum leaps with *Howards End*. For someone with no training, her instincts for the part had been honed to a razor sharpness, confirmation that her portrayal of Margaret Schlegel hadn't been sheer luck, and that she'd become nothing less than a world-class actress. Acting, she had said, was the ultimate luxury, and she was reveling in it.

Before that, however, they could bask in the glory of their reviews. *Newsweek* called *Much Ado* "the most sheerly delightful of all Shakespearean movies," stating that "Branagh shows us that Shakespeare is vibrant bodies, not just talking heads." To David Denby, writing in *New York*, "Kenneth Branagh was put on this earth to make movies out of the plays of William Shakespeare," adding that "*Much Ado About Nothing* is one of the few movies of recent years that could leave its audiences weeping for joy."

Cosmopolitan's Guy Flatley found that Ken had translated the play "in robustly cinematic style, spilling the drama out into the hillsides and valleys and streams, sweeping away scholarly cobwebs, breathing immediacy and fresh nuance into every scene and line." And *The New York Times* called it "a ravishing entertainment," pointing out that Ken had "taken a Shakespearean comedy, the sort of thing that usually turns to mush on the screen, and made a movie that is triumphantly romantic, comic and, most surprising of all, emotionally alive."

Even the English, who loved to pounce on and gnaw away at their success stories, had to acknowledge that it was "very, very good indeed. . . . In short, it is a ruddy revelation."

Writers and audiences both loved the movie. But although praise was generously distributed throughout the cast, it was Emma who was invariably singled out for her performance. Among the leading names she was one of the least proven, at least in terms of a movie career. But that didn't stop her bringing both fire and grace to the role. The "blind instinct" that led her in acting was beginning to seem infallible.

To an extent, a lack of dramatic training worked in her favor. She was less rigid in her approach. Never having been taught how she *should* do it, she was free to let herself interact with the character, to find the similarities and expand on those, as she'd done so well with Margaret Schlegel. To her the process of preparing for a role was like "asking a plumber to open his toolbox. One hopes the water will come out in a steady and convincing stream at the end of the job." So far she'd certainly been unerring. She'd been justifiably proud of her work on *Howards End*; and on the basis of the critical raves, she had just as much reason to be happy with her Beatrice. About the only reviewer in America who didn't bow in her direction was J. Hoberman in the *Village Voice*, who called her "relentlessly mannered," with an "overbright smile, ostentatiously furrowed brow, and extended display of eye-batting concern."

To almost everyone else, Emma had scored another triumph, one that confirmed that the Oscar had not been ill-awarded. "As for Thompson . . . I'll try to restrain myself," Stanley Kauffmann wrote in *The New Republic*. "She *has* elegance. She has the finest command of inflection and style. She has spirit and soul. She is the first actress since Katharine Hepburn to make intelligence sexy. She lets us understand that Beatrice, like Kate in *The Taming of the Shrew*, behaves as she does because she is employing the only means available to break out of the expected pattern—daddy's girl up for marital auction. . . . After Hero's erstwhile fiancé, Claudio, has excoriated her (and we know she's innocent), Benedick asks the shocked Beatrice, loyal to her cousin, what he can do for her. Thompson then speaks the two words with which Ellen Terry is said to have stabbed the audience with ice: 'Kill Claudio.' Ellen, thou shouldst be living at this hour—to hear Emma."

Newsweek also evoked Terry's ghost, stating that "Thompson would have delighted the great Victorian actress. . . . [She] does better; she is flashing and soft at the same time, a stand-up comic who really wants to be a lie-down lover."

Commonweal, heading its review "Much Ado About Emma," was equally effusive, saying, "This definitive performance is on film," continuing, "Thompson's 'Kill Claudio!' is limpid rage springing out of her bottomless love for her wronged cousin. It is as great a piece of acting as I ever hope to see on screen or stage.

"And must you credit me when I state that the actress does [everything] without sacrificing any of the lightness, speed, or fun of her role? No! Emma Thompson's Beatrice flourishes in Technicolor at a theater near you. Drop this magazine and go."

This unrestrained praise from the American press was merely typical, however. The critics had given many kind words to her performance as Margaret Schlegel; now they were falling over themselves to tell the world about her Beatrice. Nor was it just the men who had fallen for her. In *Vogue*, Joan Juliet Buck summarized Emma's Beatrice as "sharp but also wounded; the unbeatable British actress takes you where no one has ever gone before, under the skin of a character in a Shakespearean comedy."

With this part, Emma could let out all the emotions Margaret had been forced to keep in; in fact, that was a necessity for Beatrice. The way she did it, *Cosmopolitan* stated, was "a mercurial marvel, her voice gliding from wail to rhapsody, her vinegary expression lighting with sweet admiration, her nunnish gait giving way to something very like a jig—all in a miraculous lovestruck instant."

Even the usually staid *New York Times* went so far as to allow that "Ms. Thompson is enchanting. Looking gloriously tanned and windblown, wearing the kinds of gauzy slip-ons that today would be for après-swim in Majorca, she moves through the film like an especially desirable, unstoppable life force."

No one could have wished for more. Not only had Emma's performance worked within the context of Ken's film, but it had also been an outstanding piece of acting in itself.

It served notice that her range was far wider than most people had ever imagined, and was still growing, and also that she'd become a cinematic talent to be reckoned with. Her stagework had always merited some praise, but it was in front of the cameras that she'd come to feel completely at home. And the two were utterly different styles of acting. The former called for extended bouts of concentration, lasting two or three hours, working with the immediate feedback of an audience. Bad nights were occasionally inevitable. For movies, however, scenes and fragments of scenes were shot individually, and over and over until everything was hopefully perfect. The process was far more tedious, but what ended up in the theaters was intended to be definitive. It was the best any of the actors could do, and they had to stand or fall by that. It required the ability to be able to turn the character on and off, almost at will, which seemed to come quite naturally to Emma. This talent bloomed as her career had progressed, and she showed absolutely no inclination to return to the stage.

Although Margaret and Beatrice appeared to be at completely opposite ends of the personality spectrum, making it seem as if Emma could do almost anything, they really simply showed different facets of her own personality. If Margaret represented the English stiff upper lip and the art of compromise she saw all around her in the country, then Beatrice was the feminist inside her, who'd been there since she became politicized at Cambridge. In many ways she was the Emma who was willing to shave her head and parade around the streets, daring people to be shocked. Emma and Beatrice subscribed to many of the same ideals. Both were witty, intelligent women who had already proved their feistiness.

And that was her secret, being able to find something within each role that she could identify with and understand. It gave her a handle on the character, a place to start. She wasn't from the De Niro-Hoffman school of Method acting, submerging herself in a part and living it for the length of the shoot. For a start, that had never been the way the British worked, and as someone completely unschooled in drama, Emma had been forced to devise her own ways. On camera, she was whoever she was supposed to be. Once the film stopped running, the real Emma took over again. She'd quickly learned not only that she could trigger that switch but also how to do it very successfully.

And she'd need every bit of her skill for her next project. *The Remains of the Day* was Emma's first outing without Ken since she'd won the Oscar. In fact, *Much Ado* would be the last time they'd work together on film. Despite her assurances—"We tend to be happier when we're sharing the same routine, because you go home and have a bit of supper, chat about what's going on, and share all the same experiences. That seems to me to be the point of being married"—their work was pushing them in separate directions, ones that would eventually tear the marriage apart.

As her next non-Ken film, *The Remains of the Day* was eagerly anticipated by the industry and fans alike, all the more so because she'd be working with Anthony Hopkins again. In a way, with their newly raised profiles, Merchant-Ivory were lucky to have them in a film where the total budget was only $11.5 million.

The filming would last from September 22 to December 1, 1992, with Dyrham Park, in England's West Country, becoming the exterior of the fictional Darlington Hall (the interior scenes were shot at Powderham Castle and at Badminton House, in Gloucestershire). By that time, there was already some controversy surrounding the movie.

The book had originally been optioned by playwright Harold Pinter, who'd written his own screenplay. When Merchant-Ivory came on board, Pinter had made it clear that he did not want his script altered in any way. However, writer Ruth Prawer Jhabvala was the integral third member of the Merchant-Ivory team, and, as one executive said, "Jim [Ivory] has obviously sought some input from Ruth as a matter of course," leading to a great deal of friction with Pinter, who would eventually decide to have his name removed from the credits.

chapter nine

The characters Emma and Hopkins were set to play were far from mere reprises or variations on a theme of *Howards End*. Both Henry Wilcox and Margaret Schlegel had money, one a great deal, the other a comfortable amount. Stevens the butler and Miss Kenton the housekeeper were of a completely different social class, inhabiting the world "below stairs" as domestic servants. In their respective positions they were in the upper echelons of the working class. But although they spent they life around luxury, none of it was theirs.

"Miss Kenton, the housekeeper in *The Remains of the Day*, has decided to get somewhere in her profession," Emma commented. "And she discovers it is not her desire for motherhood that suffers, it is her desire for sex. You find her yearning for this man and they will never . . . Tone and I found it quite upsetting."

With much of the film set in the 1930s, as the clouds of World War II built on the horizon, Emma prepared for the role by reading William Shirer's *The Rise and Fall of the Third Reich*, as well as Mrs. Beeton's classic *Book of Household Management* originally written for housekeepers like Miss Kenton.

The idea of being "in service" was unusual to anyone of Emma's generation. But her own grandmother had done exactly that; for her family it wasn't too far in the past.

Although she was billed as a co-star—following her Oscar, anything less would have been impossible—in reality her role was secondary to Hopkins's. This was very much his film, a study of Stevens, just as the book had been. For the first half of the film Emma was barely on screen, and even in the second half her appearances were limited so that she seemed to be seen from the outside, glimpsed through a window, in much the way that Stevens looked at her.

She'd taken the part, although it meant no break between films, because "I just do the roles that sound interesting, basically. There's an awful lot of uninteresting stuff around, so I go for what I find engaging, or funny. . . . I don't like to be at anyone's beck and call. I don't want to feel helpless in my work, to work just for the sake of working."

Miss Kenton stood as a challenge, albeit a beautifully written one, someone who had to express a lot while actually saying very little. And Emma knew by now what would be involved in working with the Merchant-Ivory team and what would be expected of her. Those were added attractions.

Emma had done so well in the roles where there was some little thing in the character she could latch onto, but the question now was what could she find in Miss Kenton to bring her alive? They had so little in common, and in going straight from *Much Ado About Nothing*, she had to make a virtual 180-degree turn in personalities, from the fiery Beatrice to the extremely repressed Sarah.

TRUTHFULLY, Emma herself had nothing at all in common with Sarah Kenton. Emma was quite resolutely a product of the middle class, not at all repressed, and living a life she'd mapped out on her own terms rather than through other people. She'd moved on to live a grand life, largely in the public eye, not something small, hidden away in someone's boarding house or some small room in a stately house.

And that meant for the first time since she'd become a serious actress Emma would be forced to draw from the world outside herself to build her character, rather than just let the character flow through her. Ken "acted," took on the guises of the people he played. With Emma it had seemed so natural and unforced. This time, though, she built up her character with a number of mannerisms, beginning with the accent, which aped her own slightly plummy vowels while still letting the occasional "h" slide and slip, aspiring to the gentility of the middle class but never quite achieving it.

Miss Kenton was the human side that Stevens had never permitted himself. He was simply there to serve, to be a totally professional gentleman's gentleman, with no opinions about his master and certainly never a criticism—at least, none he would ever express. In the early part of the film, Miss Kenton functioned largely as his conscience, uttering the things that perhaps he felt. *His* repression was total; hers was only partial but still far greater than was reasonable for any human being. It was the idea of the British stiff upper lip extended to the working classes and taken to its extreme. Neither one could talk about their mutual attraction, even twenty years later.

When Stevens went to meet Miss Kenton, now separated from her husband, his intention had been to declare himself. He still loved her, in his own odd way. And the feelings had not vanished over time for her either. But because propriety never gave the chance, the words remained unsaid, and the occasion passed. As they parted, both showed the longing in their eyes, but they couldn't bring themselves to mention it.

For Anthony Hopkins it was a bravura performance. In so many of his films he could have sleepwalked his way through the roles, but this demanded a constant attention to detail, the type of knife-edge acting he could pull off but rarely did. His work on this would be justly rewarded with a Best Actor nomination for the Oscars, as well as a Golden Globe, a BAFTA, and awards for Best Actor by both the National Board of Review and the Los Angeles Film Critics' Association.

With no time to rest after *Much Ado*, Emma was exhausted when she began the film. Luckily, with a part that didn't necessitate her being before the cameras the entire time, she did have a number of days off and was able to drive home to London and spend a little time with Ken. In fact, her absences became a joke on the set, as she noted in her diary, extracted in *Premiere*.

"MONDAY, NOVEMBER 9

Came in to work, only to discover that I had the next two days off and could go home that night. Jim [Ivory] looked at me as I was about to breeze off again and said, 'Why does Ismail pay you so much for this? You're never here.'"

As she was being paid a good deal more for this movie than she had been for *Howards End*—understandably, since she was now a much hotter theatrical property—she replied, "'Well, think of the fee for this as the fee for *Howards End*, and the fee for *Howards End* as the fee for this, and then it works.' He laughed and said it was just what he'd said to Ismail."

The period look demanded that when not set, she wore her hair in curlers, and tucked under a corduroy hat, twenty-four hours a day, which meant that "my hair doesn't get washed for a week at a time. Makes my head itch."

The fact that it was a film about two people unable to really talk and locked within themselves didn't stop Emma and Hopkins from having fun on the set, much as they had on *Howards End*. By now they'd developed a relaxed, comfortable relationship off-camera, to the point where they'd often socialize together. He'd been an actor for many years and had worked with so many of the greats that he was "telling me stories about Olivier and squealing with delight."

"She has a terrific sense of humor," Hopkins said. "She's serious about the work, but doesn't take herself seriously. We laugh an awful lot."

"You take it for granted that you approach work with utter seriousness," Emma agreed. "Therefore you don't have to show it."

Cutting up and joking was her way of relieving the tension of the set a little, of bringing a little life into a place that often became its own hermetic world. She craved a little distraction from her character rather than constant reminders of her.

"She reads the script, gets it under her skin and leaves herself alone," commented Christopher Reeve, who had a large part in the film. "She doesn't make Great Moments; she stays light on her feet, and the emotions flow because she's not trying too hard."

The filming did contain some ironic moments. While shooting the death of Stevens's father in one of the servants' rooms, the crew was interrupted by the Duchess of Beaufort, whose house they were using, accompanied by Princess Michael of Kent and, Emma noted in her diary, "a gaggle of aristocrats and their offspring" curious to see the actors. After everyone had met everyone else, the royal party went on its way, and "as they left, the princess cried out in ringing tones, 'You've never shown me this part of the house. . . . This is the bit you must hide from your visitors! It was poignant precisely because of the shabbiness of the room in comparison to everything else. Anyway, suffice it to say that it was weird to see all the well-kept ladies in this tiny, grotty room, fluttering like great plumaged birds for a bit and then leaving us in monochrome."

Emma squeezed in her visits home, but Ken also came down to see her a couple of times, bringing some good news. His next project, *Mary Shelley's Frankenstein*, which, as usual, he was going to both direct and act in, had finally been given the green light. The visits, and the chance to be real family person again, cheered her, even if there was a "strange limbo of being not at home, but trying to relax as if we were," while being in a hotel.

For the scenes reuniting her twenty years later with Stevens, there was a great deal of work involved to age Emma. Her face seemed thinner and longer, more pinched, and she walked not as the erect, proud Miss Kenton, but as someone slightly stooped, worn down a little by her years as Mrs. Benn. She was especially pleased with the meeting in the tearoom, a "wonderful example of a scene that only the audience really feels as it's happening. The protagonists are too busy holding themselves together."

Having recently quit smoking, she made the rather foolhardy suggestion that her character smoke, and "so I sat there and smoked at least sixty filterless Players. Wonder why I gave it up. What's wrong with a tongue like a shag-pile and the breath of a moose?"

When she was working, it was a series of long days, beginning with hours in makeup and hair before going through endless repetitions of scenes for the camera, sometimes in a room "so cold that my breath is showing in great clouds as I speak. I have to suck on an ice cube before each take so the camera doesn't see it."

But as November moved toward December and the schedule was ending, she began to feel a "little green about the gills after all the intense work . . . end of school. Strange, rather nostalgic feeling. No one's much bothered by anything—pressure is letting up."

Then on the first of December, it was all over. "Cherry, the Duke and Duchess's secretary, gave me two pheasants, ready—plucked and shot on Saturday. I will roast them at home with parsnips.

"The duchess gave us all a drink at the end, in her beautiful drawing room. Jim said he had the satisfying feeling of a job well-done. I bloody hope he's right.

"Finished. Midnight. Home. Drunk. Ken in study with [first assistant director] Chris Newman, who drove back with me, talking about *Frankenstein*."

The Remains of the Day was Merchant-Ivory still very much on the roll created by *Howards End* and sweeping much of its cast along with it. In terms of period drama, the only film to challenge it that year was the adaptation of the Edith Wharton novel, *The Age of Innocence*, and there was no contest between the two.

The year 1992 had been remarkable for her. *Peter's Friends* had consolidated her comic reputation in England and had been received surprisingly warmly in America. Then *Howards End* had been the kind of knockout blow every actress hopes for, a true tour de force. And as soon as she finished filming *The Remains of the Day* she began filming a small role for the film *In the Name of the Father*.

But although her acting career was taking quantum leaps, she hadn't forgotten her commitment to produce a screenplay of *Sense and Sensibility* for Lindsay Doran. She had already been working on it when time allowed, taking what few moments she had between films to retire to her study at home to write.

As someone whose first love had been books and who, during her days as a comedian, had written her own material, it shouldn't have been too great a stretch for her. So far she'd produced two drafts. The most difficult part had been to try and establish a structure for the piece, retaining the flavor of Jane Austen while making the story flow visually as well as through its dialogue. Emma had her own strong views on Austen. To her, the works weren't girls' romances, as so many had seen them. Instead, she viewed Austen as "a cartoonist," a writer with a very vivid sense of irony in the way she looked at both society and relationships. She wanted to remove what was perceived as the prettiness, saying, "That's what's wrong with the television versions of Jane Austen. They're just—well, I find them so offensive. They're so *cozy*—there's no sense at all that they're satire. Austen is actually much closer to Cruikshank than to Sargent or Whistler or Sickert."

What she wanted to concentrate on in her screenplay was what she saw as the "real issues—money and marriage. If you haven't any money, you can't get married, and if you don't get married you'll never have any money."

Emma took the project very seriously, but because she wasn't a screenwriter by trade, she didn't have the luxury of time on her side. Acting was her main job, so it was a case of, as Lindsay Doran noted, "Emma would make a film and write a draft, make a film and write a draft, over and over again. Sometimes she'd make a film and write three drafts."

As might have been expected from the way she cataloged a character's minutiae in her own performances, using them to help build a whole person, every detail was important to her. She even contacted her former tutor at Newnham, Dr. Gooder, for suggestions as to what book of poetry one of the sisters might have been reading.

In her first draft "I dramatized the whole thing. I just wanted some starting point, because I had no idea what to do. Then you have to bash out a structure that's going to be a movie and not a novel. And that's exceptionally hard."

At times it had also been quite discouraging.

"I thought, 'I'm just asking for trouble here. I will never finish it. It will never be made.' I always felt a bit nervous about mentioning it because I thought I was hexing it in some way."

By now, however, as drafts and notes had flown between California and London, there was much greater interest in the movie business about a script based on a very English book published in 1811. Most of the executives had probably never heard of Austen, but it wasn't her name that was the relevant factor—it was Emma's. The idea of an actress who was quickly assembling an astonishing track record writing a screenplay had marketing written all over it. After Emma won her Oscar, the idea became too good to turn down. Mirage, Sidney Pollack's company, was handling it, and a buzz was beginning to spread about the idea, putting even more pressure on Emma. She *had* to come up with a workable script, and she had to work hard on it; nothing stayed hot forever.

At least when she was at home she did have the time to work on it with few distractions. With each day Ken was becoming more deeply embroiled in his new work, playing the lead in *Hamlet* with the Royal Shakespeare Company and preparing for *Mary Shelley's Frankenstein*.

This was the time, as she acknowledged later, when the first cracks began to appear in their marriage. The pair of them were working so hard, and after *Much Ado* they weren't working together but both on a number of projects simultaneously. Even on the set of *Much Ado* there had been rumors of infidelity, pairing Emma with Denzel Washington or Keanu Reeves, or even Ken with Denzel. Those were all unfounded, and all laughed off as ridiculous gossip, but rumor fueled rumor, and in time stories would start to circulate about Ken and Helena Bonham Carter on the *Frankenstein* set. Carter denied it, of course, saying, "The rumors about Ken and me started even before I had met him. They are embarrassing and completely fictional. Everybody immediately thinks that if you are playing lovers, then you must be lovers, that it can't be just acting. But when it comes to doing it on screen it's so bloody technical you just get on with it."

The gossip about them, however, wouldn't vanish. Some of it would eventually reach Emma, although she never said whether she chose to believe it or if it even mattered to her. But no one knew Ken better than she did, including the fact that before her—and including her—he'd had a habit of falling in love with his leading ladies.

True or not, and the speculation reached the stage where it seemed to be accepted as almost common knowledge, Emma simply couldn't let it get her down. She had too much to do. Still, she revealed, there were times when all the words about Ken that were flying around depressed her to the point that she could hardly get out of bed, feeling "I simply cannot fuck-ing face anybody today, because everybody hates me. But then you realize that a) it's not the case, and b) most of the public don't give a fuck."

∽

WITH true middle-class spirit and grit she pulled herself together and kept her problems, fears, and worries inside so that she could really focus on *Sense and Sensibility*. The pressure was growing to finish it, with a first reading tentatively scheduled for December 1993. Each day she retired to her study and worked.

The writing could be frustrating, but it was also oddly satisfying, so different from being an actress. It made her realize that, if she could ever produce a workable draft, she might be able to start another career as a screenwriter. That would mean she could pick and choose her roles even more than she did now, and that, as she grew older and the good parts became thinner on the ground, she'd have another string to her bow—she wouldn't be so reliant on the whims of directors and casting agents.

It was also something that offered true independence. She could work alone, answerable to no one until she presented the project. She could look and dress exactly as she wanted; no more directors criticizing her as being slightly overweight. If her face had broken out, there'd be no need for lots of makeup to cover the blemishes. And the act of writing filled an intel-lectual void within her. Her Cambridge degree was more than ten years in the past, but that didn't mean that her mind had shut down. Emma remained a person who was curious about the world, about history. She still cared very strongly about the ideas of right and wrong. Even on the set of *The Remains of the Day* she'd been active in her spare moments, writing in support of various causes that touched her heart.

She'd remained a political animal. Her involvement in the protests against the Gulf War in 1991 had been the most visible, but she was an active supporter of a number of organizations, mostly with her money—which was always welcome—but also with her name, which had become quite prestigious, and, although it was only rarely possible, occasionally with her time. The Friends of the Earth, the Campaign for Nuclear Disarmament, and a British version of Emily's List, which tried to help women in politics by giving them seed money for their campaigns, all benefited from Emma's support. She'd already served on an action committee about conditions in Central and South America. There was little she could do herself to change things in other parts of the world, but she was determined to do all she could. One thing she fully understood was the fortunate position she found herself in.

"Acting is the ultimate luxury," she said. "This is one of the luckiest things you could possibly be doing. 'Hard' is going down a bloody coal mine or living in Somalia or in a war zone. That's hard."

She was a diehard liberal, definitely on the left of the political spectrum, but hardly the radical that the British press liked to make her out to be on the occasions she fell into their disfavor. She wasn't Vanessa Redgrave, or even Jane Fonda; that kind of extremism would have been completely out of character for Emma. Her beliefs were more personally held, and her actions, at least for the most part, were far more controlled. In that regard, as in many others, she was her own version of Miss Kenton, keeping a tight rein on everything about herself and rarely letting it slip so that the deeper emotions spilled out.

She was also something of a closet intellectual, someone who chose to exercise her brain and constantly expand her knowledge of the world. It wasn't just snobbishness inherited from Cambridge but a real curiosity of the mind. She wasn't about to be satisfied with the latest Jackie Collins or Danielle Steel novel; she needed to grapple with books and ideas that would really stimulate her. And writing the screenplay fit comfortably into that. It presented challenges, not only creatively but also logistically-how to take the story and retell it best in a different format. And although it sometimes seemed as if she'd never be done with it, going through the frustration of draft after draft, the idea of admitting defeat and simply giving up never occurred to her. Having taken on the responsibility, she had to see it through.

⚬⚬

THE Oscar had elevated Emma's reputation, and then *Much Ado About Nothing* had shown the world that she was an unstoppable force. *The Remains of the Day* would confirm that, in the space of just over twelve months, she'd managed to leap from small regard to international star. Her old friend Martin Bergman called Emma "our generation's Katharine Hepburn, [with] the poise, the professionalism, the ability to perform comedy or drama with equal skill, the ability to create female characters we know and recognize and whose personalities begin with their minds rather than their cleavage."

People declared *The Remains of the Day* to be what Merchant-Ivory did best, "period drama played out in lavish European settings, with meticulous attention to detail," all done "with little wasted motion." Hopkins, "bound up in a glacier-thick carapace of dignity" was, Joanne Kaufman thought, "more frightening than even Hannibal Lecter." In the *Chicago Tribune*, Michael Wilmington summed it up as "this lovely film—bright, rich and melancholy—[that] catches you between weeping and laughing. It's a gem of twilight reverie and repressed anxiety." In the same newspaper, Gene Siskel's brief observation was that it was "one of the year's best films."

The Washington Post commented that "the cast . . . is so uniformly good, it completes the sense of seamlessness, like a perfectly realized banquet. Sit down to this and savor the human sumptuousness." *New York*, however, seemed to catch the real heart of the film in David Denby's review: "The movie has a strikingly ambiguous flavor: Ivory and [screenwriter] Jhabvala know that many of us hate class privilege yet retain an irrepressible desire for perfect order and luxury. Stevens may be a snob and a eunuch, but he's also a kind of magician; he may be inadequate in all the relations of life, but he's also admirable. So is the movie."

Emma was the female lead, but the simple fact was that *The Remains of the Day* was Anthony Hopkins's film. Anyone and everyone else playing a part was really a supporting actor. It was, in its center, a drama about one man, and that was reflected in many of the reviews.

Still, Denby wrote, "It's a relief to see Emma Thompson, after a string of Miss Wonderful performances, letting out a streak of exasperated spite.

In a moment of high comedy, she taunts Hopkins, tries to outdo him in propriety, but he freezes her out. As in *Howards End*, Thompson speaks for emotional truth and connection, and Hopkins withdraws into defensive formalities: the heroic English female, and the equally heroic, though frighteningly crippled, English male."

The *Chicago Tribune* called her "the always superb Emma Thompson" and commented on her role only in the way it touched on his. "Not only do this starchily correct pair never make love, they never kiss, rarely touch, never *talk* about love, except obliquely. Only little things . . . betray what they strive to conceal; that she adores him, that he reciprocates." And the *Washington Post* noted that "the central conflict between Hopkins and Thompson—a veritable Trojan War of implications and ironies—makes for the best moments you'll see on screen this year."

Although the reviews of Emma's performance were more than complimentary, there was little to suggest that she warranted another Oscar nomination—as for Best Actress, rather than Best Supporting Actress—for her part. It hadn't really mattered to her whether she was lead or support—this was a good script that fulfilled all her ideal criteria for female characters. Miss Kenton, for all her faults and frustrations, was a fully rounded character, perhaps even a tragic figure.

Nonetheless, another Oscar nomination was there for her, one of several garnered by the film (including, quite justifiably, Best Actor for Anthony Hopkins). And although neither of them won—Hopkins lost out to Tom Hanks in the Year of *Forrest Gump*, while Holly Hunter's and Anna Paquin's performances in *The Piano* trumped Emma for both the Best Actress and Best Supporting Actress awards, respectively—the nominations were the icing on the cake. The film had already garnered a BAFTA, Hopkins had walked away with three awards, and Emma had added to her collection of shining statuary with her own Best Actress BAFTA and a Golden Globe nomination for Best Actress in a drama.

The question it raised was why had the American movie media, and the members of the Academy, fallen for Emma in such a big way? The evidence came not just from *The Remains of the Day*, but also from Emma's relatively minor role in *In the Name of the Father*, which brought another

Oscar nomination, this time for Best Supporting Actress, as well as yet another nomination to receive a Golden Globe, again for Best Supporting Actress.

Why were they falling over themselves to pay homage to her and make this her year? She'd done excellent work in all three films released during 1993, that was quite true, but her best and most provocative part—Beatrice in *Much Ado About Nothing*—had gone unnoticed by all awards committees.

The reasons, it seemed, lay not so much in the acting as in the films themselves. Certainly, the controversial political content of *In the Name of the Father* guaranteed it publicity, perhaps more so in America with its great Irish heritage and sometimes ambivalent feelings towards the governance of Britain.

It was very loosely based on the autobiography of Gerry Conlon, one of the Guildford Four, convicted of a 1974 IRA pub bombing in England that killed five people and wounded sixty-four others. He served fifteen years of his sentence before allegations of police fabrication of evidence and brutality swept into a large enough voice to warrant a second trial of the Four, and of the "Maguire Seven" convicted with them.

That, in turn, put the detectives who'd extracted the alleged confessions on trial for falsification of evidence. Although none was ever found guilty, it cast a long shadow over police actions in Britain. And that led the London *Sunday Times* to wonder how, in the light of that legal vindication of the police, this film could be made with a "suitably heroic ending."

It was a rather naive question. Although *In the Name of the Father* was based on Conlon's story, there was also a great deal of fiction involved in the story, not only in the plot but also the chronology and courtroom proceedings; it was history remade as *Perry Mason* or *Law & Order*.

Certainly it was strange to see Emma in such a small (albeit pivotal) role, playing Gareth Pierce, the solicitor who helped effect Conlon's release by discovering suppressed evidence and arguing firmly in court. This also played somewhat fast and free with the truth of the matter; no evidence had been kept from the defense at any time, and what the real Pierce discovered was not a missing alibi for the time of the bombing but the fact that police notes about the interrogation of the suspects, supposedly taken at the time, had in fact been written later, which made them "unreliable." Nor was there any dramatic courtroom speech from Pierce. Under British law, as a solicitor, she could not appear in gown and wig before a judge. And unlike the movie, she did not represent all the members of the Four.

It could have been argued that the film was essentially entertainment and could therefore use some license. But it wanted to portray itself as hard-hitting and honest. Although it might have succeeded in the former, in the latter it failed miserably.

For Emma, a role in this film—although to call it supporting actress was perhaps a sop to her stature, given that it was little more than an extended cameo that she was able to film very quickly—appealed to that very liberal side of her politics and also offered her a chance to appear in something dramatic and contemporary. With a reputation made in period pieces, there was a faint danger of being typecast in that mold; she needed something that showed her in a modern setting, and understandably, as a strong woman. As written, the character of Gareth Pierce exposed the corrupt and lazy practices of the police and the political system that allowed that corruption to happen. *In the Name of the Father*, which would undoubtedly play better in America than England, was the ideal vehicle, even though the real Gareth Pierce had considered herself an "extremely unimportant participant" in the proceedings. And her name on the marquee, alongside that of Daniel Day-Lewis, who was still hot from *The Last of the Mohicans* and *The Age of Innocence*, would ensure a good number of tickets sold.

When the film opened in London, it provoked a storm of criticism. Even one of the defenders of the Guildford Four, unacknowledged in the movie, noted there were "court scenes which not only didn't happen, but which suggest we conduct our criminal cases on a charade basis." Robert Kee, a scholar who'd written a book about the case, said it "tells so many lies that it makes its central proposition about a miscarriage of justice questionable," while the *Sunday Times* of London wrote about it under a headline that read "The Camera That Lies."

The British papers were quite violent in their reactions, pointing out that its vilification of the British justice system seemed quite general, and that, among Americans, it could create new sympathy for the IRA, who at that time, had not yet declared their cease-fire. The reviews were directed not so much at the performances (both Day-Lewis as Conlon and Peter Postlethwaite as his father, Guiseppe, were excellent) as at its politics. One writer called it a "farrago of rubbish." Jim Sheridan, who'd written and directed, did state that he had originally filmed the appeal as it had happened, but then had decided that it needed more punch, more drama, causing a critic to reprimand him, saying, "So he's saying he refused to let the facts get in the way of a good story—isn't that what the Surrey police did in the first place?"

The film reviewers, though, operated under slightly different criteria, and in *The Times*, the "streamlining" was seen as a literary device to "suck audiences right inside its story of wrongs being righted," while the *Guardian* warned that it should be seen as a "parable based on truth [rather than] a thorough examination of the truth itself." Only the *Daily Telegraph* wondered aloud, "At what point does dramatic license shade into unwarranted distortions of the truth?" and pointed out the underlying discrepancy that existed in a film that had become fiction purporting to be "denouncing the lies of others."

The furor that erupted was, perhaps, slightly overblown, but Emma herself did nothing to calm it. When asked at a press conference whether she felt that the film could further damage the already sagging reputation of the British police, and possibly arouse sympathy for the IRA, she responded quite briefly and candidly, "I don't give a fuck."

And that sentence, in its turn, generated more controversy. From being the darling of British film after bringing home an Oscar the year before, Emma was once again *persona non grata* in the press. Granted it hadn't been the most thoughtful comment, more a foot in mouth than a reasoned response, but it hardly warranted the abuse that was suddenly heaped upon her, at least until the next juicy tidbit of news, and she was promptly forgotten again.

In America, things were completely different. Not being as familiar with the real story, the politics were glossed over, or in some instances taken at face value. But it was the film itself that was of real interest, one that the *National Review* called "a great film," with some superb performances, especially from Daniel Day-Lewis, described as "his finest opportunity to be charming, cynical, cocky, abject, childish, and finally profound. His way of aging fifteen years, both outwardly and inwardly, into a wholly new person is nothing short of stunning." And *Commonweal*, while acknowledging the deviations from reality, pointed out that "*In the Name of the Father* isn't agitprop. For all its gritty realism and headlong tempo, it's a poetic exploration on the nature of authority"—familial, political, and religious.

For *America* the political implications were almost irrelevant compared to the changing relationship between father and son as they share a cell and "uncover their past feeling toward each other, and through this mutual confession a new love grows between them."

Entertainment Weekly placed the film firmly in the line of modern cinematic political thrillers, noting that it "works with such piercing fervor and intelligence that [it] just about transcends its tidy moral design." Only *People* seemed to have doubts, finding the film too didactic and concluding that "if Sheridan didn't feel the need to pile on the pedantic subtexts, this would be an absorbing personal drama, rather than a vituperative, question-begging broadside."

Whether it was viewed as too political or too free with the truth, all the reviewers were able to agree on the quality of the performances. Work of the first order was expected from Day-Lewis, especially in a role like this, and he delivered, with "memorable" being the least of the plaudits. Of equal interest was Peter Postlethwaite's Guiseppe. *Commonweal* enthused that "there is no crack in [Postlethwaite's] characterization of the senior Conlon that shows you the actor within plugging away. I got the feeling that if I called Postlethwaite up at four in the morning, he would answer me in Conlon's gentle voice and communicate all of the man's saintliness right over the phone." The *National Review* was equally impressed, writing that Postlethwaite "etches himself into the memory with a performance of such stripped-down integrity, such self-effacing determination that you believe the actor to be drawing on resources beyond the merely histrionic . . . that blunt, blotchy pentagonal face, with its stubby nose and cluster of moles, radiates a sheer, patient, animal decency to knock your breath away."

It was everything a good supporting role should be, and it came as no surprise when he was nominated for an Academy Award for his work in the film, as was Day-Lewis.

Emma's Oscar nomination as Best Supporting Actress for her portrayal of Gareth Pierce was definitely more dubious, and perhaps owed a lot to the pro-Emma feeling that was flying around, an attempt to see that she'd at least walk away with *something* as a real tribute to a small and not especially spectacular performance. There was absolutely nothing wrong with her acting, other than there wasn't enough of it. With the exception of the climactic courtroom scene, she could have played it all in her sleep.

Writing in *New Republic*, Stanley Kauffmann, as usual, rhapsodized about her: "At first glance she is hardly recognizable, not because of her different hairdo but because she is now the center of a differently centered life from last time. The screenplay never tells us who engaged her to fight the cause she is steeped in or whether it's pro bono, but we're so glad she is doing it that we don't care. The courtroom speech in which she presents the suppressed evidence is magnificent." *Commonweal* joined his ecstatic praise, admitting that "I'm sick and tired of using this column as a camouflaged love letter to Emma Thompson . . . so let me note only that in her outburst in court during the climactic trial, Thompson's high dudgeon is done in her highest style, and that's as high as style or dudgeon gets."

And the *National Review*, calling her the "inevitable" Emma, offered praise with only the hint of carping: "Her penchant for smugness is here either in abeyance or put to good use; even the upward-scooping tone of her voice objectifies the persistence with which the underdog digs his way into recognition. Miss Thompson is not mousy like the real life Miss Pierce, but there is something very fetching about her sneer of triumph."

༄

IT would be lovely to think that Emma's awards and nominations represented a radical change in thinking for all those who judged her so harshly before, a reaction against the increasing marginalization of women and of women's roles in the film industry—exactly the thing Emma had spoken out against just the year before, causing Hollywood to studiously avoid knocking on her door with offers. That wasn't the case, however. The industry would continue to feed the public a steady diet of what they wanted to see, and what the executives hoped they wanted to see, much of which came under the heading of light entertainment, beautiful people in all manner of situations rather than the portrayal of real people by actors and actresses who actually looked real themselves, not the product of plastic surgery and endless grueling hours with personal trainers.

And one thing Emma wasn't about to do was go Hollywood, either metaphorically or literally. She had issues with her appearance but dealt with them her own way, a course that most definitely didn't include trips to plastic surgeons. Nor was she about to abandon England for the West Coast.

"I couldn't abandon English mores, and the odd angles, and this strange and twisted culture! I agree with mercantile and economic international-ism, but culturally there are such deep seams to be plumbed in each coun-try."

And the seams she could plumb in England were her real livelihood. She now had the reputation as the person who could show what it was to be an Englishwoman. "I do love England," she said. "I love the people. Even if they're not friendly, at least they're funny. The northerners. The Scottish. The Irish! God, how I'd miss the Celts!"

And if the people weren't enough reason to stay, she added, she'd just had her kitchen remodeled. How on earth could she leave after that?

But for her there could be no serious thoughts of leaving, anyway. Her family was in England, clustered in one tiny section of London, and that, as it always had been, was home to her. Emma remained very close to her mother and sister. They'd been the foundation of her life, and even mar-riage didn't change that.

In fact, that closeness helped as distance grew between Ken and Emma. Having her mother and her sister so close at hand meant support was always near. The damage was far from irreparable, however, and Emma was still considering the possibility of children, albeit with less enthusiasm than she had a year before. "I think I want kids, yeah," she said hesitantly. "I might be a bit miffed to miss out on that. But I wouldn't put my career on hold. My mum managed very well. They weren't very rich and she worked right through."

Having gone into marriage so seriously and prevaricated before finally saying, "I do," she wasn't about to abandon the relationship at the first hurdle. For her it had been a love match. And being married to an actor meant she was with someone who understood the constant stresses of her life. "I think it would be very difficult in this profession to be married to an accountant or anybody who kept normal hours and a normal life. Your schedule and your life changes from moment to moment. Not only is the traveling difficult, but sometimes you have money and sometimes you don't. It's very up and down. Sometimes you've got a set of bad reviews, and you don't want to talk to anybody. You've got to have someone who understands that."

Money was no longer a real problem for her, but bad reviews could happen to any performer at any time and could be quite psychologically debilitating, at least for a short time.

WHATEVER gap existed between Emma and Ken at this time was still small and quite easily bridgeable. Although the rumors about him and Helena Bonham Carter flew thick and fast, there was nothing in the way of evidence. The problem, she'd relate later, came mostly because of their work schedules. They hardly saw each other, and when they did, one or both of them was exhausted, having just finished another film. In a situation like, that a supreme effort had to be made not to drift apart and not to exist in a very insular world. *Mary Shelley's Frankenstein* had rapidly become a consuming project for Ken, another acting-directing job that left him drained and strained each night, while Emma was absorbing herself in a different world entirely, as she finished yet another draft of *Sense and Sensibility* and prepared for the first read—through of the script.

That took place comfortably close to home, at Kenwood House on Hampstead Heath where she'd walked so often as a teenager. It was just before Christmas, and all the actors were in a festive mood. Amanda Root—ironically, one of Ken's former loves—was playing Marianne Dashwood, with the other roles filled out by Robert Hardy, Francesca Annis, Stephen Fry, Hugh Laurie, and Geraldine McEwan. Hardy and Laurie would go on to take part in the film, but it was still doubtful whether Emma herself would take a role. As Austen had written the characters, she was too old for either Dashwood sister, and she wanted to be as authentic as possible. It would also have brought her perilously close to emulating Ken, splitting herself into two parts on the set, something she was far from sure she wanted to endure.

That aspect of *Sense and Sensibility* would remain in the air for a while longer. There was no doubt that she was now a bankable star, whose presence as an actress would bring the film even more attention than as a screenwriter.

For now, though, the read-through gave her—and producer Lindsay Doran—some clear ideas on what to do with the screenplay, where it needed to be going, things that worked, things that didn't, areas that needed to be expanded. It was, in a way, like looking at a rough sketch. There was still plenty of work to be done by Emma, locked away in her study.

And that was precisely what she did. There was still time before her next acting commitment, and she used it wisely to try and finish the next draft. Whether it was her utter absorption in that, or the differences that were growing between her and Ken, but she only visited him on the set once during the filming of *Frankenstein*.

When she finally did move away from the computer screen to act, it was for another extended period in front of the camera, beginning with *The Blue Boy*, a joint British-American production written and directed by her old Scottish childhood friend Paul Murton, whom she'd helped on his student film *Tin Fish*. A ghost story of sorts, with Emma as a pregnant woman, it was aimed at television and shown in the U.S. on PBS. *Entertainment Weekly* noted that "because the production has been shaped as a star turn for Thompson—who's certainly good—the rest of the small cast seem lost and irrelevant"—praise of a sort.

From there she made a true cameo appearance in Gerard Depardieu's *My Father the Hero*, his attempt to consolidate the success of *Green Card* and become a star in America. Emma had the role of Depardieu's girlfriend, unseen until the last minute of the movie, when she picks up the phone to hear his proposal of marriage.

And after those two, Hollywood had finally come calling. But what it was offering was a chance for Emma to exercise her comedy muscles again in something quite contemporary. And the studio was willing to pay her half a million dollars to do it.

♾

BY American film standards that was little more than pocket change, particularly to someone who had a Best Actress Oscar sitting in her downstairs bathroom. But it was far more than she'd made from the films that had given her that reputation and award. The "filthy lucre," as she laughingly called it, and the chance to show people that she could also make them laugh—America, after all, didn't really know her as a comic—was irresistible.

More than that, it took her away from her own four walls and brooding about what was going on in her marriage. Instead of the gray English weather, she'd be in California, enjoying the sunshine and putting her problems out of her thoughts for a while.

chapter ten

Arnold Schwarzenegger's last film, *Last Action Hero*, had completely flopped at the box office. In Hollywood terms that didn't mean that people were growing tired of Arnold; that was unthinkable. Instead they had to go back and look back at his successes and see what they should be doing right.

That brought two movies: *True Lies*, which teamed him with Jamie Lee Curtis and director James Cameron, who'd been behind the camera for both *Terminator* smashes, and *Junior*, a comedy that reunited him with Danny DeVito and director Ivan Reitman.

In 1988 the trio of DeVito, Schwarzenegger, and Reitman had made *Twins*, a comedy that grossed more than $100 million in the United States alone. If had that happened once, studio thinking ran, another comedy from the same group could easily do it again and return Arnold to his place among the major box-office stars.

Schwarzenegger had come across the script for *Junior* (or *Oh, Baby* as it was then known), and after he, DeVito, and Reitman pledged to work together in 1994, Reitman took the script, made some changes, and had it ready for filming.

The central comic precept was not just the idea of a man becoming pregnant and experiencing hormonal changes and childbirth, but *Arnold Schwarzenegger* going through these things.

"The concept is huge," said DeVito. "It's not just a guy with a big belly and me with a stethoscope, all aboard for hilarity. There are really interesting and great things in the movie to hold on to."

The preparatory meeting took place on January 24, 1994, just after the large Los Angeles earthquake, leaving Emma to write, "I wonder if any of us is going to live long enough to make this film."

The idea of playing Dr. Diana Reddin, whom she described as "a work-obsessed, socially challenged scientist," appealed to Emma. The role was a good, strong one, a woman whose brain was emphasized over her body, and it gave her a chance to show that under all the period costumes a comic's heart was still beating, one with a great love for slapstick.

Everything went well, and in mid-March Emma flew back to California, both for the Academy Awards (where she was up for two Oscars) and to prepare for *Junior*. Rehearsals began on March 16, with Arnold and Emma working together for the first time.

"She was looking at me from every angle, like a piece of sculpture she was going to buy," Arnold recalled. "She said: 'I'm sorry. I have to touch you. Can you lie down on the floor?' And she was rolling around with me on the floor. I was laughing my head off over the whole approach. She broke the ice very quickly, so we could get down to work."

Her memory of the incident was that it was sparked by director Reitman, although she admitted that "clearly this won't be too formal."

In early April filming had begun. By the British standards Emma was used to, her trailer on the set was huge. "I can't get from one end to the other without having a lie-down," she wrote. "Two steps leading up to a bedroom. A loo and a shower, a kitchenette and a little sitting room."

Although she tried to hide some of her awe—she was, after all, a renowned actress and should appear worldly—there was no doubt that the sheer scale of Hollywood moviemaking impressed her. There was no cutting corners, none of the scrimping and saving she'd become used to in British productions. This was luxury all the way.

One question was why, with the duo of Arnold and Danny, Reitman had felt the need to import someone like Emma. There were, after all, plenty of American actresses with big names who could have played the role.

The answer was twofold. As an Oscar winner and someone who was established as a dramatic actress in "fine" films, her name lent class to the project, which Reitman recognized that it needed; virtually the only American equivalent would have been Meryl Streep. And unlike Streep, who seemed to fade into every character she played until she was almost bloodless, Emma always possessed a force of personality. She and Reitman first met while discussing the possibility of her playing the President's wife in *Dave*, a role that eventually went to Sigourney Weaver.

Secondly, bringing in a "foreign" actress as the female lead increased the possibility for onscreen mayhem and confusion, the idea of culture clash—and of course, an international star would only help the film's chances in the lucrative overseas markets. Schwarzenegger was definitely pleased to be working with someone of her caliber.

"Studios a lot of times feel like, So we have Arnold," he mused. "We don't need any big female lead; we could get someone for $100,000. This kind of attitude is a big mistake, because I work much better if I have someone who is very strong, like Emma is, like Jamie Lee Curtis is. It helps me with the acting."

To a point, that fit with the Emma's understanding of why she'd been cast. "I think Ivan just wanted to put someone very different opposite Arnold. It was an amazing notion, and I had a bloody great time doing it."

No one was about to say that Arnold was a natural actor, and certainly not a natural comic before the camera, although he'd performed well in his action roles. But surrounding himself with those who were good did help his work and helped bring something out in him that might never have seen the light of day otherwise.

Their ways of working was completely opposite, which caused Reitman a few directorial problems. "The burden is keeping them all in the same movie. Emma is spontaneous, while Arnold moves straight ahead—just tell him what to do. Arnold punctuates each line with his face."

Being friendly and open on the set, not pulling any movie-star rank, made Emma popular with both cast and crew. She was a professional, there to work, and even have some fun while she was doing it, "a wonderfully robust, friendly character."

"She was everyone's favorite," Schwarzenegger said. "People applaud-ed her on the set. She was a fun person. A happy person. A pleasure to be around."

Only DeVito seemed to have not been totally convinced, with the rather ambiguous comment, "She wasn't the woman who everybody hated, let's put it that way."

In May, while she was in the middle of filming *Junior*, Columbia finally gave its official go-ahead to make *Sense and Sensibility*, with Taiwanese Ang Lee directing. Emma herself had gone from writing the screenplay to seriously considering the part of Elinor in the film.

"I'm too old," she said, before adding, "But we've bumped up the ages. We've had to age them for plausibility and, with makeup, I might look young enough."

So it was definite; her first attempt at screenwriting was going to make it to film. It was so overwhelming that after three years of intermittent work on the same piece it was finally going to move beyond paper. The only comment she could muster in her diary was, "Blimey."

But it gave her a renewed sense of purpose. There was still a month of shooting to go on *Junior*. She'd been in California since March, and it would be mid-June before she was able to return to West Hampstead and set to work polishing her pet project.

Her spirits were lifted to the point where she didn't even object when, during a break, "Arnold picks me up and lifts me over his head. Goes all far away for a second, says, 'Hundred thirty-six pounds, twenty-two per-cent body fat' and puts me down again."

It wasn't the super-thin body of a Hollywood actress, and at thirty-five (she'd had her birthday on the set, with Ken far away in England, prepar-ing for the London Marathon. On the day she "felt unreasonably old . . . Then I got cake and balloons, which made me feel about twelve") it was never going to be. However, Emma seemed to be finally coming to terms with her body, becoming comfortable with her appearance. When Arnold had patted her back and said, "Normally I feel bones sticking oud, bud I like dis sofness," she noted the remark wryly, rather than angrily. It was a nice irony, given that he was the man who'd initially made his reputation from his appearance.

Seeing Hollywood again had really made her think, it seemed. She'd always considered herself overweight, but suddenly she was surrounded by women who were willing to go to virtually any length of surgery to keep their youth or become more glamorous, and she had no wish to be unnaturally preserved like them. "In the West, millions of women are offering money to men to cut them open, to put foreign bodies inside them. It really has to be fought against, tooth and nail."

After years of battle, it appeared that the feminist inside had truly won out. However, she was luckier than many women in the film business—with the writing, she'd really developed a second career. "Actresses have a short shelf life," she realized. "It stops at about forty, apart from those at the very top, like Anjelica Huston or Glenn Close. An actress has to find a future for herself."

Three full months in Hollywood had her thinking quite deeply about her future. In England things were different. Actors were accepted more for what they could do than how they might look. Glamour and anorexic thinness weren't yet prerequisites for an actress; it still rested more on ability. Even so, good roles for older women weren't that plentiful. Writing would give Emma the option of another career. But more than that, it would also offer her the opportunity to create powerful roles for women of all ages.

Meanwhile, she still had to finish *Junior*. The first half of 1994 had had the strange emphasis of pregnancy for her, first with *The Blue Boy* and now this. Whether they contributed to the sense that she was thinking less of becoming a mother herself was never revealed. But the desire was definitely receding. At the same time, the distance between she and Ken was growing—not only geographically but also emotionally. They both remained wrapped up in so many projects. A year earlier she'd been able to joke that pregnancy was unlikely because "Ken's so tired. His sperm are on crutches." Now she hardly saw him for months at a time. And to a point, her screenplay became her baby. Hardly the same thing, but she'd nurtured it from conception to acceptance, she'd given birth to it after a long gestation period.

She was used to working in the British film industry, which didn't release many films—many call it little more than a cottage industry—but the ones it did put out were of a consistently high quality. Hollywood was geared like a machine, to churn out product. It was, quite literally, *the* entertainment business. When she and Ken had made *Dead Again* there, four years before, they'd had a glimpse of that. But with him as director, she'd been shielded from much of it. This time she was able to stare it full in the face. It was a town where "concepts" were more important than dialogue and where special effects—generated for huge sums of money— outweighed characterization. And by and large, it was where good roles for women remained few and far between. Her railing at the system after winning the Oscar had had absolutely no effect, although it was unlikely that it ever would.

But in being ignored by Hollywood for a while, she'd really missed nothing. Its style and hers simply didn't mesh. She remained too English to fit in to the West Coast. She liked to paint her parts with small, delicate lines. Hollywood wanted crude, broad strokes; subtlety wasn't part of the palette.

Watching *Junior*, Emma seemed to be a fish out of water. She played up the dizzy Englishwoman whose life was so centered on her work that she'd never developed any social skills. She emphasized the clumsiness and the horsy, toothy grin. But it was a performance that demanded nothing of her. She never had the chance to act, because she never really had anyone to act against. She could virtually have stayed at home and phoned her lines in.

The idea of the movie, though, had intrigued her, partly because "I thought there was a great possibility of it being deeply offensive, and I thought there's no point in doing it unless there's that possibility. It was an interesting concept. We have to start thinking about men having babies because we cannot continue having women having the babies and then bringing them up and doing all the work. It just can't go on like that. Which is partly what the movie was about."

Or it is perhaps what *Junior* could have been about, had it not chosen instead to dive straight towards the lowest common denominator, the cheap laugh. With a different cast, it might have worked the way Emma had seen it. Instead, DeVito played his standard role, surly and grasping, the unlikeliest obstetrician around, and Arnold was equally unconvincing as a research scientist.

The critics all tended to notice the "high-concept premise," but a number of them still managed to find it enjoyable. *Maclean's* thought it "weighs in at slightly more than the sum of its contrived parts . . . [the] story seems oddly credible," although the writer did admit that "the movie gets truly funny when Thompson enters a scene." *People* felt it "surprisingly calm and quietly amusing," and *Time* thought it had "a certain irresistible curiosity . . . It won't make you a better person, but it might, very briefly, make you a happier one."

The ones who didn't come away laughing, however, truly disliked the film. *Entertainment Weekly* summed it up by saying "it would be hard to imagine how a movie could be any more predictable than this one. *Junior*, I'm afraid, is the very model of what mainstream Hollywood comedy has become: a form of high-concept pacifier." And Britain's *New Statesman* blasted it, noting that "it has one measly idea and milks it for all it's worth . . . such a dreary piece of work—shoddy, smug and a little late in the day . . . the jokes are obvious, lamely executed and telegraphed miles ahead."

Inevitably, the two sides took opposite views of Emma's participation in the movie. To those who disliked it, she should never have been there at all. To the *New Statesman*, her performance was nothing more than "a surprisingly gamey turn in her briskest Joyce Grenfell mould," noting that the character was "oddly defeminized . . . by virtue of being so common-sense and English public school, with her stout-chap jumper and slacks" (also, of course, an allusion to Katharine Hepburn's typical garb in her screwball comedies). *Entertainment Weekly* thought it showed her in "I-can-let-my-hair-down-and-do-a-dumb-blockbuster mode, portraying a professor as . . . a klutzy space case."

Maclean's, which found her the comic center of the film, noted that "whenever she is offscreen, things seem dull. . . . Even the script smartens up when she is around," and that "she enlivens the comedy with the kind of dazzling, quicksilver wit she first displayed in *The Tall Guy*." And *Time* ascribed the film's "Giddiness (and most of [its] knockabout comedy)" to her, saying she offered "a lovely reminder of our screwball yesteryears."

Although the film didn't fall completely on its face at the box office, nor did it repeat the surprising success of the previous DeVito-Schwarzenegger pairing. Still, said Emma, "I got loads of money and it was really good fun."

The money, perhaps, was one of the keys. As she said more than a year later, she still hadn't spent her fee from the movie, and "from my point of view it's very freeing because if I wanted to live on the *Junior* money for two years and travel or write another screenplay or something, I can afford to do that."

It certainly wasn't something she'd have a chance to do immediately after *Junior*, however. There was still work to be done writing *Sense and Sensibility*, but that, too, would have to wait. On Saturday, June 11, two days after she finished filming her scenes in *Junior*, she flew back to England. She hadn't even had the chance to unpack and get over her jet lag before she began work on *Carrington* on Monday, June 13.

chapter eleven

Carrington was about as far from *Junior* as Emma could possibly get. It put her back into period costume, even if that period was in the twentieth century. And instead of being aimed squarely at the mall multiplexes of America, this was very much a film for the art houses.

Emma had been approached some time before about playing the title role of painter Dora Carrington, and having agreed, now found herself stuck with a full schedule. It had been written by playwright Christopher Hampton, who'd had such a success adapting Laclos's *Les Liaisions Dangereuses* for the stage, then for film as *Dangerous Liaisions*. *Carrington* would also mark his debut as a director.

Although centered around Dora—a woman who preferred to be called by her last name—it was as much to do with the men in her life, particularly the writer Lytton Strachey, the gay man with whom she was obsessively in love and lived platonically, while marrying and having affairs with other men.

"Christopher Hampton took the story from Michael Holroyd's book [*Lytton Strachey*] and that was totally about Lytton," Emma said. "And what happened to the other people in her life is completely fascinating. How to tell her life story without telling those other stories as well is a very difficult problem to solve." The solution appeared to be to make Carrington the central character but also, in many ways, the weakest character. Men would keep falling in love with her, and she would respond to that, often it seemed, merely not to hurt their feelings. But running under everything was her constant love of Strachey. Her work—at least in the context of the film—came after everything else.

"The point about Dora Carrington is that her life was an extraordinary paean of devotion to this man and there's nothing you can really do to alter that," Emma agreed. "She didn't spend enough time away from him doing extraordinary things to make you want to tell that part of the story. Everything she did related to him and related to the other men who pushed her towards or away from him."

Strachey, she felt, "offered Carrington liberty because he didn't want to own her; he was an easy person to be with. I'm sure a lot of women fall in love with homosexuals for precisely that reason—there is a form of freedom there and it doesn't confuse passion with lust. It was very difficult to boil all that down, without making this a paean of devotion, which is much less complicated than it was."

But although that simplification made for a story of sorts—really more a collection of snapshots from her series of lovers—it also had the effect of making Carrington somewhat less three-dimensional. In the film she came across as a person who loved love, someone who hated to hurt people but never wanted to be anything less than honest, both with herself and with the men in her life. In Holroyd's book, Emma said, it was clear "that Carrington was willful and perverse and treated [Gerald] Brenan terribly, absolutely tortured him. Once she gave him a whole load of Lytton's ties, a big parcel of Lytton's ties, as this kind of love gift, absolutely monstrous."

If the film was a paean to anything, it was to the days of English bohemia in all its intellectual glory, with the Bloomsbury set on the sidelines. Carrington started out a woman with strong ideas, a painter of real talent, and one who wanted to remain a virgin. Having shed that, under the persuasion of both Strachey and her longtime boyfriend, she rapidly became a very sexual being, to the point (at least in the context of the film) where sex and love—the two being intertwined for her—far overshadowed her real work.

Unlike the other characters Emma had played, Carrington had actually existed, and had often been photographed. "When something is factual, like *Carrington*, said hair and makeup designer Chrissie Beveridge, "you always want to get as close a resemblance as you possibly can, a feeling of that character, without going too much into a caricature. . . . With Carrington, the desperately important thing was her haircut."

That haircut was a bob, which she wore throughout her life, starting in 1915, long before it became fashionable for women. Indeed, that look was what had first attracted Strachey to her: He thought she was a boy.

"Emma was marvelous," Beveridge continued, "because she agreed to have her hair cut in that bobbed style, so that was her own hair. Once that was done, it was wonderful, because it was the essence of the character."

Emma's first job on the film was to be taken to a salon "where her hair was cut according to the reference photographs that were shown. And we colored it as close to the Carrington color as we could," a very golden shade. But although Carrington was also described as having "piercing blue eyes," Beveridge decided not to change Emma's own green color with lenses, but instead to emphasize other aspects of her face, "round cheeks, a rosy, healthy complexion . . ."

Once shooting began, and she became Carrington physically and mentally, a strange thing happened to Emma—she found it hard to come out of character. In the past that had never been a problem; she was level-headed enough to distinguish between reality and fantasy. But Dora Carrington had an odd effect on her.

"Someone from the press tried to talk to me while we were making *Carrington*, and I just couldn't do it" she recalled. "I was too into my character. I couldn't get out and be Emma."

It was an unnerving experience, to find herself briefly trapped in her own creation, and it forced her to take a closer look at the woman she was playing, and to admit that there might have been "more of Carrington in me than I've been admitting to myself. I always thought she was so different."

Perhaps she was too close to be able to see it properly, but there were many parallels between the young Carrington and Emma when she'd been younger. Although neither of them had been obvious beauties, men fell in love with them. In both cases, it was real, romantic love. With Carrington, they wanted to take her away and sweep her off her feet. With Emma, they'd made the big gestures—riding a motor cycle up to her rooms, for example. They both seemed to hold an innate fascination for men. The principal difference seemed to be that Carrington succumbed sexually, often as a gesture of consolation not to hurt the fragile male egos, whereas, at Cambridge, Emma had been monogamous with Simon McBurney.

Both women also believed strongly in honesty. "Emma's candor and openness are very much like Carrington's," agreed director Christopher Hampton. And there was a link in their physical iconoclasm. Carrington wore her hair in a very masculine bob, and as a student Emma had taken to clothes that de-emphasized her body, and at least briefly, shaved her head, a gesture that essentially tried to erase gender definition.

So it was perhaps no surprise that Emma should have lost herself a little in the character. There were so many elements in Dora Carrington that, consciously or otherwise, reminded her of her younger self. The most glaring difference was that Carrington had gone one step further, had actually had affairs with all these men, something the eminently sensible and, at heart, fairly conventional, Emma had never done. Emma had dabbled in the unconventional life at a time when it was easy. Carrington lived it for thirty years, in a time before the word "lifestyle" had ever been invented. So it was possible that Emma also saw some of her idealized self in her character. In statements to the press, she'd made herself out to be a great sexual adventuress, which had seemed more than a slight revision of history. The person she seemed to want to have been was, in part, who Carrington *had* been two generations before.

For Emma, "Carrington's persona was incredibly liberating to me, even though it was also frightening because it posed so many questions." At first she'd thought it was because she and her character were so different. But the longer she dwelt on it, she came to realize it was because there were so many similarities between them. Emma was more intellectual, more of an analyst: "I use words all the time to color everything. And Carrington was a visual creature. For her it was a wave of feeling—nothing to do with words."

They were also both quite resolute products of the middle class, relatively assured of where they stood in society. In Carrington's case, that had meant attending the Slade School of Fine Art and carrying off prizes for her painting. With Emma, it had been Newnham College, Cambridge, and scholarship.

"Carrington didn't like being female at the beginning," Emma theorized. "I think that was because she didn't want to be penetrated in any way—not morally, physically, or spiritually." In her own way, Emma dealt with the problems of being feminine in a very masculine world. While Carrington's response was to remain a virgin, and then, later, to take many lovers—as if she were a man—Emma chose to disguise her body and then to expose a more aggressive side of herself, to put herself on an equal footing with the males. That showed itself in the feminism of her politics, which, at Cambridge and for a little while after, tended to be extremely confrontational and direct, just like her comedy. If she presented such a strong front, there was little danger of her being perceived as feminine and weak. As she said, feminism "spurred me on to be berserk, and I wanted to get away from all those stereotypical women."

While the film dealt with Carrington, the sexual being, it didn't look at all her explorations. As her life progressed, she'd also enjoyed female lovers. But none of that time made it to the screen.

"First of all, we only had two hours in which to examine seventeen years," Emma explained, "and the main love story, upon which we had to hook everything, was the Lytton-Carrington love story. We had at least four more love stories going on with all the different men that come into their lives and relate to one or the other of them—or in some cases both of them—sexually. I think to introduce more lovers, particularly female ones, complicates the story to such an extent that people would have gone away thinking, 'Well, fuck 'em all.'"

Which was quite true. Even within the boundaries the film set itself, it was hard to keep all the nuances of the different relationships straight.

The role showed Emma making love, at different times, to several different men. She "found all the sexuality in *Carrington* incredibly moving to do. It was naked in every way, because I was using my body. *Carrington* was definitely a very sexual experience. It was very releasing." But also difficult, simulating passion in take after take. You had to approach it "with tremendous sang-froid," she said. "And humor. If you get po-faced about it, then you make everyone uncomfortable. The way to get through those scenes is to laugh a great deal and enjoy them and allow the energy to take you along." And she also had to think of the crew as "a wall of family who have to watch while you're doing it."

She even involved the others in those scenes as much as she could. "I took advice from all the boys as well. I said, 'Well, I'm coming to the last sex scene. I asked Stephen Waddington [who played Ralph Partrdige, Carrington's husband], 'What sort of orgasm should I have?'

'Oh, a silent one,' he replied."

And during the sex scene on a boat, "Nick, one of the construction boys, was down on his hands and knees two feet away from our genitalia, opening and closing a door with a piece of wood, [while] me and [actor] Jeremy [Northam] were hosing each other down with a spray gun and squealing with laughter."

At heart, though, *Carrington* tried to be a love story, with its emotions releasing very subtly, a little at a time—something Emma had already shown herself to be a master of in her work with Merchant-Ivory. The problem lay in its manner of telling the tale. Both *Howards End* and *The Remains of the Day* worked because the narratives took a linear course, allowing the characters to develop naturally and the audience to come to know and understand them. *Carrington* was more like a stage play, with a number of acts and scenes. Beyond the relationship between Carrington and Strachey, there was little sense of continuity to the film. She'd explain she'd met a new man who was in love with her. There was no sense of how she met these men, or where, or even why so many should find her so attractive. Nor, beyond seeing her sketching and sitting at an easel with a brush, was there any sense of what painting and art meant to her. It was as if Christopher Hampton chose to make the unlikely assumption that his audience would already be familiar with many of the details of her life and able to fill in all the blanks on their own.

Carrington was the obvious choice as the film's subject—her life was the one in motion. Strachey seemed perfectly content with stasis. And that made it ironic that far more about Strachey was conveyed. His character was more strongly written and more fully developed; he was rounded, while Dora Carrington remained little more than a series of sketches, gauzy and never fully present.

Carrington did, however, pose some questions that made it very relevant to the modern age, both about gay relationships, and more explicitly, as Emma noted, "that it is possible to have all kinds of erotic experiences without necessarily having that romantic relationship [which is] very, very threatening to people."

It differentiated strongly between romantic and physical love, as the bohemian set of the period had themselves. That intellectual exploration had been part of what attracted Emma to the piece in the first place, as "you get into the question of female sexuality, which has never really been understood. And because we live in a Christian patriarchy, the whole notion of women having a kind of free sexuality is threatening simply because of its inheritance."

The political implications of the film didn't move critics especially. They were more concerned with the way it looked and was acted. And most were surprisingly sympathetic towards the picture. The *National Review* agreed that it did have "a somewhat unreal quality because it is told in brief, often disjointed scenes," but praised the fact that its central points were "feelings, relationships, and talk . . ." The *New Republic* was happy to concur that "the development of the film is in character, not in drama," and found that "the finish of the story, for all its pathos, is relatively calm—a termination rather than a climax."

Maclean's was slightly less convinced by the film itself, pointing out that it "just skims the surface of its characters' lives, as if the film-maker were racing to keep up with them," and noting that, "amid all the comings and goings, the relationship at the core of *Carrington* seems sadly neglected." *Time* took a similar tack; to Richard Schickel, Dora Carrington's unusual domestic arrangements were "presented blandly," and her sexual forays "have little dramatic consequence. Mostly this is a movie in which people take soulful country strolls or wait expectantly for Lytton to lob a withering epigram." Even *Entertainment Weekly* felt that the film's "restraint sometimes borders on discomfiting detachment." However, there was a real consensus as to Pryce's portrayal of Strachey, which had earned him the top prize at Cannes, acknowledging a powerful, sometimes even overwhelming performance.

Opinion was a little more divided as to Emma's work in the movie. For the *New Republic*'s Stanley Kauffmann, who'd become her leading apologist among American critics, "no prize is good enough for her. . . . Thompson never makes us feel that she is mastering a mood or responding tellingly or providing any other individuated touches. . . . This film, for all its other brilliancies, would collapse without the central truth of her performance." *Maclean's*, too, gushed a little, feeling she brought "a discerning intelligence to the role, that of a free spirit keeping the world at bay with a blunt, quizzical candor." And the *National Review*, while highlighting the fact that Emma wasn't the "childlike" creature of Dora Carrington, said she "conveys those tomboyish qualities impressively."

Others took a harsher view. *Entertainment Weekly* thought her "deliberate acting verges on the pompous," and to *People*, very much on the mark, she just "turns out to be wrong. Her strengths as an actress are humor, intelligence and clear-eyed sanity, but not bohemian ardor. Even in her nude scenes, she seemed fully clothed." *Time* went so far as to say she "keeps undoing [the movie]. Hers is a commonsensical presence, and try as she may, she cannot catch the fever of hopeless love. . . . You want her . . . to rattle the teacups with rage."

Playing Dora Carrington had given Emma a chance to show more of herself, both literally and metaphorically. She'd made her mark playing reserved, even repressed, middle-class women. Carrington was also middle-class, and suffered from her own kind of repression, but one that was very different from Margaret Schlegel or Sarah Kenton. But it wasn't so much a variation on a theme as a theme that contained a few harmonic similarities. And she exercised a freedom, a lack of restraint in her life that those two would have found thoroughly shocking.

For all the character's wild forays, however, it was impossible that Emma could play Carrington without projecting her as being innately sensible and orderly in so many things; that was too ingrained in Emma's own personality. Carrington had a streak of tradition that she couldn't shake off and so did Emma. Carrington would cook for Strachey and act like a wife. Throughout her marriage to Ken, it was Emma who had done all the cooking at home.

It was easy to see how Emma saw so much of herself—both real and idealized—in Carrington; it was there. In a way it brought her full circle. She'd started out in show business wanting to break down stereotypes, and now she was playing someone who'd done that in her own life.

With Carrington, that lack of conformity, which partly seemed to spring from a desire to not hurt anyone, caused distress in a number of her relationships, and Emma's own relationship with Ken was continuing to deteriorate, which no doubt caused greater introspection.

He was getting ready for the release of *Mary Shelley's Frankenstein*, his biggest directing job, and was caught up in the rush of last-minute details and publicity. The two of them might have shared the same house, but as usual, they didn't see each other often. With *Carrington* finished, Emma was engaged in publicity herself for the upcoming release of *Junior*; for a little while, at least, there'd be no rest.

Frankenstein was not a success, either critically or commercially. It had been anticipated that it would bring in at least $100 million. Ten weeks after release it had only managed $22 million, leaving Ken with a major flop on his hands—the first time the Golden Boy had failed.

The pair were exhausted. They'd both done so much during 1994, and at home they discovered that their marriage was slowly crumbling. They kept up appearances, going out together, being seen in public. But these days Emma was talking even less about having a baby, which seemed to be the main barometer of her marital feelings. "I never wanted children," she said now, "but it doesn't worry me one way or the other."

It was a far cry from the statements of a couple of years before, when she'd seemed quite enthusiastic about the possibility of motherhood. Even twelve months before she'd been more or less in favor of the idea. But she knew that before that could happen with Ken the marriage needed to be on a more solid footing. The rumors about him and Helena Bonham Carter continued to buzz around. Although they were roundly denied, there was no escaping the fact that Carter had flown to New York to "surprise" him while he was there publicizing *Mary Shelley's Frankenstein*, or that she'd visited him in Tuscany where he was filming *Othello*, a trip she made, she claimed, to have her hair cut by her favorite hairdresser who was based in Rome.

And meanwhile, Emma was being spotted occasionally in the company of Anthony Hopkins. Friends said they had a "close friendship," but also whispered that it was her "revenge thing," which hit quite brilliantly against both Carter and Ken. As one insider pointed out, "Miss Bonham Carter had made no secret of the fact that she had found Tony Hopkins very attractive and had made doe-eyes at him throughout the making of *Howards End*, but he had apparently resisted her charms, so you can imagine how she felt about it."

Having been involved in the film, Emma would certainly have known about that. She'd bettered her rival, and also Ken, who was smarting under his first failure, and suddenly hearing about his wife being squired around by someone "who was viewed as an indisputably better and more bankable actor than he was." It was, the source said, "a masterstroke, playing quite brilliantly on Kenneth's and Helena's insecurities."

It was also significant that Emma, who had once stated that she could not accept infidelity—and who had briefly broken off her relationship with Ken before they were married after she'd found letters from another woman—was now fighting fire with fire, rather than walking away.

Of course, no one was about to admit publicly there was any kind of problem. Emma's publicist called the flaring rumors "rubbish." To Ken's people they were "made up," and Helena Bonham Carter stated that the gossip about her involvement with Ken was "not even worth denying."

Whatever grim satisfaction Emma reaped from her revenge, it wasn't helping her marriage continue. And perhaps more than ever before, she needed some stability in her life. She no longer wanted to be a parent, but her baby was still about to be born: The filming of her version of *Sense and Sensibility* was set to begin in April, with plenty of work to do before then. Four years had been a long gestation period, and it was finally coming to an end, leaving her understandably nervous, and now, when she could have really used Ken's support, she found herself more alone than ever.

Being Emma, though, she downplayed what was happening at home, keeping a bright and very English face on things. What occurred behind closed doors was private business, to be shared only with family and close friends. It was quite emphatically not a subject that was open for public discussion. One kept one's sadness and heartbreak inside and got on with business. Whether the stiff upper lip was the right way didn't matter; it was what she knew and she was going to stick to it.

Besides, filming would be a large enough strain. It would need all her focus. Not only was she now going to have the leading role, but as screenwriter there would also be constant calls for script revisions. For the next six months her time would not be her own. Night and day she'd be consumed by *Sense and Sensibility*.

It was a daunting prospect, given all that was going on in her life. But having been raised in a theatrical family, she knew all too well the old adage that the show must go on.

Before Christmas 1994 she'd sat down with Lindsay Doran, Ang Lee, and co-producer James Schamus to discuss her most recent draft, the thirteenth or fourteenth she'd completed. In the second week of 1995 they met again supplemented by locations manager Tony Clarkson and Laurie Borg, another co-producer, to begin hammering out the finer logistical points of the production.

chapter twelve

Emma's vision was still a little too large for the film's budget, but by the time the January meeting broke up, most of the details had been decided. One thing that she had to do was prepare yet another draft, so it was back to her house, and the study across the hall from the bedroom. It felt like the place where she'd spent most of her free time since 1991. She was alone at home and spent "the rest of January in tears and a black dressing-gown."

There was no choice except to buckle down to work, with a deadline looming large on the horizon. At least there was no repeat of the previous year's calamity, when the script had vanished into her Macintosh, and she'd been unable to retrieve it. Even technicians from Apple had been unable to find it. In panic and desperation, she'd taken the computer to her old friend Stephen Fry, who after a day, managed to locate the file.

In February the casting began. From the 1993 read-through, only Robert Hardy and Hugh Laurie remained. But others who'd joined the team a year later were also confirmed. It was a group of old friends, for the most part—Imelda Staunton, Hugh Grant ("for whom I wrote Edward"), and Harriet Walter.

By April, after a total of more than twenty drafts, most of the preparations were complete, and rehearsals were underway at Shepperton Studios. As usual, Emma kept a diary during the making of the film. It was something she liked to do, so "the jobs don't all run into one another until it's like a great big tube of toothpaste." While extracts from her previous diaries had seen publication before in magazines and newspapers, this was destined for grander things; together with her screenplay, the diaries would form her first book.

By the time it was published, in 1996, a public announcement had been made about the breakup of the Branagh-Thompson marriage. And significantly, there was no mention of Ken at all in the finished work. However, two magazines had earlier published extracts, and *Mirabella* seemed to have a less revised version of the diaries, which *did* refer (albeit briefly) to Ken. Neither was especially personal, but they offered evidence that, at the least, the couple was still communicating, even if it was just about work: "Ken's in Venice scouting *Othello* locations. He's written and finished a film [*In the Bleak Midwinter* (retitled *A Midwinter's Tale* for its American release)] in the time it's taken us to rehearse this one."

That had been on the twenty first of April. By the first of May, "Ken flew in from L.A. yesterday, worked out this a.m., rehearsed *Shadow of a Gunman* with Stephen Rea, had a meeting about the trailer of *In the Bleak Midwinter*, and saw a designer about a flyer for Cannes. 'I feel a bit sick now,' he said, sounding surprised. Mad."

For all intents and purposes, however, the marriage was over. Ken had moved out of the house, leaving Emma extremely depressed at a time when so much was dependent on her. It also left her somewhat bitter, feeling "suspicious of romantic notions of love" and offering a complete volte-face on the idea of promiscuity, saying now, "I think we're paying for the liberation of the nineteen-sixties. That everything happens freely is causing us hardship. The notion of the pill being liberating for women—I mean, it's actually liberating only for men. It's not that I'm not grateful for contraception—I am of course—but one must examine what else it brings."

The breakup was causing Emma to question some of the most deeply held tenets of her life. To compound the problem, her co-star Kate Winslet ended a four-year relationship at the same time, leaving them miserable together (Kate would move briefly into Emma's house, so at least neither would have to suffer alone).

By the middle of April, the cast was ensconced in Devon, and on the nineteenth filming began, preceded by Ang Lee's "Big Luck" ceremony, a Buddhist ritual. The Taiwanese Lee had seemed an odd choice to direct a film that was so obviously English. As he admitted himself, "What did I know about nineteenth-century England? But when I read the novel, I felt it was my destiny to do Jane Austen."

But then, suddenly, doing Jane Austen seemed to be everybody's destiny. From being someone who was viewed as a largely forgotten "women's" author, she'd spun back into vogue. There was talk of a production of *Emma*, and that novel had already been ransacked and given a modern remake as *Clueless*. Productions of *Pride and Prejudice* and *Persuasion* were underway. Everywhere you turned, Jane Austen was there.

From the problems Lindsay Doran had encountered trying to interest studios in a book that meant nothing to them, the pendulum had swung in the opposite direction, and now everyone wanted their own Jane Austen adaptation. However, it wasn't perhaps too surprising. As Emma had been saying for a few years, to anyone who would listen, "People forget Austen is a comedian, she's a satirist and an ironist of the first order, and her wit is biting and it cuts very deep."

It was also about money, the power and independence it brought, and the need for it—ideas as relevant today as they were when the book was written, late in the eighteenth century (the story originally appeared as *Elinor and Marianne* in 1795, and Austen rewrote it as *Sense and Sensibility* in 1798; the book was finally published in 1811). "I keep saying there is no real difference," Emma commented. "Human beings haven't changed that much since two hundred years ago." What had changed, she believed, was that "We don't quite know how to behave any more. I was raised to always stand up when someone entered a room. I would never start an interview without shaking hands and looking the person in the eye. A lot of social rules are disappearing and I sometimes yearn for structure."

Adapting *Sense and Sensibility* gave her plenty of scope for structure. That had been at the heart of her script—a narrative. When she undertook the project, she'd been given some tips by Merchant-Ivory writer Ruth Prawer Jhabvala, which emphasized the telling of the story.

She'd been forced to make changes of course. As she acknowledged, "The difficulty of adapting a novel is that you can't have a seventeen-hour movie."

Sense and Sensibility was Austen's first novel. Although the themes were there, Emma had to admit that "The dialogue . . . is even more arcane than the later novels. If you compare . . . the difference is remarkable."

Which meant that she also had to make changes there. To carry it all out, there was plenty she had to jettison along the way—the duel between Willoughby and Brandon, Willoughby's return to Marianne's sickbed. Some of it raised the ire of the Jane Austen Society, which complained to Columbia Pictures, leaving Emma to anticipate "picket lines, with people in mobcaps chanting, 'They never elided! They never kissed!'"

In the book, that was true; but, as she wrote, ". . . kissing Hugh was very lovely. Glad I invented it. Can't rely on Austen for a snog, that's for sure." Initially, she and Hugh had ended up unknowingly insulting Ang Lee. In their usual way of working, both had offered some small directorial suggestions. Lee had been horrified.

"Apparently," Emma explained, "in the East, the director is like a god. You never, never question them. Ever." Once the protocol had been fixed, everything was fine. But for Emma there was little time off. During the day she was usually filming her role as Elinor. In the evenings she was working feverishly to add or cut dialogue for the next day's shooting.

Elinor Dashwood was a character almost perfectly suited to her acting style, and she'd been given the chance to tailor it exactly. She was the pragmatic sister, the sense to Marianne's wild sensibility, the woman who was in control of her emotions. Even when they overtook her, she kept a firm lid on them, rarely showing the depth of what she felt. In that regard, she was somewhat of a sister to Margaret Schlegel, perhaps even more to Miss Kenton, but with more humor and laughter in her life.

In truth, Emma *was* far too old for the role. In Austen's book Elinor was nineteen, rather than Emma's actual thirty-six. But subtle makeup and good skin (despite frequent complaints about spots in different places) did a great deal to make her look eight or nine years younger, something modern audiences could easily accept.

The set did offer a few distractions from labor, though. When she wasn't busy working, there was plenty of opportunity to socialize with the other actors. In the small world of British acting, they all knew each other; many had worked together on a number of occasions. One face that was quite new though was Greg Wise, who arrived on April 30 and "ruffled all our feathers a bit."

As it turned out, he definitely ruffled Emma's feathers, as she did his. In the evenings, one person associated with the production revealed, "He was running after her like a puppy—getting her cheese and drinks. They were both smoking roll-up cigarettes and laughing. . . . At dinner, it was clear they were obsessed with each other. Emma was even copying the way he spoke."

There was absolutely nothing wrong with such flirting; in a closed, insular world like a film set, it was inevitable. Unfortunately, it happened when Greg's girlfriend, Nicky Hart (who, like Emma, was a graduate of Camden School for Girls), was visiting. When she left, the flirtation continued and, according to some, went beyond that.

"They stayed at a small country house hotel near Plymouth (the cast was based at Alston Country House in Devon)," a source said. "I think they were there for about six weeks in all. They had separate rooms, but from what I can gather they were in and out of each other's places all the time. Because they were working very late into the evening six days a week, the only time off was at night or on Sunday. They also went for walks together. But Emma has kept it very, very quiet. . . . It was just like 'What a bizarre situation I'm in.'"

Obviously she was in a vulnerable position—alone, with a marriage that seemed over, surrounded by the constant stress of making and scripting a major film—so when the chance arose, it wasn't the sensible girl who said no, but the adventuress who replied yes (in spite of her recent reserved comments about promiscuity). However, she was circumspect about the affair for the duration of filming. There was no big splash; it was kept quiet and secretive, mostly between the two of them and a small circle of friends.

After all, nothing could be allowed to interfere with the business at hand. The film had to come before anything and everything else. There was a strict schedule to be kept, and a budget. However bad or good Emma, or anyone else in the cast, was feeling, things had to continue.

Ang Lee proved surprisingly adept at extracting subtlety from his Western actors and seemed to have an innate understanding of the proprieties of English society at the time, so convoluted and heavy with the rigors of class structure. And perhaps because of his ancestry, he seemed to feel comfortable with the intricacies of the film's family relationships. "I thought that Ang's sensibilities were true and very accurate about human nature and particularly about female nature," Emma commented. "He's so good on the relationship between people in a family which we don't examine much because we are so hung up on boy meets girl. We don't represent moms or sisters or all the other human relationships that involve love and betrayal and despair. These stories are of prime importance and should be told more often."

The Dashwood women felt poor, or at least in straitened circumstances, with only 500 pounds a year to support the four of them. And after the munificence they'd known, it didn't seem like much. But in reality, it was more than enough to leave them very comfortable, at a time when a member of what was deemed the "middle class"—a white-collar worker in today's terminology—would have to keep his family on 100–150 pounds per annum. By those standards they were in luxurious circumstances. None of them had to consider work. Even if their lives weren't a constant series of balls and mixing with the cream of society, neither were they liable to be walking around in rags and seeking the charity of the Poorhouse. For Marianne and Elinor, the major aim in life was to catch a husband, and preferably a rich one.

With the liberties Emma took in her script, and the additions and deletions from the novel, she produced a screenplay that unfolded at a steady pace, never lagging, and one that was rich in both Austen's natural laughter and drama. "Emma understood the humor in every character—she is very funny herself," Lindsay Doran said. "But she also saw the pain that surges beneath the surface." For the production, the costumes, furnishing, even the sheep were correct for the time. Jane Austen herself could have walked onto the set and felt at home. Being utterly authentic about those trappings gave a better feel. But Doran commented, "Although the film was shot perfectly in period, the story itself transcends the time. When we fall in love, we all have to work out our capacity for emotion, how much to reveal, how much to conceal. These are very modern concerns, too."

What this English cast, under a Taiwanese director and an American producer, captured was a wonderful story, marvelously acted. It had everything an audience could want in an English film: drama, love, glamour, and glorious West Country scenery. And above all, excellent performances from everyone involved. For the most part they were stalwarts of stage and screen who could be relied on to be excellent. But even the newer faces—Kate Winslet and Emilie Francois, as the younger Dashwood sisters—proved to be excellently cast.

After finishing his part, Hugh Grant (as reticently attractive in this as he had been in *Four Weddings and a Funeral*) left to begin publicizing his new movie, *Nine Months*. That publicity tour included his infamous jaunt to Los Angeles, which resulted in his arrest for consorting with a prostitute, an event that gave tremendous amusement to the rest of the *Sense and Sensibility* team. Headlines like "Hugh Dirty Dog" circulated in the New York tabloids, with much worse running in the newspapers in Britain.

When Emma was questioned as to how she felt about the incident, she replied brightly, "I thought it was wonderful. It seems a perfectly reasonable experiment in human behavior. If I was him, I might well have done the same thing. It's none of our business anyway," continuing, "If Ken were to go strolling down the boulevard looking for a blow job, I'd think, 'Well, that seems to be a perfectly reasonable thing to do, if you have the urge.' It's certainly not something I'd take personally."

Of course, these days it was mattering less and less to her what Ken might do. The interview gave her a chance to say that, in lightly veiled terms, and to stir up a little controversy at the same time. It was hard to believe that an avowed feminist could fully approve of prostitution, with its exploitation of women, or of any man who frequented one, whether it was a friend like Hugh or an estranged husband.

Anger was behind the words, anger at Ken. Even if she had Greg Wise for consolation and friends around, that was hardly the same thing as a working marriage.

๛

When the production wound up, early in July, it was like another family falling apart to her, all the more so because they'd largely been her support for the last several months, at a time when she needed people around her, and also because they'd brought her creation to life in front of her eyes. For the wrap party, Lee gave a Chinese banquet, and Hugh Laurie's band played. "For everyone, it's been uniquely happy," Emma wrote in her last diary entry. "I am in a right old state of gratitude." And it truly had been a special experience with lots of fun and laughter, plenty of work, a little romance to ease the loneliness, and a long labor over.

There was a great deal of anticipation surrounding the film's release. It stood at the vanguard of the Austen revival, as it should have, given how long Lindsay Doran had been fighting to make it. Only the slightly dour version of *Persuasion* had preceded it. And more particularly to critics and moviegoers, it had a screenplay by an actress, something largely unheard-of in the past—certainly for a major release.

By the time it opened, Emma and Ken's marriage had officially and publicly collapsed, so doubtless some went looking for clues to her feelings in the words she'd written. But there was none to be found. As always, there was a separation of public and private life; she was a professional.

A great deal rested on how well *Sense and Sensibility* did at the box office. Lindsay Doran had years of effort invested in it, and other studios, with their Austen adaptations due out or in various stages of productions, looked eagerly at the bottom line to see how they might fare. It would have been unfair to have expected a blockbuster on the order of *Star Wars*, and indeed, the film didn't go breaking attendance records. It was an entertain-

ment with some depth, no violence or special effects, and a story that largely unfolded through speech. It was driven by character and words rather
than action. That qualified it as a classy product in Hollywood's eyes,
along the lines of Merchant-Ivory (who had expressed some interest in it
a few years before), the type of thing the British always did so well.

In the end, it proved to be a bigger film than people had anticipated,
drawing in a diverse and gratifyingly large audience. The initial reviews
helped spread the word, and soon word of mouth praise was bringing people to the theaters. There seemed to be little doubt that it would be in line
for all manner of awards, even in a year that had brought any number of
excellent movies to the screen.

For the critics, it was like manna from heaven. They had something literate and articulate to discuss and compare with the novel, as well as
Emma's dual role in the production. Since *Howards End* she'd proven to
be a consistent favorite with reviewers. Any writer worth his analytical
salt, it seemed, sat down to discuss the film and its acting.

Writing in *National Review*, John Simon felt it "capture[d] the essence
of the novel. . . . The film truly looks right. It also plays right." To *Variety*,
"the Austen party continues with this classy, entirely enjoyable comic
melodrama that is bound to be so well received . . . one can only complain
that it's almost too much of a good thing." In Canada, *Maclean's* decided
that "it gives Hollywood a lesson in how to make a romantic comedy" with
"the framed elegance of a Merchant-Ivory film." Not surprisingly,
Commonweal rated it among the great adaptations, noting that "Lee's subtle directorial touches can be relished at second, even third viewings."

In the *Los Angeles Times*, however, Kenneth Turan called it "the
audience-friendly, Hollywood version of Austen, easygoing and aiming to
please." He was willing to concede, though, that "at day's end . . . it seems
churlish to complain about a film that creates so much good feeling by its
fail-safe close. The sensibility may be a bit off, but there is more than
enough sense involved in this mid-Atlantic Austen to make up the
difference." To the *Washington Post* it offered "rapturous romance," which
was "not only laugh-out-loud funny but demonstrates how little
humankind has evolved in matters of the heart."

In America there was a general love of Emma Thompson and almost anything involving her. She seemed to represent something quite exquisitely and perfectly English, refined, honed, intellectual, and funny in the way people wanted all the English to be. That offered an overall sympathy to her movies. At home it was altogether another story. At different times the press had loved and hated her, and the reception for *Sense and Sensibility* would depend on which phase they were currently stuck in.

Luckily, the barometer seemed to be on "like." *Empire* summed it up as "a beautifully crafted, witty, moving film likely to overcome even the stiffest Austen prejudice." And the *London Sunday Times* declared it "by far the best match of Austen's own that the screen has seen . . . beautiful, but never self-preeningly pretty."

Quite understandably, Emma came under particular scrutiny for her work, assessed this time both for her writing and her acting. For someone who was still essentially a novice at screenwriting, she managed to draw plenty of high praise. *Variety* characterized *Sense and Sensibility* as a "shrewd, highly humorous adaptation," and *Maclean's* was ready to hail her as a "Renaissance woman" whose work "captures the sly wit of Jane Austen's 1795 novel with a lively, literate, script. . . ."

In England, the *Sunday Times* pointed out how Lee "has worked a neat alchemy with Thompson's script, a labor of love that took her four years to write. Together, they have forged a tone for their film that is both ironic and indulgent. . . ." Elsewhere, others were happy to note "The bright screenplay is skillfully attuned to Austen's ironies, with Thompson laying a few extra of her own on top," although the reviewer found herself wondering "if it was also her deliberate ploy to make the women in the film so exceptionally engaging and the men really rather dull." *Empire* found plenty of joy in Emma's writing, saying, "Thompson has done a dazzling job in bringing out the comedy of the work. The script bubbles with lovely comic vignettes. . . ." However, it was *Commonweal* that made a true celebration of her work, putting her on the cover with "A Toast to Emma Thompson's *Sense and Sensibility*." Richard Alleva wrote at length about the adaptation, gushing with praise. In his view "what's up there on the screen is satisfying in itself. But if you do return to the book, you may be astonished by Thompson's expansions and curtailments. And you will certainly be struck by her complete understanding of what this novel is really about."

In addition to comments about her screenplay, there were also plenty of effusive words about her performance. *Empire* downplayed a little, merely noting that "Thompson leads with assurance as the responsible elder sister who bottles up her emotions for the sake of others." The *Gannett News Service* offerred: "Thompson gives a terrific performance as the spirited and logical Elinor, capturing the inner longing and pain while displaying a calm exterior." For *People* it was difficult to choose between "Thompson slowly uncorseting her emotions or Winslet learning to rein them in."

New York was willing to go further, stating "Emma Thompson, whose high intelligence never spins into eccentricity—she has a grip on common emotions as well as common sense—anchors the movie just as Elinor anchors the book."

The *National Review* chose to highlight the scene "in which Elinor unburdens herself to her sister, beating her chest as she does so. There's no hint of melodramatic chest-beating in the act; you can hear the hard rap of knuckle against ribcage too clearly for that. She seems to be beating her pain back in, as much as letting it out, or perhaps giving back her heart some of the hurt it's given her. It's one of the most inspired things I've seen her do; she's caught Jane Austen in a single gesture."

As John Simon concluded, "Miss Thompson has been remarkable in most of her many films, but—improbably—she keeps getting better. Just when you think she has reached her acme, she goes ahead and tops herself." And he finished with a quote from literary scholar W. P. Ker that seemed to best sum up not only Emma's performance but also her screenplay: "There is no name for the dominant quality in Miss Austen's work, except perhaps intelligence."

As in her best work, Emma was not only the narrative heart but also the moral center of the film. Unlike Margaret Schlegel, or especially Miss Kenton, as Elinor she did get to blossom; one could anticipate a happy-ever-after life for her. And as John Simon had noted, her work did keep improving. She *should* have given a masterful performance in *Sense and*

Sensibility; no one knew the script better than she did, after all. Even so, she was able to invest Elinor with a startlingly luminous quality. She unashamedly tugged at the audience's heartstrings, but did it in a such a subtle way that it never seem manipulative or even obvious.

Emma's trademark, as much as she had one, was to color her characters with quiet shades and gestures, using the small things to build a personality, to take things from her own life and transform them into something for the role. With the gradual disintegration of her marriage, she had plenty of fodder for a broken heart and a reflective personality.

It certainly helped that the rest of the cast was uniformly excellent; there was little to fault in any performance. It highlighted the difference between the English and American approaches to a film; in England (even with American money) there was a large pool of talent who had the opportunity to work *because* they were excellent actors, even if they were not leading names. In America the name was far more important than the ability. The more big names in the cast list, Hollywood thinking seems to run, the greater the chance of box office success.

If Emma's performance in *Sense and Sensibility* didn't seem quite as transcendent as her work in *Howards End*, it was no fault of hers or even of the film. In truth, one was the equal of the other. But having pulled it off once—three times, really if you allowed for her work in *The Remains of the Day* and *Much Ado About Nothing*—she'd established a standard to live up to. She could add to the canon, but surpassing it would have been virtually impossible, certainly within the rather strict confines of Austen.

The mere fact of equaling her best, though, was quite remarkable. Her great roles—and her playing in them truly warrants the word—of Margaret Schlegel, Beatrice, Elinor, and even the relatively contemporary Miss Kenton, all moved beyond the time and place of their setting to speak directly to the heart and mind.

She'd already established herself as probably the leading British actress of her generation. Her work in *Sense and Sensibility* set the seal on that title and proved again that she was able to temper the "serious" acting with a comic froth that made her characters even more rounded and human.

With this film, she'd also given a gift to herself, something that was, in effect, another life. The plaudits for her writing meant that more script work would undoubtedly be offered to her, whether in England or elsewhere. She now had a career apart from acting, and one that might last considerably longer. She'd noted caustically that the roles for actresses tended to diminish considerably past the age of thirty-five, and for parts of any substance that was true. Young and beautiful generally remained the order of the day—exactly the thing she'd railed against in 1993 at the Oscars. Even if things had improved slightly, it certainly wasn't enough to accommodate a generation that was getting older. As a writer she could avoid the competition for the few parts available and could even make a real difference by creating some from her own pen.

The film critics seemed to be in no doubt that she had the ability to do it, and at the box office *Sense and Sensibility* performed every bit as well as anyone could have hoped. Without a doubt, it was award material, and early in 1996, as she had three years earlier, Emma campaigned on behalf of the movie—and herself.

Towards the end of 1995 she'd done something that earlier she'd sworn she'd never do—spent some time at an American health farm. This time, however, it wasn't to lose weight. The stress she'd been living under had already taken care of that. It was simply a chance to get away from everything, to clean out her system. The year had been punishing—the split with Ken, six solid months of work on *Sense and Sensibility*, followed by the publicity for both that and *Carrington*. It was a tremendous amount of work. She needed a break. Returning clear-eyed and healthy, she gave a long interview to *Vanity Fair*, which featured her on the cover dressed, for some reason, as Saint Joan, and included a couple of fairly daring photographs of her by Annie Liebowitz.

It was all very high-profile stuff, and the February issue of the magazine appeared on the newsstands shortly before the Academy Award nominations, timing that couldn't have suited her, or the film, better.

By then she'd already collected her first trophy, at the Golden Globes held on January 21, 1996. Emma had been nominated for both Best Actress and Best Screenplay, Kate Winslet for Best Supporting Actress, and the film as Best Picture (Drama). With the awards being seen to an extent as predictors of the Oscars, they'd grown in importance, and a win in one or more categories would stand things in good stead, as well as increase the box-office takings.

Neither Emma nor Kate won for their acting (Sharon Stone was named Best Actress in a Drama for her work in *Casino*, and Mira Sorvino was Best Supporting Actress for *Mighty Aphrodite*). But Emma didn't leave empty handed. Not only was *Sense and Sensibility* named Best Picture (Drama), but she also won for Best Screenplay.

In her speech, a good portion of which was an entertaining diary entry Jane Austen might have written after attending the awards, she defended the current vogue of Austen adaptations, pointing out that "It's okay to keep going back because the things they're about are still universal today," before adding, with some small venom, "For example, we're still falling in love with the wrong men."

But the Globes were still seen as the minor cousins of the Oscars, now two months away. When those nominations were announced, *Sense and Sensibility* was in the running for seven, including, almost inevitably (given its mixture of both quality and commercial success), Best Picture and Best Supporting Actress (for Kate Winslet's bravura performance). And, like the Golden Globes, it was possible for Emma to hit twice, as she was nominated for both Best Adapted Screenplay and Best Actress.

On March 26, it was the usual event of glitter, glitz, and glamour. Surrounded by what seemed like acres of cleavage, Emma was dressed conservatively but classically in an Armani outfit of a long white skirt and beaded cardigan ("Mr. Armani sewed each one of these sparkles on himself," she joked to reporters). Unlike her last appearance, there was no Ken to accompany her this time; instead, she brought the person closest to her, and who'd been with her the last time she won—her mother.

In a year when the Academy's sympathies seemed strongly with *Braveheart*, *Sense and Sensibility* didn't have much chance of becoming Best Picture, and once again Kate Winslet found herself losing out to Mira Sorvino. For Best Actress, though, Emma seemed to have a very strong chance; in the end, that went to Susan Sarandon for her work in *Dead Man Walking*.

Where there really was no competition, however, was for Best Adapted Screenplay. There might as well not have been any other contenders. Hollywood had always loved making film history, and that Oscar made Emma the first actress ever to win Academy Awards both for acting and writing.

It was nonetheless an obvious thrill, and she reached the podium a little breathless and wide-eyed. But after a moment or two, the British sang-froid reasserted itself as she began her humorous acceptance speech with the words, "Before I came, I went to visit Jane Austen's grave in Winchester Cathedral to pay my respects and tell her about the grosses. I don't know how she would react to an evening like this, but I do hope she knows how big she is in Paraguay."

Unlike her first appearance at the Oscars, where nerves had left her awestruck and tongue-tied at the parties that carried on through the night, she was now an old hand. Instead of seeking out stars, she'd become a center of attraction herself, going on to the Columbia pictures bash at Dria's, where it was noted, she "spent long stretches sitting on the lap of *Sense and Sensibility* co-star Greg Wise."

Although a highlight, the Oscars weren't the end of the award season. Less than a month later, back in London, Emma found herself at the BAFTA awards. And for once she didn't win an award for her screenplay—it went to the other big British film of the year, *Trainspotting*. It was impossible, though, that *Sense and Sensibility* could win nothing, and Kate Winslet finally was given a Best Supporting Actress award. The movie itself was voted Best Film, and Emma won as Best Actress. Finally, she'd received everything it was possible to win for the movie, a full vindication of all the facets of her ability. And as she'd deliberately not signed for another film, she could take the time to rest, read, and slowly recover, and to work out what she really wanted to do next.

chapter thirteen

To the public at large, the Golden Couple truly shattered on October 1, 1995, when Emma Thompson stood outside her house and recited a statement about the collapse of her marriage to Ken. The couple, courting publicity even in sadness, had hosted a brief press conference the day before to announce "with sadness" that they'd decided to part.

The roots, of course, went back almost to 1992 and the way their careers had both taken off—generally in different directions. That much, though, they'd been willing to endure: other couples survived it. Even when Emma became a far bigger international star than Ken, things hadn't fallen apart. His joy for her, and all the awards she kept winning, had seemed to be genuine, as was her belief in him as an actor and director.

When she opened her door to talk to the reporters who'd assembled outside the house, her face was drawn, exhausted, her eyes hidden behind glasses. She was dressed in old blue sweats; she looked tired and depressed, stumbling through some prepared words: "I can't even string a sentence together this morning. I'm sorry. . . . I'm feeling pretty ropey. I didn't sleep at all. It's been rough." At the same time, she said that there was nothing she could add to the statement released the previous day, where the cause of the breakdown was given simply as: "We have drifted apart. The separation is entirely amicable but it is painful for both of us." In spite of persistent questions, she refused to add anything, saying, with extreme equity, "Because Ken's not here, it's not fair to say any more."

There had been attempts to save the marriage. But although the major problems were deep-seated, the more immediate obstacles were the lovers each now had and showed no signs of relinquishing.

In the middle of September, according to a friend, Ken and Emma had taken a weekend in France to discuss their relationship, and whether it could continue. "Unfortunately, they couldn't work things out," the friend said. "In fact their differences were such that the subject of a quickie divorce even came up. As soon as they got back from France, [Emma] was seeing Greg again."

For the press, news of the breakup was like manna from heaven. Reporters and photographers stayed on the trail of Ken and Emma, capturing their every move. "That day," recalled Hugh Grant, who'd been under journalistic scrutiny himself since his Hollywood faux pas, "I could hear the sound of knuckles scraping against concrete as the British press left my flat and head for Hampstead."

The details emerged very slowly. Understandably, neither Ken nor Emma was eager to dissect the breakup for the British public, so one never took to blaming or accusing the other. In that regard the civility of British manners continued to reign supreme. Whatever there was in the way of dirty linen wasn't aired.

For a long time, said an associate of Ken's, "There was a feeling . . . that the marriage could still be saved. It is true that Helena was infatuated with Ken, but she was making all the running [doing the pursuing], and he was by no means clear in his own mind about where he wanted to go. Everyone was very busy at this point, no one had really thought it all out." During Emma's trip to see Ken in Italy, the source continued, they had a "long and amicable conversation" about the state of their marriage. "They both accepted that all their problems stemmed from the fact that their work was keeping them apart for too much of the time. They spoke very seriously about trying to make more time for each other, even having children."

Certainly Emma had been willing to make the time to be with Ken. After *Sense and Sensibility* she turned down a role opposite Daniel Day-

Lewis in *The Crucible*. Ken, however, needed a success after the major flop of *Mary Shelley's Frankenstein*. The pressure was on him to come through with something strong.

The affairs, according to psychologist Dr. Dorothy Rowe in the *Daily Mail*, were largely attempts to gain notice from each other, and to prop up insecurities. "It is a very common situation for a couple who have been married for a bit and are starting to feel neglected and unappreciated. They both evidently felt the need to demonstrate to the other that they were still attractive to successful, talented people of the opposite sex. The other parties they involved were, I suspect, just pawns in their long, drawn-out battle."

But if it was a battle, it wasn't a very conscious one. Even as the affairs were continuing, so was the dialogue of making everything work. One friend admitted that "[Greg] even offered to step aside to allow her the space to see if she could sort out her marriage troubles with Ken."

By then, though, they were resorting to last-ditch attempts to hold things together. According to some reports, Ken had moved out of the West Hampstead house several months earlier, although at the end of September he was still insisting that he lived in the marital home, and when asked if his marriage was over by Dawn Alford and John Chapman from the *News of the World*, Ken replied, "I respect your interest but it's not the case"—this comment being made after he spent the night at the home of his secretary and her husband.

It was Dawn Alford and John Chapman who broke the story of the failing relationship and Emma's affair with Wise in the *News of the World*. There seemed to be little doubt that both Ken and Emma were aware that the article would surface, and so the conciliatory tone of previous press statements ended, to be replaced by the formal announcement of their separation, to coincide with the article.

By then of course, it could no longer be denied. In the *Daily Mail*, Tim Walker asserted that they had been "rushed, if not panicked" into informing the world of their breakup, after hurried consultations with close family and friends. One reason given for them having held back in the first place was that they had planned to wait until Emma's sister had married in

October—to actor Richard Lumsden, who'd played Robert Ferrars in *Sense and Sensibility*—in an attempt to stop the event becoming a media circus. But it was also to give them time to reflect on the gravity of their actions, to see if it was what they *really* wanted.

As it turned out, circumstances forced their hands and put them under a microscope of publicity. Other than Emma, who could only manage a few words to the press on her doorstep, everyone was tight-lipped. Approached by a reporter, Greg Wise offered, "Print what you've got, mate. Print what you know." And Phyllida Law, who was spending a great deal of time across the street consoling her daughter, merely said, "I regret . . . I just can't comment."

The dust took several weeks to settle. Richard Briers, the British actor who'd worked with Ken and Emma on a number of Renaissance productions, suggested that, "You must understand that all of the people who are involved in this are at the height of their profession and the pressure on them is intense. It is simply not possible for them to have relationships in the way that the rest of us have them. Their commitments mean they are hardly ever on the same continent together. They are in a very different world and have to be judged by different standards." But, he added, "You don't have what they had and have it just end. I think at the very least they will always be friends, but it's not inconceivable they could get together again. I'd certainly love to see that happen."

By November, just a month after the split had been made public, Ken had moved into a Surrey mansion he'd bought for almost a million pounds, guarded by careful security arrangements and located on a private road. It was reported in the *News of the World* that he and Helena Bonham Carter "chat endlessly on the phone and snatch time together whenever their busy schedules allow. His pet name for her is 'Helsa.'"

One friend said that now "[Ken and Helena] can admit their true feelings for each other—at least in private. They have always been soul mates. Now they are much more. He loves her intelligence and toughness and builds up her confidence. He thinks she's wonderful and extremely talented. . . . He seems to be waiting for the fuss about his marriage break-up to die down before doing anything more about it. But they are staying in

close contact and have even talked about setting up home together."
(Which, according to *Parade*, they finally did in 1997 when Helena moved
into Ken's London flat.)

At the same time, though, Bonham Carter would only allow that "My
relationship [with Ken] extends to a friendship."

Phrases like "loves her intelligence and toughness . . . thinks she's wonderful and extremely talented" were ones he could easily have applied to
Emma, and not only in the early days of their courtship and marriage. The
difference, perhaps, was that Helena's career hadn't eclipsed Ken's the way
Emma's had. In anything between Helena and Ken, he would remain the
senior partner, both in terms of age (Emma was a year older than Ken) and
business.

To an extent he remained the Golden Boy, but the glow had tarnished a
little since the heady days of theater productions in London and the
success-on-a-shoestring of *Henry V*. The critical and commercial failure
of *Mary Shelley's Frankenstein* had definitely moved him down a few
notches in the industry's estimation. People were still waiting for him to
fulfill the vast early promise and live up to being a man who could confi-
dently write the first part of his autobiography at the age of twenty eight.

Emma, on the other hand, had continued to shine brighter and brighter.
When she made her move from comedy, nobody had anticipated that she
had such a large dramatic talent. The way she'd developed, and the fact
that she'd been mostly able to keep her ego in check and her feet planted
on the ground, endeared her to people, and most certainly to Americans,
for whom she embodied the best English qualities.

Ken and Emma had always insisted that there was no jealousy between
them, and that they were completely supportive of each other. Was that
possible, however, when the pupil (as Emma had been seen in the early
days of their marriage and working together) had outclassed the master?
He was driven to succeed, a workaholic. Emma showed some ambition,
but things seemed to flow to her quite naturally. As Ian Shuttleworth
pointed out in the *Evening Standard*, "He has come from far humbler origins than she and has always had to work harder for all of life's goals. She
has always been able to take the broader view."

In the late eighties, and even into the nineties, the couple was being compared to Sir Laurence Olivier and Vivien Leigh, which seemed to occasionally appeal to Ken. Emma, though, was far more pragmatic: "I think people are always looking to build up new heroes," she explained to journalist David Wigg, "and this thing of us being the new Laurence Olivier and Vivien Leigh has been created—we never set out to do that. The comparison is just not fair. We are bound to suffer by it. It's very flattering, but it is also faintly ridiculous because we couldn't really be less like them."

That was certainly true. Ken might have shared a few traits with Olivier—they'd both run their own companies, had brought *Henry V* to the screen, and had been actor/directors—but that was as far as it went. Emma had absolutely nothing in common with Vivien Leigh. However, the press, in seeking newsworthy comparisons, had never been beyond hyperbole. The tag had stuck and had been dusted off and dragged out again with each film they made together, which again was largely erroneous since the real Golden Couple only ever filmed *Fire over England* together.

After a while Ken and Emma even stopped trying to shake off the comparison and just ignored it. But inevitably, with the split, they found themselves compared to another famous couple—Richard Burton and Elizabeth Taylor. Would they follow in those footsteps instead—find they couldn't live without each other and reunite?

It was all ridiculous speculation, but it filled the column inches and brought in readers eager to hear the latest doings in the private lives of celebrities.

ꝍ

It was notable, but hardly surprising, that it was Ken who moved out. They'd bought the house together, but in many ways it had always been more Emma's than his, whatever the wording on the deed might have been. It was *her* neighborhood, the place she'd lived all her life. *Her* mother was across the street, literally just a few steps away. The area, all the surroundings, were as familiar to her as her own face. It was a part of her security to be able to return there, to see people she'd known since she was a girl, to have her mother slip across for a cup of tea and a chat. If she'd been forced to move, all that would have been taken away from her. The semidetached house perfectly suited her sensible personality. It wasn't flashy or pretentious, even if it did have a couple of expansive touches inside; not too many of the places in her street could boast an elaborate shower and an Oscar in the downstairs bathroom. With its net curtains and standardized appearance, it represented English suburban conformity, the type of blending—in that had often suited her, once she'd outgrown her brief rebellious phase, and an indication of why she'd been able to play her greatest roles so well—she didn't just understand them, she *was* them.

Unless he'd be feeling very vengeful, Ken would not have robbed her of all that. And if he'd tried, she'd have probably fought tooth and nail to stop him. With one thing collapsing, she needed the comfort of another around her.

The Surrey mansion he moved into instead really seemed more his style, upmarket instead of suburban, the home of a wheeler and dealer, of someone important. It befitted the stature bestowed on him by both the press and his own ego.

For Emma, it was a time when she needed all her anchors, the surroundings she knew, her roots. To Ken, the separation offered a chance to show who he really was and how he saw himself.

But who was really to blame for all that happened? Before their marriage, Emma had stressed the importance she placed on fidelity, and from the reports it would seem that Ken fell from that state of grace first. By then, though, was it even an important issue to Emma? She'd certainly brushed off Hugh Grant's soliciting a prostitute and had even said she wouldn't have blamed Ken for doing the same. Was that a major shift in attitude or simply another way of saying she didn't care any more? Most likely it was the latter, just as, to a point, was her involvement with Greg Wise. He was, as one friend put it, "a breath of fresh air."

Reduced to its basic point, they'd grown in different directions. It was always hard to admit, and possibly the affairs were what made them realize it and come to their senses. Most certainly Emma, in spite of her fling, wanted the marriage to continue. From the example of her own parents, who were together more than a quarter of a century before her father died, she'd seen that it *could* work. And for her own not to implied a failure on her part, something difficult to swallow, most particularly for a person with social proprieties at her core and a person who had, by and large, known only success and stability during her life.

A few months later, after the initial shock had worn off, she was a little more open to discussing the topic of her split with Ken, while cautioning in the *Los Angeles Times*, "I didn't approve of being invaded by the press and don't appreciate being asked what it's like by people I don't know, because I wouldn't dream of doing it in return. It's rude. And it's not meant to be rude and I understand why it's done, but I just think that the only way of dealing with it is by reiterating again and again that my personal life is not for public consumption. It is not reasonable to require that of me."

But at the same time, she could come out and say, "It's always a tremendous mistake for actors to get involved with someone they're working with—it can be very confusing. What is so exciting to me about acting is that you can have this wonderful charge, this connection, with somebody and then say, 'Ni-night! See you in the morning!' It's like borrowing a child for a half-hour: You can enjoy the best bits and then you don't have to take them home."

It was an interesting statement, not only in the light of Ken's alleged actions but also her own affair with Greg Wise, which was continuing, although she perhaps was beginning to feel a little ambivalent about it. He was, after all, younger than her, which might have been an ego boost of sorts. But like Ken, he didn't have her education and erudition and might not have been able to offer the intellectual stimulation she needed.

Certainly, the media hounding wore her down. "Oh, don't ask me about that," she complained theatrically to *The European Magazine*. "It plunges me into despair," before admitting, "Actually, it's all right. I'm fine *really*, thank you."

By the time *Film Review* cornered her on the subject, she was not in the mood to talk about it any more. "The bottom line is that I wouldn't dream of asking [a reporter] about their personal life because I know it would be rude. If they were my friend, I would say, 'I hear you've been having a bit of a hard time. Are you okay?' I do not agree because one's job involves publicity, because one has to go out and bang a drum for the work that you do, that you should be selling your life. I'm astonished what people will say on *Oprah*. I think there was a generation of movie stars, certainly in the forties, where the studios wanted that side of it because it was part of being a movie star, the Elizabeth Taylor/Richard Burton angle on things. And if you make that a part of your life and that's how you want to present yourself, and you're able to give that of yourself, then do it, but I think it's very difficult to live with and very destructive. I'm just an actor, actors don't really matter, we're just performers."

In all fairness, Emma had rarely given many details of her private life. But then, she hadn't been asked for them. However, from her earliest days in the business she'd been very open in talking to the press, almost eager to offer her views on so many subjects, from politics to romance, that asking for her comments now was a natural response.

Also, like it or not, she was a celebrity, and Western culture has become celebrity driven. People wanted to know what had happened with Ken and Emma, much as they'd wanted to know about Burton and Taylor or those stars of an earlier era. By placing themselves in the public eye and asking for approval, they'd become something close to the public's proprietary children, and now they wanted their privacy; it was hard for the public to let them be. And with no studio system to carefully censor what was available to the media, it was inevitable that they'd want it all.

Who could blame her for feeling defensive when asked over and over again why her marriage had broken down? It hammered home the point that it *had* failed, that she and her husband were no longer together—not the most pleasant fact to be constantly reminded of. And though Ken might be able to say in *Vanity Fair* that, "Not even a grain of failure in any sense could be attributed to Emma. . . . She's been absolutely magnificent throughout. She is able to remind herself, and me, that what's happened to us has happened to a trillion people in much more difficult circumstances. The price we have to pay—and in the grand scheme of things it's rather a small one—is the public spotlight," the words didn't make the harsh facts go away.

In that same *Vanity Fair* piece, Emma did finally open up a little about her feelings, saying, "Ken will always be family. That's a given. There has been a metamorphosis, perhaps. I don't know yet. . . . I committed every molecule to my marriage, so relinquishing it has been very hard. It's been like breaking your fingers as you let go. But that's perhaps important in itself. . . . Certainly it was like sitting on a time bomb. . . . If you like, the pain sort of started such a long time ago. Three years. I know I'm steering into a calmer place. Despite the pain, one comes through it."

Unlike so many of her words to the press, it was a rambling speech, unrehearsed, unprepared, and therefore decidedly honest, slowly gathering the thoughts and letting them out. "Marriages stop," she admitted. "Marriages change. People are always saying a marriage 'failed.'. . . Failure is terribly important. Perhaps that's what I'm saying: the notion that failure is a negative thing is wrong."

At the same time, she'd set limits as to how much she'd tell. When asked if there was an aggrieved party, she replied, "Well, even if there were, I wouldn't tell you. Our separation had nothing to do with anyone else." And when questioned on her affair with Greg Wise, she felt, "That's a separate issue"—as if it wasn't directly connected to the marriage breakup. And perhaps it wasn't. By the time they met, things appeared to be largely over anyway.

Even a child, that issue over which she and Ken had flipped and flopped for a number of years, would not have been likely to keep them together, and now she claimed she had "no feelings of that sort."

An era had ended. As with anybody else going through the same process, it would take her a long time to work through all the issues within herself. And possibly she did feel some sort of blame; it was a relatively common feeling. But on the outside both she and Ken were putting a very civilized face on the whole proceedings.

It had yet to come to court, but it seemed more than likely that all the legal details would be hashed out beforehand. Almost certainly Emma would keep the house. Although she was well able to afford a mansion similar to Ken's, the chances of her wanting to leave West Hampstead were slim. "I used to think I would never grow up if I didn't move," she said. "But I don't think it's where you live that makes you grow up. In some ways, it's accepting staying where you come from, and then moving up from there."

Quite possibly the divorce really would be entirely amicable, and that in time they *would* become good, close friends. For now, however much they protested that they were "family" or close, grains of anger had to rankle to some degree. Only time would tell the final story.

All the awards in 1996 essentially closed a chapter in Emma's life. And now, there was one thing she needed above all else—some time off, time to herself. Since *Dead Again* she'd kept up a fairly steady, often hectic pace. Not as grueling as Ken's perhaps, but with nine films and endless drafts of a screenplay it had been more than enough. In the light of the split, some space was vital to her well-being. There had been talk of her being involved with a number of movies—*The Horse Whisperer* with Robert Redford, *The Well of Loneliness*, and others—but she realized that she needed a full year with no commitments, merely a chance to live, and above all, to read. It remained one of her constant pleasures. She'd reached a stage in her life of feeling that "too much fiction is bad for you," and it was time to go back and rediscover the joys of nonfiction.

She'd become far more successful than she could ever have imagined when she took her first serious role in *Fortunes of War*. From being a comedian stretching her wings she'd become internationally lauded, moving in rarefied circles, on the Hollywood "A" list, her house positively cluttered with awards and statuettes. In her career she'd truly blossomed. At the same time, she hadn't been able to have it all; the center hadn't been able to hold. Her personal life might no longer have been in tatters, but it remained fragmented. She needed to gather those fragments together before she could really move on, both in her life and work.

Although she never referred to it in her published diaries, much of the trauma of the breakup had occurred during the rush up to, and making of,

Sense and Sensibility. She'd had to be able to put all that baggage aside every time she stood in front of the camera, or sat down at her computer, making her work even more impressive that it had otherwise seemed.

Now with everything over, and nothing on the horizon, was a perfect opportunity to duck out of the public eye and become herself—even discover who she really was. After so many years in so many roles, it was time.

chapter fourteen

Emma officially announced her year off in May 1996, while speaking to the children at her old primary school. But it had been evident for some time that she'd decided to take time away from work. Interviewed in *The European Magazine* before the 1996 Oscars, she'd noted that she resented the pressure to "go on and on. It inspires greed, not for money but for stimulation. And gosh, when I get to the end of my life I'll think what the hell did I do? It's all gone. . . . I think it's time to look at a tree."

Something else she was eager to do was deflate the impression that all her nonacting pursuits were intellectual, pointing out that, "I do all the old-fashioned things, to be honest. I like to cook. If I need physical activity, I make something from a big lump of pastry. I like to read. I have a piano, so I tinkle a bit. I write letters; I'm quite a good correspondent." She took great pains to try and point out how essentially *ordinary* she really was, emphasizing elsewhere that "I love all kinds of things. Working, reading, cooking a meal. I like watching *Star Wars*. I'm a perfectly normal human being. And I always have been. I really couldn't have had a better time. And if I died now it wouldn't matter."

Barring her sudden demise, though, there are a number of questions about what Emma might do with the rest of her life. Obviously, writing a successful screenplay has expanded her working options exponentially within the movie business. After completing it she'd talked about wanting to write an original screenplay (as opposed to an adaptation), partly for her own satisfaction but also because "I don't think things will change until we get more women writing. . . . You hope you'll be able to produce material that will redress the balance. It's ridiculous to think that when women pass the age of forty-five they cease to be interesting or evocative or sexual. It's an insult."

Whether she would become a writer exclusively would remain to be seen, although in *Film Review* she did speak of a time "later, when I'm older and I've waved my final farewell to the theater," confirming that then "I'll write roles for women—good female roles. Later on I'll have lived a bit more and I might have something to offer up."

Although she has in the past enjoyed some anonymity by going out in ordinary clothes and without makeup, looking for all the world like an everyday woman instead of an international film star, the lure of the glamour can be very strong. And to ignore acting would be to deny her major talent. When she appeared at a book signing in Los Angeles, promoting her *Sense and Sensibility* screenplay and diaries, six hundred people were in line by the time the store opened. They were there to see Emma Thompson—the actress who'd become a writer. After a few years away from the cameras, Emma the writer would be unlikely to draw that kind of crowd. But that in itself seemed an attraction in 1996, after all the months of press.

"I regard it with a certain degree of jaundiced skepticism at the moment," she explained in *Film Review*, "and certainly if it were to snowball into anything worse, I'd stop acting. . . . If being famous takes your life away, then stop being famous, walk away, it's simple . . . I would stop and write and really concentrate on that. I think fame is poisonous. You have to be very careful. . . . It can really knock you for six, and I'm old enough now not to think, 'Hey, I'm great.' Too much attention doesn't make you feel very well."

In America—unlike England, which seems to merely tolerate her—she's viewed, even revered, as an icon of British acting. Granted, that's partly because Emma has appeared in so many period dramas, which appeal to a country that has yet to fully establish its own traditions, and also because her characters have tended towards the genteel and middle class, with the social graces and urbanity so many Americans wish they had. Most Americans identify Emma strictly as a dramatic actress and are not familiar with the stage that the British can't seem to forget—that of a brash, young comedian who wanted to shock and be noticed. For better or worse, she did both there, and she's never been fully forgiven or rehabilitated. Even after two Oscars, the admiration for her in the British press is somewhat grudging.

And to be fair, at times she's been her own worst enemy. Some of her statements have been delivered off the top of her head and seemed far too precious, pretentious, or deliberately controversial. When interviewed by *The Advocate* she was asked if, were she to take a role in *The Well of Loneliness* "or something else where you play gay, what actress would you like to be in love with?" Emma replied, "Oh, God, well, lots of women. . . . I think that because of my masculinity—I've got a lot of masculinity—I would probably put myself with someone very feminine, overtly feminine like Michelle Pfeiffer. Actually, I find Michelle fantastically attractive. I'm always kind of rushing up to her and kissing her on the mouth because she's so delicious. She's so-o-o delicious. But oh, God, it could be any number of women, actually. . . ."

In itself, that was fine; she answered the interviewer's question honestly and fully. No limits had been placed on her fantasies or ideas. But the quote was on the record (albeit in a magazine whose primary audience was the gay and lesbian community), and it was a weary Emma with her guard down who was talking, not the sensible schoolgirl. Emma's repeated comments regarding Michelle Pfeiffer were making it obvious that she saw her as a feminine icon—to the point that her ideas about Pfeiffer could be sexual. Inevitably, the British press picked up on the remark and had a field day with it, wondering in a headline "Why Can't Emma Thompson Stop Talking About Sex?"

Those kind of statements, however, tended to be the exception rather than the rule—one of the reasons they seemed so glaring. Her words tended to be considered at length, even occasionally rehearsed, before an interview. In America, at least, she had a reputation as a strong, intelligent, articulate woman.

ONE possibility for the future is that Emma might move into politics. While it's something she's never mentioned, there's a tradition of sorts for British actresses to be politically involved. Vanessa Redgrave, Julie Christie, and Glenda Jackson have all made politics an important part of their lives. Since Cambridge Emma has been an activist, not so much with her time, since that has been limited, but with her money and her name, supporting a number of causes. Not surprisingly, the woman with her roots set firmly in the suburban middle class hasn't been as radical as Vanessa, although when "I protested about the Gulf War at a time when I thought my country had literally lost its mind, I was castigated both by the press and people I knew and got a tiny, tiny taste of what folks like Vanessa Redgrave have gone through."

Although Glenda Jackson has made the transition from actress to Member of Parliament—in fact, she represents the district in which Emma lives—Emma is not so certain she wants to follow in those footsteps: "I confess to being deeply, deeply uneasy by celebrity politics. I'm a member of the Labour Party, and I'm constantly asked for endorsements. It makes me feel peculiar."

At the same time, she doesn't rule out the possibility entirely. She understands that the level of work and commitment would be high and remains uncertain "whether I've got the stamina. And also I value my privacy, truly."

Were she ever to stand for Parliament, it would inevitably be as a Labour candidate. She's been a staunch supporter of the party since she was at university, along with the Campaign for Nuclear Disarmament, Friends of the Earth, and Greenpeace. They may be the standard causes of the bleeding-heart liberal, but her support for them has been long-lasting, as has all her political involvement. She's sat on committees discussing women's issues. Her film diaries have often showed her writing politically oriented letters in her free time on the set, and now that her name carries real international weight she's realized that being involved is more important than ever.

The involvement won't stop, that much can easily be predicted. It's too much a part of her now. Whether it will go further and prompt her to throw her own hat in the political ring seems, ultimately, to be unlikely. Between acting and writing she has two strong career options already, one that can glide quite easily into the other, and she seems quite content with those. Writing, in particular, offers so much for her to explore.

As a writer she has the luxury of money—the half million dollars she was paid for *Junior* remains in the bank—and time to write. Anything she comes up with will almost certainly be bought on the strength of her Oscar and will very likely also be made. She's already proven herself to be a sharp, insightful writer with a deft comic touch; the only question is whether her own material can measure up to her adaptation.

Whether she'll begin that original screenplay during her year off remains to be seen. After so much time running from film to film, and so much sheer pressure of work, she may simply take the chance to relax at length. At the same time, there is some force inside that drives her, and she may well not be able to just sit still for that long.

Although she's been willing to attribute her career to a series of "happy accidents," it's also true that the drive has been there since she really discovered performing while at Cambridge. Without it, she would never have become a stand-up comic, had her own television show, or found her acting legs on *Fortunes of War*.

Certainly it was reinventing herself as a serious actress that saved her. She'd made a reputation of sorts as a comic, which was hurriedly ruined by *Thompson*, such a total disaster in the eyes of both critics and the public. By then her work on both *Tutti Frutti* and *Fortunes of War* had made people realize that there might be more to her, and indeed, she seemed to realize that her real future lay outside comedy.

There's no denying that Ken was a catalyst in drawing out her real talent—*Much Ado About Nothing*, the last film they made together, remains a highlight among her screen appearances—but too much credit shouldn't be given to him. The majority of her great work, and certainly the performances that brought her Oscar nominations, was created away from him.

It's often been said that Emma always plays a variation on herself, and to a large degree the statement is true. She's been at her best when she's done exactly that. But her power of transformation is such that the viewer sees no real similarity between her roles. At heart they may have a great deal in common, but on the surface there seem to be vast differences between, say, Elinor Dashwood and Margaret Schlegel. And that is a great deal of her art, finding the nub she can understand, putting it in herself, and then disguising it under a flurry of other things. It makes her no less of an actor than a DeNiro or Hoffman, those great proponents of the Method. In some ways her achievement is larger, coming to the profession as she did armed only with instinct, as opposed to their rigorous training.

She's become acknowledged as Britain's leading actress. And although that's an impressive title for a country that's produced a wealth of talented actresses, it's also well deserved. She's been able to capture the English personality in her work better than any other actress—the repression and sublimation, the stiff upper lip, and the emotions that occasionally boil over. She can take something that is essentially middlebrow, like *Howards End*, and make it into something more—she can find the art in it quite naturally it seems.

That, perhaps, is what people see more than anything, certainly well beyond the looks, the voice, or anything else. And it's why she's been honored so much. There's an integrity about her work. Even in *Junior*, bad as that film was, Emma's presence was able to nudge the film above the lowest common denominator it seemed otherwise headed for.

It's also proven true in her writing. Her adaptation of Jane Austen was not only entertaining but also a wonderful study in family relationships.

The great temptation would be to call her an alchemist, transforming base materials into gold, and within her own work she does seem to exude that ability. It establishes her in the tradition of fine British actresses (and now fine screenwriters); we're simply lucky enough to see her on the big screen.

Ultimately, though, it must be remembered that she's mortal, a woman. We tend to think of our celebrities, particularly in the movies, as we see them—much larger than life—and treat them that way. They've become the new pantheon of gods and goddesses. At the end of any day, though, they're human, with failings, foibles, and virtues. Some who consider themselves godlike might exist in the more rarefied atmosphere of the Hollywood Hills, but even they go through the same daily routines as the rest of us.

Emma Thompson has always wanted to be treated in an ordinary manner. She may have established herself to a point where the fickleness of fame can't really touch her, but she's remained grounded in the everyday—the price of a pint of milk, the crowds at a Tube station. Even her occasional grandiose statement is decidedly human—who hasn't puffed themselves up at times, only to be soundly deflated?

The love-hate relationship the British press maintains with her ensures that she'll never get too big for her boots. "I've been very fortunate," she said, "but if they've made the odd snide remark, I'm sure it's no more than I deserve."

It's an accidental path that's led her to two Oscars and worldwide acclaim. Whether anyone chooses to call it luck or fate or whatever, it's happened. Emma's return to film will be a relatively low-key one. A family affair, Emma will star in *The Winter Guest* with her mother. The film will also mark the directorial debut of actor Alan Rickman, whom Emma has worked with in the past on various projects with Renaissance. *The Winter Guest* is expected to be released in the fall of 1997.

From a career that seemed to be teetering on the edge of extinction Emma managed a Phoenix-like rise, a real reinvention. That reinvention will continue when she plays American Susan Stanton, the wife of Governor Jack Stanton (John Travolta), in Mike Nichols's film adaptation of Joe Klein's (writing as "Anonymous") *Primary Colors*, which is expected to be released sometime during the first half of 1998. Both big-budget and decidedly Hollywood, it's an odd turn for her to take, but with co-stars like Travolta, Jack Nicholson, and John Malkovich, it can only raise her profile and help break down the "period-drama" image that surrounds her. The question, of course, is how convincing will she be? Emma and England remain intertwined in people's minds; if she can change that, she'll have pulled off a very powerful piece of acting indeed. But only time will tell.

◈

As some have noted, the unifying theme of her performances, both as actress and writer, is intelligence. It can blaze, smolder gently in the background, or shine through on the page. But inevitably it's there. And in the moments it combines with honest instinct, Emma Thompson has the ability to set a theater alight. Whatever she chooses to do in the future, intelligence will always be a part of it.

◈

Of course, her life isn't even half over yet—she has yet to reach middle age. The picture of her life is far from complete; indeed, her options seem to increase exponentially with each passing year. All a biographer can do is look at the past, attempt to put it into a framework of sorts, and speculate about the future. Since her life is still being lived, any conclusions must be temporary, subject to endless changes and revisions.

One thing stands quite immutable, though, and that is her talent. Emma Thompson has proven herself beyond a shadow of a doubt to be one of the leading actresses of her generation; some might argue of all time. She may become one of the industry's great screenwriters, too, but it's for her appearances in front of the camera that she will most likely be remembered. Even if she were to make no more films, her reputation and place in film history would still be assured.

appendix

emma thompson

Tutti Frutti (1987)
Fortunes of War (1987)
Thompson (1988)
The Winslow Boy (1989)
Knuckles (1989)
Tin Fish (1990)
The Blue Boy (1995)

ALSO, GUEST APPEARANCES ON:

Carrott's Lib
Saturday Live
The Young Ones
Cheers

RADIO

Three Plus One on Four (1982)
Saturday Night Fry (1987)
Hamlet (1992)
King Lear (1994)

STAGE

Lady Audley's Secret (1976)
Aladdin (1978)
All's Well That Ends Well 1979)
Travesties (1979)
Nightcap (1979)
Woman's Hour (1980)
The Snow Queen (1980)
An Evening Without (1981)
The Proposal (1981)
The Cellar Tapes (1981)
Beyond the Footlights (1982)
Short Vehicle (1983)
The Big One (1984)

Me and My Girl (1985)
Look Back in Anger (1989)
A Midsummer Night's Dream (1990)
King Lear (1990)

TRAINING VIDEOS
Managing Problem People

SCREENPLAYS
Sense and Sensability

references

BOOKS

Branagh, Kenneth. *Beginnings*. New York: W. W. Norton, 1989.

Shuttleworth, Ian. *Ken and Em: A Biography of Kenneth Branagh and Emma Thompson*. New York: St. Martin's Press, 1994.

Thompson, Emma. *The Sense and Sensibility Screenplay and Diaries*. New York: Newmarket Press, 1995.

PERIODICALS

"Never Look Back," by Kevin Sessums, *Vanity Fair*, February 1996. "The Americanization of Emma," by Rachel Abramowitz, *Premiere*, April 1992. "Prince of Players," by Mark Huisman, *The Advocate*, February 20, 1996. "Emma Thompson," *Vogue*, June 1993. "Much Ado About Emma," by Gabrielle Donnelly, *OK*, July 1993. "Day by Day," by Emma Thompson, *Premiere*, December 1993. "A Hampstead Socialist Tackles Schwarzenegger," by Brenda Maddox, *The New York Times* November 20, 1994. "Beyond the Cringe," by Ian Parker, *Independent*, September 3, 1995. "Greg and Emma left the house . . ." by Dawn Alford and John Chapman, *News of the World*, October 1, 1995. "The Prime of Miss Emma Thompson," by Lynda Lee-Potter, *Daily Mail*, June 13, 1988. "Life is Sweet," by David Gritten, *Empire*, December 1993. "Emma Thompson's

Family Business," by Russell Miller, *The New York Times Magazine*, March 1993. "Robbie Coltrane/Emma Thompson," Emma Thompson interviewed by Robbie Coltrane, *Interview*, May 1993. "The Untold Story of Emma Thompson," by Sandra Parsons, *Daily Mail*, March 16, 1993. "Sensible English Heroine," by Marcelle Katz, *The European Magazine*, February 29, 1996. "Emma Makes Sense," by Judy Sloane, *Film Review*, March 1996. "Emma Thompson, Sensibly," by Jan Stuart, *Los Angeles Times*, December 10, 1995. "Emma Thompson," by Judy Wieder, *The Advocate*, September 19, 1995. "Classy, Sassy Emma Thompson," by David Gritten, *Cosmopolitan*, December 1993. "Emma Thompson," *Empire*, October 1995.

acknowledgments

This book may have been conceived privately, but its gestation would have been impossible without the help of many, many people. As always, my great thanks and respect to Madeleine Morel, a truly wonderful, tenacious agent. Macy Jaggers (now a happy mother) proved to be an editor with a sympathetic ear and a stout belief in this project, as did her excellent successors, Holly McGuire and her assistant, Stacey Sexton.

In Seattle, I'm indebted first and foremost to my wife and son, Linda and Graham, whose love and support help me keep going day after day, and who make it all worthwhile. Also to Dave Thompson, as good a friend as a person could wish for, and Dennis Wilken, who's always been glad for me and never jealous. Stephanie Ogle at the excellent Cinema Books proved to be a remarkable resource, as always, and introduced me to Julie Atwood, who was more than generous in letting me borrow and sort through her huge collection of Emma Thompson cuttings. I appreciate everything you've all done.

In England, an award for service far above and beyond the call of duty goes to Jonathon and Judy Savill, who not only housed and fed a relative stranger but made him feel at home (and thanks to Michael and Andru for the connection!). Jonathon connected me to some valuable sources, most particularly Peter Trowell, Dawn Alford, and Tracy Schaverien, who couldn't have been kinder if they'd owed me money . . . no thank yous would be enough to show my gratitude.

Certainly I can't forget Kevin Odell and Dani Byrne, who also helped make my time in the Smoke much easier. And Ian Shuttleworth, who had himself written about Ken and Emma, was willing to take time to discuss the couple with me, a very magnanimous gesture.

Further north, the people at ACT and University Library in Cambridge were very helpful on my visit there and didn't mind their brains being picked a little.

Given that there's no support like a family, I'm grateful to have had the chance to spend time with my parents, Ray and Betty Nickson, constant inspirations, and my sister Lee and nephew Greg, a time as welcome as rain in the desert, and I lapped it up eagerly. As I did the beer when bending elbows with Mike Murtagh. Cheers, mate!

All of the above gave of their time and expertise to help me on this project, in their different ways. Others preferred to be anonymous, for various reasons, and to them I also extend my gratitude. The failings of this book are not because of anything any of you gave me, but merely because of my writing.

Index